THE
JESUITS

THE JESUITS

HISTORY & LEGEND OF ❧ THE SOCIETY OF JESUS

❧ ❧ ❧ ❧

MANFRED BARTHEL

TRANSLATED & ADAPTED BY MARK HOWSON

WILLIAM MORROW AND COMPANY, INC. • NEW YORK 1984

Copyright © 1982 by Econ Verlag GmbH

English translation copyright © 1984
by William Morrow and Company, Inc.

Originally published in the Federal Republic of Germany in 1982
by Econ Verlag under the title Die Jesuiten

All rights reserved. No part of this book may be reproduced
or utilized in any form or by any means, electronic or mechanical,
including photocopying, recording or by any information storage
and retrieval system, without permission in writing from the
Publisher. Inquiries should be addressed to William Morrow and
Company, Inc., 105 Madison Avenue, New York, N.Y. 10016.

Library of Congress Catalog Card Number: 84-60446

ISBN: 0-688-02861-6

Printed in the United States of America

BOOK DESIGN BY LINEY LI

FOREWORD

In 1948 Christmas fell on a Sunday. The Free University in the Dahlem district of West Berlin had just wound up its very first semester the week before. It was cold and damp, as it is every December in Berlin, only this year there would be no coal or heating oil. All the radiators were turned way down or, in our case at the university, shut off altogether. That was the winter of the Soviet blockade of West Berlin, and for the first time in history a city under siege that had no access to the sea was going to be supplied exclusively from the air. We students from the East Zone were sitting it out in our furnished rooms; our windows, badly in need of putty, looked out on a vista of bombed-out apartment blocks (if we were lucky) that was even more desolate against the gray December sun. Distractions meant a lot to us, and we didn't get too many. One of the few that was available just then was the Christmas service for the students at the university, so off we went.

The Protestant service began about ten in a university building in the Gelfertstrasse. The seminar room on the first floor seemed even colder that day than usual, for which the scrawny, scantily decorated Christmas tree that someone had stuck up in the front of the room was primarily to blame. Standing right beside a blackboard scrawled with formulas of some kind, and already beginning to shed its needles, it looked dismally out of place.

The Protestant chaplain was obviously feeling the cold as badly as any of us, but, being a good Lutheran, he didn't let it distract him from the exercise of his pastoral duties. He read us the beginning of the Gospel According to St. Luke, and he read the story of the Nativity, first verbatim, then with commentary, as we had been accustomed to hearing it at Christmas since we were children. Perhaps he thought that, as philosophy students, he owed us a detailed account of the material facts of the case, but while he was waxing theological, we were philosophically freezing to death.

By the time our little holiday observance was over, it had started to rain again, hard, so four of us decided to stay on for the Catholic service, which was to follow immediately. Of course we were quite convinced that the Gospel According to St. Luke has long since given up its secrets and there was nothing new that the Catholic chaplain could tell us. As it happened, we were quite wrong.

A thirty-year-old man of average height and build—"a normal consumer," as the ration cards used to read back in those days—propped up his soggy umbrella in the corner, muttered something about what rotten weather we were having, rubbed his hands together a few times, felt the cold radiator, took note of the pathetic Christmas tree, and began, not exactly a sermon, but a litany of complaints.

"The university could certainly have spared the money for a decent tree. It would have been nicer, and more appropriate, to have the radiators working so that we could at least have a little *external* warmth on this festival of light and reconciliation. So what? That's the way it should have been, of course, but there you sit, not exactly bursting with impatience to hear what the man up there—myself, I mean—has got to tell you. Because you just don't believe that anyone can help you out with words alone. Especially not somebody who wears his collar backward and hasn't got anything to offer you but a bunch of words that are already two thousand years old. Maybe my Protestant colleague was right simply to read the Christmas story to you—just as if nothing at all had happened in the last two thousand years, in the last six years of the war, in the last few months, since we started worrying if we *didn't* hear the drone of those big two-engine jobs overhead, just the way we used to worry before that when we *did.* In fact, a lot of things, an infinite number of things, have happened since then. Most of you are sitting here now because the border's sealed up tight and you can't get home—or maybe because you don't feel like going back out in the rain just yet."

The man in the black sweater was not the least bit put off by the involuntary gulping noise that I had not very successfully tried to stifle. He went on:

"There are more reasons for taking part in divine services than the simple desire to avoid getting cold and wet out in the street when you could be staying cold and dry in here. But whatever reasons prompted you to join in this celebration—you all have only one and the same real reason for coming here. We feel lost and unsure of ourselves in this world. This uncertainty is not some kind of metaphysical concept, something thought up by Heidegger or any of that crowd, but something very real. It will start up again tomorrow, when we count the handful of marks that are supposed to see us through this Christmas season and into the New Year. And when one of us walks down the Kurfürstendamm in his old army greatcoat, past all the people with their Christmas packages and past the shop windows where the simplest little knickknack starts at ten or twelve marks, I can readily understand it if this world's tough hide, whatever it is that makes it so easy for people to forget so fast . . . I can understand it if whatever that is starts to get to you.

"But then you just happen to glance across the street and maybe there's somebody walking along over there who's so much like you, he could be your brother. His coat's worn out and he's dying for a cigarette, just like you, but with a pack of Camels going for eight marks a throw he just hasn't got the wherewithal. And take a closer look, this fellow who looks so much like you"—and here the man in the Roman collar paused artfully (artfully enough to have made him the envy of every poor actor in the Berliner Barlog Ensemble)—"that man across the street is one of us. And not only that, he might just as easily be Jesus Christ himself."

Of all the sermons I've heard in the course of my life, this is certainly the one that has stayed with me the longest. I've forgotten the chaplain's name. He was the first Jesuit I ever heard speak. A German Protestant of my generation had scarcely any opportunity to come into contact with members of the Order. That was one of the lesser absurdities perpetrated by the rulers of the Third Reich—in whose upper echelons, by the way, there were more Roman Catholics than in any previous government in Germany, as well as many of the most spiritually impoverished, most brutal adversaries that the Order had encountered in the course of its long history—and this, as we shall see, is saying quite a lot.

The relationship between National Socialism and the Society of Jesus was, like so many aspects of that half-baked, indigestible ideology of the master race, full of contradictions. In 1941 a secret communiqué of the Wehrmacht High Command classified the Jesuits as "unfit for military service." But on November 8, 1941, the High Command informed its field commanders on the eastern front that "with a view to our rapprochement with the Vatican, you are to assist Jesuits [already active] in the occupied territories in the furtherance of their missionary activities." In his book *The Secret War,* published in England in 1953, a former SS officer, Walter Hagen, made the claim that Jesuit Superior General Wlodomir Ledóchowski was even prepared to take part in an *ad hoc* anti-Bolshevik coalition with the Waffen SS (the dozen or so black-uniformed SS combat divisions that made up the elite of Hitler's armies), though Hagen did not produce any documentary evidence to support this charge.

It is true that certain formal similarities existed between the organizations. SS Reichsführer Heinrich Himmler had accumulated an enormous archive of material on the Order, and when the time came, he set up his "Death's Head Legions," the Waffen SS, along similar lines, at least in theory. According to Walter Schellenberg, a former SS general who served on Himmler's personal staff, the upper echelons of the SS were sent on retreat once a year, to Wewelsburg Castle in Westphalia, in imitation of the "meditations" devised by Saint Ignatius Loyola, the founder of the Order. Wewelsburg was very much to Himmler's taste—a picturesque castle on the Rhine that took its name from a previous tenant, a medieval robber baron called Wiwel von Büren. The subject of these knightly meditations was the usual Nazi hodgepodge of bogus medievalism and esoteric "wisdom" of every description—the Holy Grail, the Teutonic Knights, everything from the Jesuit Rule to the ritual hocuspocus of the Ku Klux Klan. All of this was crammed into a kind of yearly refresher course in Nordic ideology and solemnly discussed afterward around the great oaken round table in the baron's great hall. (Hitler himself did not take any of this too seriously, and on one occasion, according to Hitler's *Table Talk,* he sardonically referred to Himmler as "our very own Ignatius Loyola.")

Others were not amused, however. After the abortive attempt on Hitler's life in July 1944, hundreds of "conspirators" were paraded before the People's Court in show trials presided over by the infamous Dr. Roland Freisler. When it was disclosed that one of the defendants, Count von Moltke, had had some contact with a Jesuit provincial, Freisler thundered out, "No true German would be caught dead in a ditch with one of those fellows! . . . As for myself, if I find out that a certain city is harboring a Jesuit provincial, why, that's almost reason enough not to go there." Curiously enough, though, the story persists to this day that Dr. Goebbels, Hitler's Minister for Propaganda and "Popular Education," was an alumnus of one of the five Jesuit colleges in Germany. This is not true, as it happens, but it is a kind of backhanded compliment to the Order that the apostle of the Big Lie was assumed to have learned his trade in one of their academies. Even today the word *Jesuitical* is not entirely positive in its connotations, to say the least. Dornseif's *German Thesaurus* (1954 edition), for example, contains a long list of synonyms, including "two-faced, false . . . insidious, dissembling, perfidious . . . mendacious, sanctimonious, insincere, dishonorable, dishonest, untruthful . . ." The English word, only slightly less disparaging, conjures up a whole realm of deceit and dissimulation, roughly bounded by such phrases as "making the weaker argument appear the stronger" and "I had my fingers crossed all along." The French have a proverb to the effect that "whenever two Jesuits come together, the devil always makes three," and the Spanish likewise: "Don't trust a monk with your wife or a Jesuit with your money."

Clearly the Jesuits have had their share of enemies ever since the Order was founded, and it is to their credit that these have almost always included the greatest minds of the age; quite often it is simply their admiration for the accomplishments of the Order that has inspired the most passionate opposition. Even during its occasional lapses from grace, the Order has always represented an elite group within the body of the Church—a point on which all its more discerning critics are completely in agreement. "Let us hope," Loyola once wrote, "that the Order may never be left untroubled by the hostility of the world for very long." This wish has been amply fulfilled for over four centuries and—if the latest news from Rome is to be believed—should hold true for another century to come.

Since the Church Militant has now become a forum for all sorts of dialogue across the aisle, the Jesuits have sought to find a place for themselves and their Order in this postecumenical scheme of things. Some of the younger Jesuits have called the Order's very right to exist into question, just as they have tried to search out the real spiritual significance of all the established dogmas and institutions of the Church. In the Netherlands, where Jesuit theologians have been especially audacious in suggesting radical changes of course for the Order and the Church as a whole, one Jesuit residence is supposed to have a sign posted by the door: "Will the last one leaving the Order kindly remember to turn out the lights." (Apparently the Jesuits are not alone in their plight, since this story is told about the Dominicans as well.)

Without the Jesuits, runs one line of argument, Christianity would never have become a true world religion. And without the Jesuits, runs the response, there would only be a single Christian Church today, instead of two—the reformed Catholic Church envisioned by Luther, Calvin, Zwingli, and the other great leaders of the Reformation. It is commonly supposed that the Order was founded in response to these pressures for reform within the Church, but in fact Loyola seems to have been almost totally unaware of the activities of Luther and his colleagues. It would be much more accurate to say that the careers of both Luther and Loyola are reflections of a new age in which the individual, the individual soul in this case, has finally become a figure of some consequence, free to read and interpret the Scriptures in his own language, to be judged by the purity of his faith rather than the outward show of piety, free—in Loyola's own words—"to find God always, whenever I wish to."

The last five centuries can provide no better example of the influence that a few thousand individuals could have on European thought and cultural development than the Jesuits, though in this context it scarcely matters whether it was felt directly—through their achievements in philosophy, science, and education—or indirectly—as a result of the bitter intellectual controversies and counterattacks their activities always provoked.

When Loyola sent his protégés out onto "the battleground of faith," he gave them as their watchword a text from St. Paul's First Epistle to the Corinthians: "I am made all things to all men, that I might by all means save some." The historian Egon Friedel has drawn up a fairly comprehensive list of what this entailed. "They were," he writes, "the most brilliant courtiers, the sternest ascetics, the most self-sacrificing missionaries and the sharpest traders, the most devoted footmen and the shrewdest statesmen, the wisest confessors and the greatest impresarios, the most gifted physicians and the most skillful assassins. They built churches and factories, sponsored pilgrimages and conspiracies, proved theorems in mathematics and stated propositions in church dogmatics, worked to suppress the freedom of enquiry and made a host of scientific discoveries. They were—in the broadest possible sense of the term— truly capable of anything."

Certainly they did turn their hands to almost every learned profession or skilled pursuit—scholar, artist, technician, astrologer, geographer, interpreter, or physician. And if they became involved in any kind of intellectual controversy, they were quite able to match wits with the greatest scholars of the age. But, of course, this ideal of universal competence was only pursued as the means to an end—to demonstrate conclusively that theirs was the only true knowledge, the only true faith. Not since the height of the Order's golden age has the world seen such a brilliant display of entrenched, dogmatic inflexibility.

No other order was as much concerned with the affairs of this world, and no other order has suffered so much persecution at the world's hands, as the Jesuits. Accordingly it seems only fair to assess the Order's successes and failures according to strictly secular standards. The first question is whether the Order's successes outweigh its failures. There are those who regard the Jesuits as among mankind's greatest benefactors, and those who regard them as a gang of intellectual terrorists and troublemakers who have only one true homeland (the Vatican), serve only one master (the Pope), and recognize only one law—the orders of their General; all other moral and civil law they heedlessly trample underfoot in order to carry out his commands. The best reply to this sort of accusation that I have come across was written by a Mexican Jesuit in 1970: "When the Jesuits are on the side of progress, they are being opportunistic; when they oppose it, they are reactionaries. If they cast a critical eye over their own activities, then they are being hypocritical; if not, they're being snobbish. If they close one of their schools, they're irresponsible; if they don't—corrupters of youth. If they minister to the rich, they're exploiters; if they work among the poor, they're communists. And whatever else they might do, they're branded forever as disciples of Machiavelli."

Who were they, who are they really? Since it is not to easy to provide a clear answer to this question, both hostile and friendly investigators of the subject tend to rely heavily on catchphrases and canards. The Jesuits, formerly "the Pope's light cavalry," have been upgraded to the Vatican "Rapid Deployment Force," their squadrons presumably in a state of perpetual alert, with one hand on the rosary, the other hand on the ripcord, ready to spring into action the moment the Holy Father picks up the Black Telephone. The unseen power of the Order has always provided a fertile field for speculation: the untimely deaths of countless popes, the St. Bartholomew's Day Massacre, infant crown princes snatched in their cradles (e.g., King James II's notorious "warming-pan baby" in 1688), enemies of state succumbing to undiagnosed maladies or disappearing into underground dungeons, like the Man in the Iron Mask—all of these were said to be the special province of the Jesuits.

Both John Wilkes Booth and Lee Harvey Oswald were also said in their turn to have been "tools of the Jesuits," but the most preposterous accusation that I have encountered was made by a certain Edmond Paris in his book *The Secret History of the Jesuits,* namely that *Mein Kampf* was written not by Adlof Hitler but by a Jesuit by the name of Stämpfle.

Mr. Paris does at least make one thing very clear—that he himself never actually got around to reading Herr Hitler's impenetrable masterwork. But behind such lurid and ridiculous accusations as these lurks the more conventional image of the sinister, scheming Jesuit that has been instantly conjured up by such phrases as "faithful unto death," "fanatically loyal to the Pope," and, most sinister of all, "the end justifies the means." How much truth is there, if any, to this four-hundred-year-old stereotype? Were the activities of the Jesuits a spur or a hindrance to spiritual awakening, both within the Church and outside it? How much influence did the Order actually have on European political life? This book will try to provide the answers to these purely historical questions, and also to examine the situation of the Order in the world of today and its prospects for the future.

Here, I would like to thank those individuals, institutions, libraries, and archives all across Europe who have assisted me in the task of assembling and sifting through the source materials for this book. The sheer number of my collaborators and the special nature of their duties and positions oblige me to thank them collectively rather than individually in this space. Nowhere did I find that a door had been closed to me, and in several instances I was given access to documents that had hitherto been slighted or overlooked altogether, which may provide a few unexpected revelations even for specialists in the field.

DR. MANFRED BARTHEL

CONTENTS

In one of the first encyclopedias ever published, the *Staats- Zeitungs- und Conversations-Lexicon* of 1759, the entry un- der *Jesuits* reads as follows:

JESUITS, or of the Societate Jesu, are religions of the Romish Church, which the Concilium Tridentium [Council of Trent] calls clericos regulares, and their founder was Ignatius Loyola, a Spanish nobleman, who forsook the worldly profession of arms for the habit of a cleric in 1534. Pope Paul III granted them a charter in 1540, and his successors favored them with many enviable privileges. Apart from the customary three monkish vows of poverty, chastity, and obedience, they take a fourth as well, which is to do the work of missionaries and devote themselves to the propagation of the Roman Catholic faith. They do not maintain a choir, and they are generally engaged in giving instruction in the sciences to the young. They are also much given to quarreling with the other Catholic orders, especially the Dominicans, on account of the conversion of the Chinese. In England they were obliged to quit that country altogether, and in France also on account of the Constitutio Uni- genitas they are fallen into disgrace both at court and amongst the other religious.*

* "The conversion of the Chinese" refers to the so-called Chinese rites controversy, for which see pages 197–199. "Constitutio Unigenitas" (the title of a papal bull) refers to an earlier controversy as to whether the Pope or the French king was actually the supreme head of the French Catholic Church, in which the Jesuits were naturally estranged from "the court and the other religious" in France.

Both the Jesuits and their founder began to incur the hostility of other religious orders very early on. Here, a Spanish Dominican called Tomás de Pedroche, writing in 1553, just a few years before Loyola's death, provides a highly subjective critique of Loyola's *Spiritual Exercises* for the Archbishop of Toledo:

. . . as everyone knows, this Ignatius, or Iñigo, de Loyola was summoned before the Holy Office as a notorious heretic. As one of the *Dejados* or *Alumbrados* [Spanish heretical sects—the "Abandoned Ones" preached a doctrine of complete detachment from worldly things, the "Illuminists" believed that a Christian should be guided by his "inner light" rather than by the teachings of the Church], this Ignatius, or Iñigo, fled to Rome to escape the wrath of the Inquisition. Thus, it is well worth noting and reflecting that this same Ignatius, or Iñigo, has fashioned these exercises of his more in accordance with the inner promptings of his heart and the inspiration of the Holy Spirit than from books. This smacks, and more than a little, of the fundamental error of the *Dejados* and *Alumbrados,* who have cast aside and hold in contempt the revelations that can be found in books and uphold only what the Holy Spirit says to them in their innermost hearts, and whatever the Divine Spirit says to them, they take to be infallible truth.

It is also worth noting and reflecting that Loyola was *acquitted* by the Inquisition, though with the caution that he should not take up his vocation until he had completed his religious studies. He spent the next seven years getting his master's degree at the Sorbonne and did not even get to Rome until almost a decade later. Since the *Dejados* and *Alumbrados* were condemned as heretics and ferociously suppressed by the Inquisition, Father de Pedroche, a Dominican, seems to be motivated by something quite different from a spirit of friendly competition in drawing this parallel between Loyola's *Exercises* and the Illuminists' doctrine of "inner light."

PART ❧ I

A Knight for Christ—
the Mission of Ignatius Loyola

. . . at the present time there is no single instrumentality that was fashioned by God for the extirpation of the heretics that is mightier than your holy Order

—Pope Gregory XIII's Address
to the Fourth General Congregation, 1581

For the which reason it would be better for them to be called not Jesuits [Jesuiter] but Jesus-Haters [Jesu-Wider], Jebusites, Esauites, or Jezebelites, and take their name from the company of prophets of Jezebel, that is to say, the false prophets of Baal, and of the companies of the Pharisees, the Samaritans, and such other Devil's apostles as these . . .

—from a pamphlet written by
the Stuttgart court chaplain
Lukas Osiander (1534–1604)

The Conversion of Squire Iñigo

The dozens of surviving portraits of Ignatius Loyola depict him variously as a warrior, a man of God, a second Saint Paul, the majestic Superior General of his Order, and as a humble, repentant sinner. Apparently none of these really shows us the man himself as his closest associates knew him in his lifetime, since the Jesuits would not accept any of them as a genuine likeness of their first General. Perhaps the closest approximation was painted from Loyola's death mask by Sanchez de Coello, court painter to Philip II of Spain; it shows us Loyola as executive rather than apostle, and his friends must have noticed immediately that the artist had not captured the radiant persuasive power of his features and the fiery light in his eyes.

And why did the founder of the Society of Jesus turn out to be such an elusive subject for the portrait painter? His friends believed that this was because in the sixteen years that he had guided the destiny of the Order his own personality had been entirely consumed by the faceless, impersonal organization of the Order itself. The man and his creation were one and the same; they were no longer even distinguishable. (And, perhaps more to the point, he had steadfastly refused to sit for his portrait—even those that were painted during his lifetime were based on sketches and fleeting impressions only.) Certainly a more comprehensive index to Loyola's public personality can be found in the enormous cache of letters and administrative communiqués he left behind: There were over seven thousand letters alone, dictated or written out in his own hand; sometimes as many as thirty were sent out in a day, and each of them had to be read through twice before he would affix his signature.

The Dominican Father de Pedroche, otherwise the most unreliable of sources, was at least correct in reporting that Loyola's given name was "Iñigo." Loyola was a Basque, and "Iñigo" is the Basque version of the Spanish given name "Eñeco." His full name was "Iñigo Lopez de Oñaz y Loyola," as is quite well attested in the magistrates' records of the period, since the young squire Iñigo de Loyola was hauled before them pretty regularly for nonpayment of debts or as a result of some gambling scrape or amorous escapade. He first took the name "Ignatius" when he signed the matriculation roll at the Sorbonne in 1534. His namesake, Saint Ignatius of Antioch, who was martyred in Rome in 107 A.D., was a fairly peripheral figure in the medieval calendar of saints, so perhaps Loyola chose "Ignatius" as a more cosmopolitan equivalent of "Iñigo," or perhaps simply because the saint's day, October 17, happened to be the same as his birthday. (This is merely conjecture, since we don't know the exact date of Loyola's birth, only the year—1491.) Fourteen ninety-one was otherwise not very eventful and is probably most notable in European history as the year before 1492; in fact Loyola's oldest brother sailed with Columbus on his second voyage (in 1493). It was traditional for the oldest sons of Basque noble families to go to sea, though they really did not have a great deal of choice in the matter of a career. About the only acceptable alternative was for them to attach themselves to some noble court as a squire and take up the profession of arms, as did Ignatius himself and two of his brothers. The Basques were especially prized as soldiers, shepherds, seafarers, and administrators, and widely despised as brawlers and ruffians; both their admirers and detractors conceded that they took all the honors for endurance and tenacity. There is a famous story of a Basque petitioner who sat patiently in the antechamber of an important personage, a cardinal, for fourteen hours with nothing to eat or drink until the great man finally gave in and agreed to see him. (The petitioner's name, of course, was Ignatius de Loyola.)

The Loyolas were one of the two dozen famiies that made up the *parientes mayores,* the Basque landed gentry, which is to say that they had a great deal of pride, a great many children, and not very much land. Iñigo was the youngest of the brood, though some disagreement exists as to whether he was the eleventh of eleven or the thirteenth of thirteen. (His most recent biographer, Father Paul Imhof, S.J., mentions five sisters and seven brothers.) The Loyola family seat is well worth a visit if you ever find yourself in the Spanish Pyrenees. Take the coastal road from San Sebastian toward Bilbao, head inland at Zumaya, and before long you will have arrived in the province of Guipuzcoa. Between two tiny market towns called Azeoita and Azbeitia in a green mountain valley is the castle of Oñaz y Loyola, though actually the word "castle" sounds a trifle pretentious for this sturdy farmhouse built around a courtyard, with a lower story of dressed stone and an upper story of wood. But even so, the family had their own coat of arms, which they had carved into the stone over the main gateway: a stylized representation of two wolves springing away from each other, while between them hangs a kettle on a chain. The heraldic meaning of all this was no doubt perfectly clear at one time; today it is simply something for the old-age pensioners to argue about over their fourth glass of strong Basque red wine in the cantina in town on market days.

We know very little about Iñigo's family. His mother died when he was born, or shortly afterward, and his seafaring older brother's wife, Magdalena de Araoz, took charge of his upbringing. Iñigo left his father's house at an early age to seek his fortune, but Magdalena was to exercise, at least indirectly, a decisive influence on him during the early stages of Iñigo's metamorphosis into Ignatius. That is to say that it was she who introduced books (two of them) into the Loyola household, which many years later were still the only two to be found in the castle. It is perhaps no exaggeration to say that at no time in history has a dearth of light escapist fiction had such profound consequences for the future.

At the time we are speaking of, however, Iñigo was not a great reader. He seems to have preferred dancing, fencing, and riding, and, as we have seen, he had already developed into a bit of a rake and a ruffian. More specifically, he was repeatedly brought up on such charges as statutory rape, inflicting grievous bodily harm, and slander, and there is a notation in the records of the archbishop's court at Pamplona, which was celebrated for its leniency, describing him as "treacherous, brutal, and vindictive." This is not to say by any means that young Squire Iñigo was especially vicious or depraved. Manners were fairly rough in those days, even by the standards of our own permissive age; as the Protestant historian Heinrich Boehmer explains it, speaking of the sort of plain, unaffected habits of speech that were current among the women of

Luther's time, "the tenderest young virgins had about as much sense of propriety as a Hamburg fishwife of the present day." Moreover, for young men of Iñigo's age, the history of the world seemed already to have come to an end with the first decade of the sixteenth century. There were no new wars to fight, no discoveries to be made; someone else had already done it all. The Moors had long since been rooted out of their last Iberian stronghold in Granada, and the fame of the great Columbus was already being eclipsed by that of an upstart called Vasco da Gama, who had sailed around the southern tip of Africa and found a new route to the Indies for Portugal. King Charles was not only king of Spain, the Two Sicilies, Burgundy, and the Netherlands; in 1520 he was crowned in absentia as Emperor Charles V and was perhaps the first monarch who could truthfully claim that the sun never set on his empire.

What was there left to do for a young man of gentle birth and martial upbringing in this age of boring universal peace? Pass the time at court with amorous intrigues and tournaments, a hundred years before *Don Quixote,* in which each participant won the favor of the unattainable noble lady to whose service he was pledged. Iñigo could look forward to an undistinguished career at court; in a year or two he would be married off to a moderately eligible young lady-in-waiting, and from then on he would just get a little older, a little fatter, and a little more complacent with every year.

Then, suddenly, Squire Iñigo disappeared from court. Most of his biographers do not even attempt to explain why his career, to which he had already devoted ten years of his young life, was curtailed so abruptly. The rest speak of complicated rivalries and intrigues that forced Iñigo to give up his place. I found one source that suggested that Iñigo had actually fallen into disgrace because of an ulcerated nose (*ozena* is the medical term), which in those days was commonly supposed to be the result of secondary syphilitic necrosis. It seems likely enough that the dissolute young Squire Iñigo might have contracted syphilis (which had been epidemic throughout Europe for the past twenty years), and we might be tempted to conclude that Ignatius's early biographers had conspired to suppress this disagreeable evidence of their subject's youthful folly. (But before we follow this chain of inference any further, it may be helpful to recall that twentieth-century medicine is not necessarily as confident of its diagnosis as sixteenth-century moralists evidently were, and according to one recent authority [1951]: "The pathogen which causes this atrophy of the nasal mucosa cannot be identified with certainty." And certainly the pathology of Squire Iñigo's nose is totally irrelevant to the subsequent accomplishments of Ignatius de Loyola.)

Whatever the real reason for his departure from court, Iñigo is next heard of as the youngest officer in the life guard of Duke Antonio Manrique de Nájera, the viceroy of the kingdom of Navarre. This, as it turned out, was all to the good, since a French army crossed the Pyrenees to invade Navarre in 1521, and Iñigo found himself in the thick of things. Something was finally happening in the little world of the Basque gentry. The ostensible purpose of this campaign was to depose the current king of Navarre, who had been set on his throne in the first place by Charles's predecessor, but what the French king, Francis I, really had in mind was to inflict a crushing defeat on Charles on his own territory that would tip the balance of power throughout Western Europe (then heavily weighted in favor of Charles and the Hapsburg Empire). At first things went according to plan. The French army successfully stormed a number of fortified towns, and even received the capitulation of Pamplona, the chief city of Navarre and a place of great strategic importance. Only the citadel above the town still held out against them; Iñigo de Loyola, as an officer of the viceroy's guard, was a member of the garrison.

The French forces outnumbered the defenders by five to one, and the commandant was inclined to ask for terms; his senior officers agreed that it would be futile to try to hold out any longer. This was before they were subjected to a fiery harangue by Ensign Iñigo de Loyola that dealt primarily with knightly honor and the baseness of surrendering a fortified place without a fight. This was on Monday, May 20, 1521, the first time (that we know of) that Iñigo demonstrated his extraordinary powers of persuasion, and as is often the case with military men, a few well-spoken words on the subject of duty, honor, and country weighed much more heavily with them than the irrefutable logic of the situation. All the officers of the garrison immediately changed their minds and rushed to defend the citadel against the French.

When the French commander realized that the commandant of the citadel was not about to come out to parley, he ordered a six-hour bombardment, fire at will. In those days the science of ballistics was still in its infancy; artillerymen had only just mastered the basic principles involved—point the front end of the gun at the enemy troops, the back end at your own. With a bit of luck most of the cannonballs (which were still being made out of stone) would make it out of the barrel—there was no question of sighting or elevation—and after that they were on their own. Thus we can be sure that it was an especially lucky shot that struck one of the citadel's defenders, Ensign Loyola, shattering his right hip and breaking his left leg below the knee. Actually it seems almost fitting that Iñigo, who was raised on the chivalric ideal of hand-to-hand combat and knightly prowess, should be put out of action, as the whole idea of knighthood would be before too long, by a handful of powder and a random cannonball.

The French, who had taken the citadel after all, were now in a position to make their own chivalric gesture—the garrison was allowed to march out with what were called the full honors of war, which meant, in Iñigo's case, that he was carried on a litter to the family castle of Loyola by an honor guard of French soldiers. The entire journey, over very rough terrain, took two weeks, and the surgeons who treated him obviously did not have much confidence in their handiwork—on their advice Iñigo was offered the sacrament of extreme unction on June 28. Five days later his fever broke, and he began his long convalescence.

Since he would be confined to his bed for several months, Iñigo naturally asked for something to read, about the only distraction available in those days for a bedridden young man with two broken legs. And naturally he would have preferred to read chivalric romances, which, like their modern namesakes, were the most popular books of the day (only somewhat more respectable), all written very much according to formula and full of the same sort of clean-limbed heroes and trembling, virginal heroines that, along with Cervantes and *Don Quixote,* did so much to give chivalry a bad name. But, as you may recall, the only two books to be found in Castle Loyola had been brought there by Magdalena de Araoz when she married Iñigo's oldest brother. The first of these was *The Life of Chris.,* written by a German Carthusian called Ludolf of Saxony; the second a popular version of the Golden Legend called *Flos Sanctorum* ("The Flower of Sanctity") by Jacobus de Voragine, in other words, the lives of the saints. Since devotional and inspirational works of this kind were almost as prevalent in Spanish households of the period as chivalric romances (insofar as they were prevalent at all), the presence of these two volumes in Castle Loyola at this critical moment in Ignatius's career does not seem like too much of a coincidence. But in this context, however, it might be best to recall the words of Albert Schweitzer: "Coincidence is the pseudonym that the good Lord uses when he does not wish to be recognized." At any rate, this was the beginning of Iñigo's first serious attempt to come to grips with the doctrines of the Catholic Church; before that he had simply gone to mass and to confession and was quite content to leave it at that.

But at this point Iñigo came to a decision that suggests at first that he had not yet entirely turned his back on personal vanity and the things of this world—though it would serve very well as an example of bullet-biting Basque stoicism and determination. The bones of one of his legs had knit badly, and Iñigo was left with a bony protuberance below his left knee that was covered with scar tissue. Not a pretty sight, perhaps, but certainly not anything that would have caused him pain or other physical problems in later life, or so a number of military surgeons have assured me. A man who has already been given extreme unction, who has had what Othello would have called a "hairbreadth scape i' th' imminent deadly breach," would probably tend not to be too particular about the esthetic aspects of his recovery. But Iñigo preferred to put himself back in the hands of the quack surgeons who had treated him earlier, and they simply sawed off the offending lump of bone, scar tissue and all, while their patient, of course, was fully conscious. And finally, when the bone began to knit again, it became apparent that one of his legs was going to be shorter than the other. He attached a heavy weight to his left leg, heavier than the cannonball that had done the damage in the first place, in the hope that after many weeks of this self-inflicted racking, the leg would be stretched out and the damage undone. (In fact, probably as a result of this strange procedure, Iñigo would walk with a limp for the rest of his life.) Nevertheless, he seems to have been quite delighted with the way things turned out. "I can dance again!" he is said to have exclaimed in triumph.

All this seems to imply that Iñigo's state of mind at the end of his convalescence can only be described as frivolous. In fact it is incredible that he could have endured so much for such a superficial motive as personal vanity. A more attractive possibility is that Iñigo, like so many of his generation, shared the great dream of the High Middle Ages—the promise of uniting faith and power, spiritual and temporal authority, Pope and Emperor, in a single person. The Christian knight who would serve this ideal would surely have to have both a sound body and a pure, devout spirit. The unity of this world and the next, of knighthood and sainthood, was Iñigo's personal ideal, as it remained that of Ignatius.

In the meantime Iñigo analyzed and reflected on what he had read in his two spiritual handbooks. He discovered that certain passages were a source of comfort to him while others left him feeling desolate, as if he had been plunged into the void. He learned, naturally enough, to read selectively, to forge a kind of partnership between writer and reader. During those weeks that he lay on his sickbed, he began to grope his way toward the perfection of a spiritual exercise that would later be known as "the distinction of spirits" in the Jesuit spiritual lexicon. This became the basis for his own apostolate, and also the essential motivation of the Order itself. Jesuits understand this to mean, with various individual interpretative shadings, that one should present oneself to the world not *as* oneself but in imitation of Jesus Christ by means of one's service to mankind. It may have been this great spiritual (or psychological) transformation on the part of its founder that later gave the Order such a profoundly individual character. The external form that the Order was to take had already coalesced by this time, at least as an idea. Iñigo had envisioned an elite order of knights that, unlike the knightly orders of the Middle Ages, would find their battleground exclusively in the struggle for men's souls. Its members would follow the banner of Christ like knights following the banner of their liege lord—in his *Spiritual Exercises* Loyola speaks explicitly of two opposing armies, one of them under the banner of Satan, the other under the banner of Christ. Finally, *The Spiritual Exercises* themselves, at least in their more mechanical aspect, can also be traced back to this period, when Iñigo began to keep meticulous written records of the progress of his physical recovery. (It is perhaps worth noting that Loyola's handwriting was remarkably smooth and fluent, which, graphologists report, indicates both inner serenity and great strength of will. Apparently he had taken some trouble to learn a flowing italic hand that would make his love letters seem all the more impressive to the maids of honor at court.)

In early 1522 Iñigo set off on muleback from Castle Loyola to the shrine of the Virgin of Aranzazu, the patron saint of the Basques, where he took a vow of chastity, and then set out for the Benedictine abbey of Nuestra Señora de Montserrat, northwest of Barcelona. For three days and nights he searched his conscience, and then before the celebrated image of the Black Madonna of Montserrat, the protectress of Catalonia, he swore to dedicate himself to the service of God. He felt that the only purpose that remained for him in life was to do penance, and accordingly he presented his mule to the abbey, gave his doublet, tunic, and Basque beret to a beggar, and left his sword and scabbard hanging in the chapel of the Madonna, where so many others had left their crutches. Now his only possessions were a monk's cowl, a gourd that he used as a drinking cup, and a pilgrim's staff. For the next several months he lived as a hermit and a mendicant outside the little town of Manresa, some fifteen miles from Montserrat. He wandered the countryside at night, lost in prayer, whipped himself bloody with a scourge studded with iron barbs. Just as he had been willing to endure unspeakable agonies the previous year to restore himself to the ideal of a well-made Christian knight, now he made his life a perpetual torment until he was finally convinced that his soul was dead to the allure of this world. Squire Iñigo no longer existed—but Ignatius, the founder of an order that would come to be renowned for its austerities, had still not come into being. During this intervening period Iñigo believed that he could now die contented, since he had "richly earned the reward of eternal salvation through his penitential exercises." Fasting and scourging, illness and delirium, had brought him to the threshold of enlightenment, and these experiences "made such a strong impression on me that it was as if I had become a different person, and as if I had a totally different intellect than I had had before."

During his convalescence at Loyola he had developed his own system of notation so that he could record his progress on a kind of grid; while he was living in Manresa and Barcelona, he adapted this system so that he could monitor and record all of his emotions and "illuminations"—whether he had merely sobbed while mass was being sung, or whether he had wept, or whether he had actually been transported by "a flood of tears and sobs." The raw power of his intellect becomes apparent when Iñigo, still more accustomed to wielding a broadsword than a quill, tries to systematize his record of his ecstatic visions by means of a kind of simplified verbal code in order to keep from being overwhelmed by them. Above all he wants to remain in control, even when dealing with the irrational and the transcendent, or at least, failing that, he wants to get it all down in writing. Most of his visions do appear to be fairly straightforward and to draw on a simple and restricted vocabulary of symbols. He sees "something white," for example, "like three of the keys of the clavichord or an organ," and he interprets this as a vision of the Trinity. "Something white, not very big and not very small" is his mental image of Christ's communion with mankind, and Christ himself appears to him repeatedly as "a glowing ball, a little bigger than the sun."

Some of Loyola's biographers have seen this primitive double-entry system of the soul as a kind of preliminary study for *The Spiritual Exercises.* It seems to me that the two have just as much (or as little) in common as Goethe's *Urfaust* does with the great work of his maturity or Shakespeare's *Titus Andronicus* with *Hamlet.* There is too much distance between the hermit of Manresa, the zealot of Barcelona, and the great administrator and Superior General of the Order. A few examples will help to make this clearer:

- Iñigo hoped to bring himself closer to God by fasting and self-mortification.

  Ignatius felt otherwise. The Order emphasized self-discipline rather than self-mortification, and in its first statutes, adopted in 1539, Ignatius decreed that the brothers should abstain from "scourging themselves, going barefoot or bareheaded, eating certain foods, doing [excessive or self-imposed] penance, wearing hair shirts, or practicing other forms of self-chastisement. . . ." All penitential practices that tended to "sap one's strength" were strongly discouraged.
- Iñigo felt that every bite he ate beyond the bare minimum necessary to sustain life was sinful.

  Ignatius stipulated that the brothers' dining tables should be properly cleaned and the food both good and plentiful "as in the houses of gentlefolk."
- For Iñigo the highest goal of man was to lose himself completely, to merge with the Godhead. His ideal was the monk, who turns his back on the world, the hermit (which is what *monachos* originally meant in Greek).

  Ignatius made it very clear in the first of the statutes of 1539 that the Jesuits were not going to be a contemplative order; they would not retire into monasteries to spend their days in chanting and prayer. They would remain in the world.

Next Year in Jerusalem

Iñigo's next project, which he went about with typical Basque obstinacy and tenacity, was to set off on a pilgrimage to the Holy Land. It was no longer the goal of most adventurous young men to visit the holy places of Jerusalem as it had been a century or two earlier, and those who were simply eager to escape the poverty and monotony of their homelands usually preferred to sign on board a merchantman bound for the Indies or the New World. The future was there, after all; Jerusalem was medieval, passé. Martin Luther put it very clearly, as he always did, when he observed that "as far as God is concerned, Jerusalem and all the Holy Land is not one whit more, or less, interesting than the cows in Switzerland." And this is not to say that nothing was going on in Europe at the time: The entire continent, from the Oder to the Tagus, from Norway to Sicily, was in a fine ferment. Open warfare was about to break out between the peasants and the nobility in Germany; Luther and Zwingli were waging a pamphlet war against the excesses of the "Romish" Church, and the Turks had just driven the Knights of St. John from Rhodes and chased them back to Malta, the last Christian stronghold in the Mediterranean.

Nevertheless, Iñigo was determined to go to the Holy Land. It is none too clear why a thirty-year-old man who had served as a diplomat and a soldier should have been so naive about the political realities of the situation. He seems simply to have refused to believe that the Turks, who still allowed Christian pilgrims to visit Jerusalem, would not tolerate any sort of proselytizing or missionary activity—which is precisely what Iñigo had in mind, a one-man Christian crusade to reclaim the Holy Sepulchre.

A Parsifal, a Peter the Hermit, or a Don Quixote, for that matter, could hardly have gone off as haphazardly or as ill-prepared as this cadaverous begging friar from Barcelona. Of course, it might be said (and some of his biographers have done so) that his boundless trust in God encouraged him to believe that he would encounter some helpful Samaritan who would set him back on the track if he went astray. Perhaps so, but it could also be said that in later life Loyola seems to have learned not to depend on Him for quite so much. And in fact Iñigo eventually found a ship that would take him to Palestine. The Franciscans, who looked after the Latin holy places in Jerusalem (as they still do today), were hard pressed to convince him that his missionary ardor was commendable but misplaced, and his sojourn in the Holy Land would last no longer than any of his fellow pilgrims'. Like the others, he visited the Mount of Olives, but the standard pilgrim's itinerary, as he explains in his *Autobiography,* was not enough for him. He also wanted "to see the stone from which Our Lord ascended into Heaven," in which the imprint of the feet of Christ were still to be seen. The reason for Iñigo's special interest in this sacred relic is typical of his passion for exactness, even in matters of the spirit; he was curious to see what direction the footprints were pointing in, and thus whether Christ's Ascension had taken him to the east, the west, the north, or the south. The Franciscans decided that he had seen enough of Jerusalem, and before long he found himself back on board another vessel, outward bound, equipped for the journey with little more than his pilgrim's staff and his drinking gourd, though he had the presence of mind to fill a small casket with an assortment of stones, shards, and dried flowers he had collected from various spots that Jesus was supposed to have visited.

This strange episode is usually given short shrift by Loyola biographers, which to my way of thinking is a mistake. Iñigo's journey to the East (seemingly undertaken in much the same spirit of improvisation with which young people would set off for India or Nepal a decade or so ago) was not just the result of a naive and unworldly obsession; this was an idea that he never really abandoned and certainly continued to take seriously throughout his life. Eleven years later, on Ascension Day, August 15, 1534, he and six of his fellow students at the Sorbonne swore an oath in the chapel of St. Dénis that they would all one day make the pilgrimage to Jerusalem. Things worked out rather differently, but these seven were to become the hard kernel of the Jesuit Order, and if everything had gone according to plan, Ignatius and his companions would have devoted the rest of their lives to the conversion of the unbelievers of Palestine. Many years later, after the Order had already won its renown as the "Holy Lance of the Church," Ignatius was still drawing up an ever more ambitious plan—it is symptomatic of the ways in which his own life and personality had evolved that he was now calling for a vast crusade to reclaim the Holy Land from the Turks by force of arms. Instead of the apostolic spark of a single mendicant friar, he now believed the job would require a vast armada of a hundred ships (financed by an emergency crusading tax that would be levied on all of Christendom). In the course of half a lifetime Loyola seems to have abandoned the simple faith of the Children's Crusade for the megalomaniac zeal of a sixteenth-century crusader like Philip II of Spain, but the idea behind it remained the same all along.

When Ignatius returned to Barcelona—he was thirty-two years old by now—he decided he would be more effective serving God in a more conventional way; he decided to enter the priesthood, even though by training and temperament he was much better suited to be a crusader. At first he attended a school with some two hundred other students (the youngest of them was barely ten), picking up splinters from the unplaned wooden benches and trying to absorb the rudiments of Latin grammar and syntax. Otherwise Iñigo's ascetic manner of life was unchanged— he scourged himself three times a day, prayed for six hours each day (not forgetting his customary midnight observances), attended mass three times a week, and went to confession every Sunday. This fanatical young man who cut the soles out of his shoes and went barefoot even in winter soon began to attract a young, idealistic following in Barcelona. Women of all classes were fascinated by his extreme austerities, and soon the Inquisition began to take an interest as well. He was twice brought before the inquisitorial court, twice detained for questioning, and was denounced as a heretic no less than ten times. It was finally decided that he should complete his studies elsewhere, preferably someplace outside the inquisitors' jurisdiction and someplace where his sort of behavior would not attract quite so much attention.

The Montmartre Oath

Late in the year 1527 Iñigo set out for Paris, leading a pack mule that carried his precious library (which is to say, everything he owned) on its back. At that time the Sorbonne was the gathering place of students and scholars from all over Europe, the academic metropolis of the Western world. There were over four thousand students enrolled there when Iñigo arrived, and the whole Latin Quarter was in a state of philosophical unrest. The anticlerical spirit of Erasmus wafted through the lecture halls, and the great Humanists' new editions of Latin classics and the writings of the Church Fathers had left the old-style Scholastics and Catholic apologists with a great deal of explaining to do. "Anyone who learns Greek is a secret Lutheran!" was the war cry of the Catholic students, since Luther's German translation of the New Testament was based on Erasmus's revised Greek edition. These unruly passions often spilled out into the streets, and on Pentecost of 1527 a gang of Protestant students had knocked a statue of the Virgin off its pedestal. Erasmus, like many another great scholar of years to come, had tried to remain aloof from all this conflict and eventually ended up being stranded in no-man's land.

Ignatius, as we must call him from now on, was enrolled in the Collège de Sainte-Barbe, which was affectionately nicknamed "the asshole of Mother Theology," since apparently in spite of the new spirit of Humanism that was sweeping through the lecture rooms, the students were still breathing a danker, medieval air in the dormitories and corridors. One of Ignatius's immediate predecessors on Sainte-Barbe's weary benches was a Swiss student called Jean Chauvin, who later returned to his native Geneva and began to preach a very austere brand of Protestant theology that came to be known (from the later form of his name) as Calvinism. Certain parallels between the administrative structure of the Calvinist academy in Geneva and the constitution of the Society of Jesus suggest that these two great adversaries may have both had the familiar routine of the College of Sainte-Barbe in mind as a model. The idea that Ignatius Loyola and John Calvin must have attended some of the same lectures, perhaps even sat in the same row, is certainly compelling, but there is another matter, one that is generally slighted by Ignatius's biographers, that seems to me to be of greater practical interest. Namely, how did Ignatius pay his tuition, and what did he live on during his seven years at the Sorbonne? Living in Paris was not cheap, even for students, who were usually subsidized by the various monastic orders. But since Ignatius was not on the best of terms with the Inquisition when he left Spain, he certainly could not have counted on these to look after him. He seems to have had a number of well-wishers and admirers in Barcelona who sent him a small stipend—but never quite enough apparently, since he was obliged to go off on fund-raising expeditions to Flanders and London to ask for alms from the merchants in the Spanish trading colonies there.

Before long Ignatius had gathered a small circle of close friends around him—they might almost be called converts or disciples, since it had been his intention from the outset to recruit them for the great enterprise he was determined to carry out. The first of his companions to be won over was one of his two roommates, Peter Faber (Pierre Favre), born in 1506, a Savoyard peasant's son with an enormous appetite as well as an unslakable thirst for knowledge. Ignatius offered to supplement Peter's short rations out of their meager housekeeping fund and treat him to a lavish feast on the proviso that Peter would devote himself to prayer and meditation just as rigorously as Ignatius did himself. Peter Faber lived up to his part of the bargain, and eventually became one of the leaders of the infant Jesuit Order.

Ignatius had to devise a very different strategy for his other roommate, a Spaniard called Francisco de Jassu y Xavier, who was born in Navarre in 1506. Francis Xavier was the perfect type of the good-looking, pleasure-loving undergraduate—charming, athletic, musical, witty, successful with women, and naturally a little vain from being lionized and fussed over so much. Ignatius finally wore down his resistance by tirelessly sounding that favorite theme of sixteenth-century moralists— the emptiness of the pleasures of the flesh, the transitoriness of all worldly things. Perhaps surprisingly, Francis Xavier not only proved receptive to this message, he ultimately became "the Apostle to the Indies," the first and most successful of the Jesuit missionaries to India and Japan, and was canonized by the Roman Catholic Church. On all his travels Francis Xavier kept with him a slip of paper with the names of his six original comrades written on it so that, symbolically at least, he would never be separated from them. He treated Ignatius with such deference that he actually knelt when he was composing a letter to him or reading one of his replies.

The third member of Ignatius's Parisian circle was Nicholas Boabdilla, another Spaniard, who was born in 1509. As with Peter Faber, Ignatius is said to have won over Boabdilla by appealing to his ruling passion, which was billiards. Ignatius would only agree to play on the condition that Boabdilla would reciprocate by participating in a session of spiritual exercises for every game he lost. Ignatius had already proved himself adept at putting into practice a maxim that was later adopted as the watchword of the Jesuit Order—"To be all things to all men, so that they may be all things for all men"—though perhaps it would have been better if Ignatius had been a less accomplished player. Boabdilla turned out to be a fairly irascible character, and on one occasion, for example, Ignatius was compelled to recall him from a mission to Germany because his brusque, unpleasant manner had already made too many enemies. Boabdilla survived all his comrades: He died in 1590, at the age of eighty-one.

The Portuguese Simon Rodriguez, born in 1510, and the Spaniard Alfonso Salmeron, the youngest in the group, born in 1512, both played more distinguished roles in the early history of the Order. Salmeron's name is even mentioned in the archives of the Elizabethan secret service, since informers had identified him as one of the organizers of the Catholic underground in England. Ignatius's closest personal friend of the six was Diego Lainez, a Spaniard of Jewish extraction who was born in 1512. Lainez seems to have been very impulsive and hot-tempered by nature, and Ignatius always treated him much more severely than any of the others, during the early days in Paris and afterward as well. In retrospect this appears to have been part of a protracted rite of initiation, since shortly before his death Ignatius chose Lainez to succeed him as General of the Order. The intemperate Lainez made a remarkably evenhanded and judicious General.

And as we have seen, on Ascension Day, August 15, 1534, Ignatius and his six bearded young companions—they ranged in age from eighteen to twenty-six—made their way across the city from the Latin Quarter to the hill of Montmartre and the crypt of St. Dénis. There they took their vows of poverty and chastity, and they also solemnly promised to make a pilgrimage to the Holy Land. If a year's time had passed and they had been unable to fulfill their vow, they would then petition the Holy Father to set them some other task to carry out. At this point Ignatius and his comrades had no clear intention of founding a new religious order (in spite of what the history books might tell you), and their desire to serve God by serving his people was almost as vague and ill-defined as it was impassioned. Montmartre was chosen not so much for its associations with the martyred St. Dénis as because it was the poorest neighborhood in Paris. The municipal gallows was located on the crest of the hill, which tended to keep rents low, and even after the gallows disappeared, it was the cheapness, to say nothing of the squalor, of the neighborhood, not the splendid view from the steps of the Basilica, that made Montmartre the artists' and students' quarter in the nineteenth century.

The Montmartre oath may have caused a mild stir among the theology students at the Sorbonne, but the real news of 1534 involved more consequential personalities, such as Luther and Henry VIII, as well as the Pope, Clement VII, and the question of what he proposed to do about the other two. Luther's German Bible had just been published in its entirety (the New Testament had appeared separately in 1522), which was about to turn the steady torrent of defections from the Roman Church in Germany into something more like a deluge. Henry VIII had made good on his threat of many years' standing, and the Act of Supremacy, passed by Parliament in 1534, established the Church of England as a totally independent entity (and finally authorized Henry's highly problematical divorce from his first wife, Katharine of Aragon, and left him free to marry Anne Boleyn). It must have been clear enough in Rome that more was going on here than could be explained simply as the result of the frustrated ardor of a lovesick monarch. The swaggering tone of the following letter, sent by Henry to Pope Clement, certainly suggests that papal supremacy, in England at least, had become purely a matter of political and diplomatic expediency, even before the final break occurred: "Make the King satisfied with regard to his marriage in order to avoid the injurious consequences for the Church that will unquestionably ensue if his wishes were to be thwarted." (This document was kept in the secret archives of the Vatican, safe from historians' prying eyes, until 1981.)

Both of these events were to have portentous consequences for the Jesuit Order in years to come, but for the moment Ignatius and his compatriots were only concerned with finishing up their studies and setting out for Jerusalem. All seven had qualified for the master of arts degree (though this was more like the equivalent of a Ph.D. today), and in October 1537 they rented a dilapidated empty house in the countryside between Venice and Vicenza, where they planned to wait for a ship that would take them to the Holy Land. They made good use of this time "by preaching in hospitals and in the poorer quarters, and teaching children to say their catechism," or as Ignatius himself described it, "They each went to a different place, and at the very same hour of the same day they began to preach. Then they cried out in loud voices for the people to draw near and waved their caps in the air. The sermons that they preached caused a great sensation in the city, and not a few of those who heard them were convinced to lead a pious life." Other accounts say much the same thing, but with all due respect, it seems hardly likely that Ignatius and his colleagues could have been up to much in the way of preaching at this point. None of them was really competent in Italian, certainly not fluent enough to sway a crowd of unbelievers or even to get the simplest point across. (Even in later life Ignatius's difficulties with Latin and Italian were notorious.) So we can suppose that though they may well have caused a sensation and the reactions of the crowds may have been most encouraging, it is doubtful that the long-term effects were quite so impressive.

However, they were certainly more effective in their work with the poor and the sick, especially those afflicted with what were generally referred to as "loathsome diseases." Cleansing sores, draining abscesses, and other tasks of this kind, beloved of medieval mystics because they exactly symbolized their disdain for the world and the flesh, recommended themselves to missionaries in particular, since not only were these patients even more shamefully neglected than others, but also because working among them had a kind of morbid glamour that was certain to attract notice. It was probably not coincidental that the Theatine Order, founded in 1524, was the first to make Venice the focus of its charitable and humanitarian activities, since the Queen of the Adriatic, with some 12,000 registered prostitutes out of a population of 162,000, certainly qualified as a priority patient, both from the moral and the medical standpoint. The Theatine Order—which eventually was to provide the Church with more than two thousand bishops—was strongly motivated by the desire to reform from within, and their constant efforts to surpass themselves in the performance of good works won them an excellent reputation among all sectors of society. (This combination of elitism and ambition was sure to appeal to Ignatius's Basque instincts.)

By the time Ignatius and his companions had been in Venice for a year, it was obvious that their pilgrimage to Jerusalem had become a political impossibility. The Turks and the Venetians had been drawn in on opposite sides of the struggle between the French and the Emperor Charles V (the Venetians were allies of the Emperor, who also ruled over most of Italy). So, just as they had agreed to do in the chapel of St. Dénis, they were obliged to "offer our services to the Pope," though none of them had any idea what this would actually entail. Despite the constitutional vagueness of their enterprise, their first year together in Venice had only intensified their feelings of solidarity. Ignatius and his six original companions had been joined by several Frenchmen by this time, and they agreed that their little community should not be broken up even if they were to be separated by their new assignments. They resolved to found an order "that the community might survive."

THE FOUNDING OF THE SOCIETY OF JESUS

Conditions were certainly favorable for the founding of a new religious order, or indeed for almost any kind of reformist tendency within the Church. The consensus seemed to be that something would have to be done to prevent vast numbers of the faithful from becoming even more embittered and disillusioned. Accordingly a special commission of cardinals was assembled to draft a report on the abuses and errors that were prevalent in the Church. (Some say, though this is probably too good to be true, that this was the origin of the phrase "cardinal sins.") In any case, the cardinals quickly discovered that they had their work cut out for them. Among other things, a great many bishops were living with their mistresses, and far from their dioceses; ordinary diocesan business was transacted by secretaries and paid subordinates. Many priests insisted on cash on the barrelhead before they would perform any of the rites of the Church for their parishioners; many of their churches were more like warehouses or brokerage houses than houses of God. And as Cardinal Contarini tartly observed, many convents were no better than brothels, in which "self-styled nuns engaged in indecent pastimes to inflame the desires of their clients." Even the popes were taken to task for trying to rule like absolute monarchs.

And since it is not so easy to correct such abuses when they have become ingrained in existing institutions, the papal Curia encouraged, as never before or since, the establishment of new religious orders. We have already met with the Theatine Order, founded in 1524. They were followed by the Capuchins (1528), the Barnabites, and the Ursuline Order of nuns (1535), and the Hospitallers of St. John of God (1537). It was not all that surprising that Ignatius and his companions should have decided to turn their missionary fellowship into a more permanent sort of institution.

"We divided up into three or four groups and set out on the road to Rome. I was with Favre and Lainez," Ignatius later recalled in his *Autobiography* (which was actually a collection of reminiscences transcribed and prepared for publication by Father Luis Gonzales da Camera in 1553). In November 1537 they crossed the Milvian Bridge and entered the city of Rome, where Pope Paul III had occupied the Throne of Peter for three years. Before his accession Alexandro Farnese was better known to the people of Rome by his nickname, "the Petticoat Cardinal"; he was so called because his priestly vow of chastity was probably the one he took least seriously. His sister, the beautiful Giulia Farnese, is said to have had a great deal to do with his rapid advancement through the hierarchy, since she was commonly supposed to have been the mistress of Pope Alexander VI (Rodrigo Borgia, who reigned from 1492 to 1503). Ignatius was quick to realize that in this sort of atmosphere his cause was unlikely to advance very far without an influential friend at court, and it seems only fitting that the uncrowned queen of Rome in those days was Donna Costanza Farnese, who was also the Pope's illegitimate daughter. Ignatius is said to have persuaded her to intercede for him and his friends. Finally, by haunting various anterooms and causing as many strings to be pulled as possible, Ignatius succeeded in winning Pope Paul's approval. *"Hic est digitus Dei!"* ("This is the fingerstroke of God!") the Holy Father is supposed to have exclaimed when he was first presented with the plan for a new religious order that would combat the spread of the Lutheran heresy. On another occasion he is said to have taken leave of Ignatius and his companions after an audience with the words "Italy is become the true Jerusalem, since ye would set about this great work in God's church." Like most memorable remarks of this kind, these were probably thought up by someone else altogether at a later date—for one thing, the original statutes of 1539 are only marginally concerned with the role of the Order as the prospective scourge of the Lutherans. It is difficult to imagine that a flinty-eyed old politico like Paul III—as Titian's famous portraits certainly show him to have been— would have had much time to spare for a little band of fanatics like Ignatius and his friends. Though he was not nearly as irreligious as certain aspects of his private life might imply, Pope Paul was primarily a diplomat. The situation was not quite as precarious as it had been a dozen years earlier (when Rome itself was sacked by a mercenary army that the Emperor had neglected to pay off), but the French were still at war with the Empire, the Turks were rampaging through Central Europe and had already appeared at the gates of Vienna, and the Venetians were preparing their fleet to sail against the Turks.

It was the responsibility of one of the papal chancelleries to examine Ignatius's petition in detail and, more important, to investigate the petitioner himself, since the old accusations of heresy had recently been revived by the Inquisition. However, Ignatius and his friends were given a clean bill of health and were finally certified to be "reforming priests" in good standing who had been making themselves useful in various capacities all over Italy. Ignatius had originally drafted the statutes of the Order, the so-called *Formula Instituti,* on June 24, 1539, and on September 3 this document was orally approved by the Pope. But it was not until September 27, 1540, over a year later, that the new order was formally authorized by the bull *Regimini militantis ecclesiae* ("On the Supremacy of the Church Militant"). (The word *bull,* by the way, comes from *bulla,* the Latin word for "bubble" or "capsule," which refers to the special lead seal that is affixed to a papal edict. Not every bull has won undying fame, and a great many of them might be considered, at best, curiosities of social history—such as the bull issued by Paul's mentor, Alexander VI, which prescribed that a monk's tonsure had to be at least the size of the papal seal. This was presumably necessary to prevent monks from rearranging their hair and trying to pass themselves off as laymen, probably for reasons that even a Borgia pope could not bring himself to countenance. A papal bull had to bear some twenty signatures in order to be technically valid, which meant that it was just about impossible to keep its contents from leaking out before it was actually promulgated. Thus, for more consequential matters, the Vatican came to prefer the breve [Latin *brevis,* "brief"], which only required two signatures. The decision to dissolve the Jesuit Order in 1773, for example, was announced in such a breve.)

The Order as originally constituted was a "minimal society," as Ignatius called it, which meant that although his enemies in the Curia (and he had quite a few of them) had not succeeded in having the project suppressed altogether, they had managed to impose a very critical limitation—the Society of Jesus was to consist of no more than sixty members. Ignatius managed to circumvent this very neatly and jesuitically; only sixty brothers would be permitted to take all four vows, but the Order would accept an unlimited number who had not taken the fourth vow.

As a matter of fact, when Ignatius first drew up the statutes of the Order in June of 1539, he already had the name "Societas Jesu" firmly fixed in his mind—a martial designation for a *"compañía"* that "will do battle in the Lord God's service under the banner of the Cross." The word *Jesuit* never appears in his writings, however; he preferred to speak of "the most humble society of Jesus." The name "Societas Jesu" was regarded as the height of presumption by many clerics, since it seemed to imply that other Christians were *not* of that exclusive company. Ignatius simply replied, "Since we acknowledge no other leader than Our Lord Jesus Christ, it is fitting that we have come together as the compañía Jesus Christus." Nevertheless, the name continued to be a thorn in the side of many good Catholics, and some years later, in 1590, Pope Sixtus V decided to change the "offensive" name "Societas Jesu" to the less controversial (if less euphonious) "Ignatine Order." The General of the Order at that time, a resourceful Neapolitan called Claudio Aquaviva, wrote to the Pope that, for his part, his own conscience and the respect he bore for the memory of Ignatius Loyola would not permit him to undertake such a change on his own, but, of course, if the Holy Father still felt it to be advisable, then how could it possibly be otherwise? (That was the gist of it, at any rate.) The Pope went ahead and ordered the decree to be drawn up; Aquaviva instructed his novices to make a novena, a nine-day cycle of prayer, as a sign of Christian resignation to the inevitable. The Pope died on the ninth day of the novena, without having signed the decree, and his successor, Urban VII, decided simply to leave things as they were.

However, in 1620, the archbishop of Paris tried to convince his sovereign, Henry IV, that this "overweening and provocative name" should no longer be tolerated within the borders of Henry's kingdom. Henry was a Protestant by upbringing, a pragmatist by conviction who had found it well worth his while to trade in his religion for a kingdom ("Paris is worth a mass" was the way he put it.) He may not have ordinarily had much sympathy for the Jesuits, but, unlike almost everyone else in the seventeenth century, he was willing to tolerate a certain amount of diversity in matters of religion. "Some of my worthy peers," Henry wrote back to the archbishop, "are Knights of the Holy Ghost. There is also an Order of the Holy Trinity, and in Paris we have a congregation of nuns who call themselves the Daughters of God. Since we have all of these among us already, how could we possibly object to a Society of Jesus as well?"

Today the pros and cons of this issue are somewhat obscured by the fact that it is sufficient for a Jesuit to identify himself by the simple initials S.J. to proclaim his membership in the Society of Jesus—or, as the old seminarian's joke has it—the Society of Jesus Christ, S.J. (Incidentally the word *Jesuit* seems to have been around for many years before the Society of Jesus ever existed: the German Carthusian Heinrich Arnoldi of Saxony, who died in 1470, speaks of the *Jesuiten*, the hosts of the blessed who have won eternal salvation through the intervention of Jesus Christ.)

In early April 1541 the members of the newly established Order met to elect their first General. In the first ballot Ignatius received eveyone's vote but his own; he declined the nomination. The second ballot brought the same result, but only after his confessor (a Franciscan friar) made a personal appeal to his conscience on behalf of the others would he consent to serve. This was on April 19, 1541. (The crucifix and mosaic image of the Madonna before which Ignatius knelt to pray after his election can still be seen today in the choir loft of the Church of San Paolo fuori le mure [St. Paul Without the Walls].) Historians of many persuasions have puzzled over the question of why Ignatius twice declined the office to which he had been elected unanimously by his comrades. Certainly this was a fitting conclusion to his two decades of struggle and self-denial and no less appropriate to his apostolic calling and his sense of mission. Why then did he decline? It has sometimes been suggested that it was really Diego Lainez who deserved the credit for the creation of the Order and that Ignatius was accordingly reluctant to usurp the place that was rightfully his. Ingenious perhaps, but totally implausible—this is squarely contradicted by the record of every day of Ignatius's life, from his vigil before the Virgin of Montserrat to the day of his death.

It seems most probable, in fact, that Ignatius was guided by a realistic appraisal of his own physical capacity to carry out the duties of the office, rather than by any motives of false modesty or some sort of crisis of confidence. He was already fifty years old—an old man by sixteenth-century standards (his colleague Lainez died at fifty-three). Ignatius certainly realized that the first General of Order would have an enormous task ahead of him, but that he would be serving strictly as a desk officer, an administrator rather than as an apostle among the masses of the people or a missionary in the field. Perhaps he was reluctant to abandon his career as a missionary so soon after it had begun. But once he was convinced to take on the job, he went at it with superhuman energy, despite his failing health (gallstones and chronic heart trouble). Not surprisingly he turned out to be the sort of general who demands as much from others as he did from himself and was meticulously concerned with the most trifling details of his command. "I would very much like to know," he once remarked, "exactly how many fleas are tormenting my brothers at night."

After sixteen years of tireless activity he had built up an international organization of a totally distinctive character, created, in other words, in his image, so that every word that was spoken, every deed that was undertaken, every breath that was drawn by a Jesuit could have only one purpose—the advancement of the Roman Catholic Church. Ignatius himself hardly slackened the pace even on his deathbed, and it is instructive that he died without receiving extreme unction or the Pope's blessing, as it turned out, simply so that the day's official correspondence could get out on schedule. On Tuesday, July 28, 1556, the sixty-five-year-old invalid, in the throes of a critical gall-bladder attack, still managed to dictate a packet of letters. He received Holy Communion on that day, and on Thursday his secretary, Juan de Polanco—"my hands and my feet," as the bedridden Ignatius called him—discussed the next batch of letters, which were destined for the Spanish province (for administrative purposes the Order in Europe was divided into thirteen provinces—there were over a thousand members by 1566). In the afternoon Ignatius asked that the Pope be sent for to give him his final blessing, but Polanco suggested that this could be postponed until the following day, since they still had so much correspondence to get through. Ignatius answered, "I would rather it were today than tomorrow, but do as you think best." Polanco decided to give priority to the Spanish correspondence.

A nursing brother had kept vigil at Ignatius's bedside ever since the onset of his final illness. Early the next morning, Friday, July 31, he heard Ignatius's voice raised in prayer but thought little of it, since Ignatius was accustomed to pray at night whenever he had difficulty sleeping, and the brother decided not to disturb him. Apparently Ignatius also did not wish to give any trouble, since he died silently before dawn, at some time between five and six o'clock.

Just sixty-six years later, on March 12, 1622, the newly canonized St. Ignatius Loyola and St. Francis Xavier were welcomed into the company of the 1,848 blessed saints of the Roman Catholic Church. The ceremony in St. Peter's turned into an unprecedented display of ecclesiastical pomp, pageantry, and extravagance; as an eyewitness described it, "The central aisle of the basilica when everything was almost in readiness was overflowing with a great gathering of the faithful. A flourish of silver trumpets opened the ceremony, then the Sistine Choir began to sing. The walls were covered with tapestries, and from the cupola hung gigantic banners painted with the likenesses of the new-created saints. The fact that these two were chosen to be canonized, as well as the pomp and splendor of the ceremony itself, was an expression of the reborn spirit of the Catholic Church, of the triumph of the Blessed Virgin over Luther and Calvin." (Luther and Calvin would probably not have been terribly surprised by all this, but Ignatius Loyola would have been profoundly chagrined.)

It was at about this time that the way in which Ignatius is portrayed, both verbally and pictorially, ceases to be recognizably human and finally becomes a kind of indistinct, venerable blur, like one of his ecstatic visions at Manresa. Two excellent examples of this trend can still be seen in Rome—the first is the ceiling fresco in the Church of San Ignatio, the second Jesuit church to be built, in which Ignatius's ascent into heaven is rendered with a lavish baroque palette. The second is the statue in St. Peter's of a very militant St. Ignatius trampling underfoot a grotesque monster that probably represents error and unbelief (and the heretical views of Luther and Calvin in particular). Ignatius is the only one of the many saints in St. Peter's nave who is taking such a strong line against unorthodoxy.

Pope Paul IV (not to be confused with Ignatius's original patron, Paul III) responded to the news of Ignatius's death by saying, "The Jesuits have lost their idol." Then he is supposed to have added, sotto voce, "Ignatius ruled over the society like a tyrant." Paul was not the only one who felt this way. Nicholas Boabdilla, the hot-tempered billiards player of Ignatius's student days, addressed a memorial to Pope Paul shortly thereafter in which he gives a remarkably outspoken critique of Ignatius's strengths and weaknesses as General, and the current leadership of the Order. He begins by touching briefly on the *Constitutions* of the Order:

> Ignatius alone drew it up, and he put in, as he always did, just what he thought fit. . . . It is a labyrinth of confusion, so bewildering that the superiors [of the Order] have never been able to understand it; most of them have simply ignored it. . . . The Society has been given so many privileges and freedoms by various apostolic [papal] bulls that the name Jesuit has fallen into disrepute. . . . After the great Ignatius's death, there were three [evidently Lainez, Polanco, and Hieronymus Nadal] who tried to mimic him, down to the smallest particular, so that once again the reputation of the Society was injured by it. . . . No doubt Ignatius was a wise man, but he was still only a man, and, as your Holiness knows, he was not to be dissuaded from holding certain opinions. Let us retain only the good ideas and not be too stubborn about defending the bad ones.

The actual purpose of this document, as may already be clear, was to persuade the Pope that now that Ignatius was gone the affairs of the Order should be managed by a consortium of the five founding members who had survived him. Boabdilla did not make any headway with this not entirely disinterested proposal at the time, and the memorial itself had been lying forgotten in the Vatican archives for some four hundred years when Pope John Paul II finally got around to curbing the power of the Superior General by installing Father Paolo Dezza, whose official title was "papal delegate," as the acting head of the Jesuit Order in 1981. This was a kind of slap on the wrist—or rather more like a sharp tug on the reins—that is without precedent in the history of the Order and is certainly not envisioned in its statutes or *Constitutions*. How much of an effect this will have on real power exercised by future generals and the structure of the Order itself will probably not be apparent for many years to come—it is part of the Jesuits' iron-fist-in-the-velvet-glove approach to strategic and disciplinary matters that changes of this sort are scarcely noticed when they occur. What really went on at the extraordinary convocation of Jesuit provincials that took place at the Villa Cavaletti in Rome in early 1982 is still cloaked in diplomatic obscurity. It is certainly not clear how the eighty-year-old "Father Legate" intends to exercise his commission from the Pope, which gives him a very free hand, since it merely instructs him to "oversee the administration of the Order until such time as a new general should be chosen." In the meantime the Father Legate's path has not been entirely free from pitfalls, some of them apparently having been dug especially for him (a subject we will be getting back to in our final chapter).*

---

*On September 13, 1983, the Thirty-third General Congregation elected Father Peter-Hans Kolvenbach, rector of the Oriental Institute in Rome, as Superior General of the Order and accepted the resignation of both Father Dezza and the "Vicar pro tem" Father O'Keefe (who was widely regarded as General Arrupe's chosen successor). [Tr.]

PART ❧ II

ESPRIT DE CORPS—THE FIRST PRINCIPLES OF
THE SOCIETY OF JESUS

You may find every imaginable kind of Jesuit, including an atheist, but you will never find one who is humble.

—*Denis Diderot*

You must realize that man does not only serve God by praying; otherwise all prayer that did not go on for twenty-four hours a day would be too short.

—*Ignatius Loyola*

The Meek Shall Inherit the Earth—the Four Vows

The standard catchphrases that have attached themselves like reliable echoes to the word *Jesuit* over the centuries—"blindly obedient," "fanatically loyal," and so on—like most echoes, are inclined to be deceptive. Such phrases as these do not really tell us very much about what is unique about the Order; a more suitable watchword, in fact, was coined by one of Loyola's original companions—*contemplativus in actione*—and the Society of Jesus was intended from the beginning to be an order, unlike any of its predecessors, in which the emphasis was very much on the active side of things rather than the purely contemplative. As Ignatius himself expressed it, "There will be no harm done if the others surpass us in fasts and vigils and other austerities. . . . Instead I would very much wish that true and perfect obedience, together with a voluntary renunciation of the individual's own will and judgment, should be manifest in all those who serve in the Society of Jesus." In practice this meant that the Jesuits differed from the other orders in various external ways as well. They did not wear a distinctive habit, they were not cloistered (i.e., they did not live in monasteries), and consequently they did not chant the liturgy or participate in communal prayer of any kind. (Prayer and meditation was and is strictly an individual matter with the Jesuits.) Ignatius also intended to break away from the old monastic tradition of scholarship; "neither studies nor reading aloud [as many monastic orders did during meals and during the evenings] in the Society of Jesus" runs a notation in the first draft of the statutes of the Order. However, the pursuit and transmission of knowledge became one of the Order's main concerns before too long; there were already twenty-nine Jesuit academies in existence within twenty years of Loyola's death.

There were also four basic organization differences that distinguished them from the other orders, and these deserve a word or two of explanation on their own. First, the *compañía* was to be headed by a Superior General, which in itself was nothing new, since the Franciscans and the Dominicans had generals of their own; these, however, did not enjoy the almost unlimited power of the Jesuit General. The second difference involves the notorious fourth vow, by which Jesuits who have completed a long probationary period (more on this shortly) simply pledge "particular obedience with regard to apostolic missions," though the original version that was incorporated into the *Formula Instituti,* the spiritual prospectus of the Order in 1539, is both more explicit and considerably more elaborate: "We pledge ourselves to obey every instruction of the Pope of Rome, to go in whatsoever direction he might choose to send us . . . even if this should take us among the Turks or any other infidels. We are prepared to go even unto the realm that is called the Indies or among heretics or unbelievers of any kind. . . ." This may seem more than a little quaint to us today, especially since the authors' apostolic fervor seems to have far outstripped their real awareness of the world outside. (The mention of the Turks and the "realm called the Indies" probably taxed their knowledge of geography to the limit.) There were also certain priorities to be observed; missionary work among the heathen—Ignatius was clearly still haunted by his vision of the earthly Jerusalem—took precedence, and the heretics are quite a bit farther down on the list.

This "special vow" of obedience to the Pope is still very much in force, and Pope Paul VI was not above exploiting this for its full propaganda value. When General Pedro Arrupe was granted his first audience with the newly elected pontiff in 1965, the Vatican press office released a photograph of Arrupe on his knees before the Apostolic Throne, as if to say that even if the Jesuits had gotten a little bit out of hand during the days of Vatican II, at least their General still knew his place, namely, prostrate at the feet of the Holy Father. It is also part of this tradition that no Jesuit ever criticizes the reigning pope, though of course the key word here is "explicitly." In cases where the Order and the Holy Father are not getting along too well, as sometimes happens, the precedent was suggested by Ignatius himself; a group of Jesuits who wanted to publicly criticize Paul IV were admonished by their General not even to mention Paul by name, but simply to lavish all the praise they could manage on his undistinguished predecessor, Marcellus II.

The Order has not always shown such restraint, however, especially if it is felt that the current Pope has trespassed flagrantly on some special preserve of theirs. When Sixtus V made it known that he was about to issue a bull expressing his disapproval of the Jesuit theologians' interpretation of certain points of doctrine, General Claudio Aquaviva forgot his fourth vow altogether and resorted to outright intimidation. "If Your Holiness," he wrote, "should inflict such a humiliation on the Order, then there is no way that I can guarantee that ten thousand Jesuits will not pick up their pens to attack this bull in a manner that is certain to prove detrimental to the prestige of the Holy See." This is an unusually candid admission of the power of the Order—as well as an expression of the pride that its members take in their preeminence in the realm of publicity and controversy as well as theology.

As for the third organizational difference, a Jesuit is expected to remain a Jesuit and not to accept any other ecclesiastical office or any higher rank that is not bestowed by the Order. When a Jesuit is made a bishop or a cardinal (as was Augustin Bea by Pope John XXIII), then the word invariably runs through Jesuit circles that "the Pope's got something against the Order; he's just made one of us a cardinal." Numerous exceptions to this rule have been made at one time or another on the grounds of urgent necessity. The Counter-Reformation Pope Gregory XIII (who reigned from 1572 to 1585) was unwilling to deprive himself of the slightest tactical advantage in his struggle against Protestantism, so he decreed that every papal legate should have a Jesuit adviser on his personal staff.

Finally, the fourth difference: The Jesuit's cure of souls is not sharply defined and his activity is certainly not restricted to the parish and the pulpit. The boundaries of his parish extend to wherever the soothing influence of the Church is needed, and the Jesuit's pulpit might be the roof of a camper, a scaffold on a construction site, or the speaker's dais of the UN General Assembly.

Stronger than Convent Walls—the Four Vows

As with other religious orders, the prospective Jesuit must undergo a period of testing and instruction called the novitiate. But unlike other orders, the Jesuits have also installed a second screening process by which candidates are reviewed before they are permitted to take their first three vows. In one memorable case a Flemish novice called Cornelius van der Steen was turned down by the selection committee solely on the grounds that he was too short and slight to make a Jesuit. The committee informed van der Steen that they were prepared to waive the height requirement, but only with the proviso that he would learn to recite the entire Bible by heart. The story would hardly be worth telling if van der Steen had not complied with this rather presumptuous request, and under his Latin name, Cornelius a Lapide, he became one of the greatest biblical scholars of his time (which was around the beginning of the seventeenth century). Today the Jesuits are hardly in a position to set quotas or turn away otherwise qualified candidates on such frivolous grounds; in fact, in Europe at least, the Order seems to be on the verge of extinction. In 1983 the two Jesuit seminaries in Germany had a total enrollment of thirty; in Spain the total number of novices has decreased by 90 percent in recent years. Only in the Third World has the Order really managed to replenish its ranks from year to year. Still, the Jesuits are not about to relax the strictness of their entrance requirements, which have remained relatively constant since the days of Cornelius van der Steen. To use the language of the help-wanted columns and the industrial psychologists, they are still looking for "spiritually advanced, mature young men (eighteen or over) of sound judgment, good leadership qualities, able to give and follow orders, with a history of good relations with family and significant others, ability to participate fully in life of their community, and the capacity to love."

The Jesuit's novitiate lasts for two years, twice as long as in the other orders, and in general the Jesuit's progress from one plateau to the next is painfully slow. Twelve years after he has been accepted into the Order (which would make him at least thirty), a brother is finally permitted to take the fourth vow, which earns him the title of "professor." This is purely a sign of spiritual rather than academic attainments, since the vows are called "professions" in ecclesiastical language, though it is true that the letters *S.J.* after one's name are still regarded as a more convincing badge of intellectual achievement than *Dr.* or *Ph.D.* At any rate it takes longer to become a Jesuit "professor" than it does a surgeon or a psychiatrist.

Until recently the novitiate was a kind of prolonged forced march in the course of which the novice could never break out of step or look off in any direction but straight ahead. In 1942 a German Jesuit called Father Rudolf Mayer could still write from his prison cell that "the routine of life inside reminds me of the days I spent as a novice at Feldkirch." Here, in fact, is a typical daily schedule from the seminary at Feldkirch from the year 1900; the comparison seems to be valid at least to the extent that both are total institutions in which the inmates' lives are seamlessly planned and very little is left to individual initiative.

5:00 A.M.	Wake up
5:25	Devotions in the chapel
5:30	Meditation in the common room
6:30	Mass
7:15	Breakfast—strict silence is observed—followed by bedmaking and other household tasks
8:45	*Instructio* by Pater Magister (instruction in the rules of the Order by the master of novices)
9:30	*Opera*—helping to prepare the midday meal, setting places in the refectory, working in the garden, cleaning, dusting, and so on
10:15	Coffee, followed by devotions
10:30	Devotional reading or sacred studies
12:00	Reading from *The Imitation of Christ*
12:15	Examination (of one's conscience, i.e., a meditative technique devised by Loyola) and prayer of thanksgiving
12:30	Midday meal (reading aloud, service at table); devotions, followed by recreation in the garden (with Latin conversations twice a week)
2:00	Rosary

2:30	Instruction in Latin and Greek
3:15	Athletics and gardening
4:15	Coffee
4:45	*Instructio*
5:30	Evening meditation
6:15	Litany and collect
6:30	Dinner, recreation
8:10	The master of novices reads out the subjects for the next day's meditation; examination
9:15	Lights out

(Twice a week novices were permitted to go out walking between two and four, and once a week they were permitted to go on short excursions into town or to go swimming, beginning at eight in the morning.)

Actually there is a sound psychological basis for this totally prepackaged existence, as may become clearer after reading this letter written by General Vitelleschi to the provincial of the Rhineland, Johannes Cooper, in 1628: "Your Reverence wishes to have a novice to whom saints and angels have appeared at times kept occupied with so many tasks that he could not possibly have the time to entertain such fancies. The master of novices should entreat him to pray to God that he might be spared such dangerous and not infrequently deceptive visions in future." The novice also receives instruction in the *Constitutions* of the Order, which is, in effect, the code by which all of his conduct will be governed for the rest of his life. Part of this work in particular, the *Examen Generale,* is the novice's constant study for his two years at the seminary, and he will be tested almost continuously on his mastery of its contents. During this time the novice must also select the form of prayer that he finds most congenial to his particular temperament: he must find his own place within the Order and in the larger context of the Church. Above all he must do a great deal of thinking about what it means to submit to the Jesuit Rule, since the Society of Jesus is an authoritarian or (to put it more politely) a highly structured, hierarchical society.

The novice's routine of *opera* and *instructio* is occasionally varied by what is called an "experiment" (which in Latin means something more like "experience"), working for a short time in a hospital or factory, but the most important event of the novitiate is the four-week-long exercises, the same ones devised by Loyola, which we have already encountered and which we will be getting back to shortly, since they deserve a chapter all to themselves.

After two years the novice is ready to take the three initial vows of poverty, chastity, and obedience, and he also makes a solemn undertaking to join the Order after he has finished his education. Now the candidate is known as a "scholastic," and any further training he might receive in a secular university or professional school is supposed to deepen and enrich his spiritual understanding. When the scholastic has finished his education, he embarks on the "tertiate," a period of several months in which the accumulated experience of some ten years in the Order will be proved and tested all over again. The high point of the tertiate is the so-called great exercises, essentially a reprise of the final passage rite of the novitiate. At the same time the candidate is preparing to take his final vow, which at long last will make him a full-fledged member of the Society of Jesus. Many scholastics with an academic or scientific background spend a few years teaching at a Jesuit "college," actually a private academy, of which there are six, for example, in Germany and Austria alone, and even those who have strong reservations about them on other grounds generally concede that academic standards are very high indeed. Many of these instructors rejoice in the title of "*scholasticus formatus*," which sounds like fairly serious business but only means that the bearer is a newly hatched probationary Jesuit, between twenty-three and twenty-five years old, who has not even been ordained into the priesthood.

A great many candidates, of course, do not even make it this far, and may simply part company with the Order at some point along the way, at the instigation of one or both parties. The process is relatively straightforward up until the time that the candidate has actually been ordained, and the Order does not have any way of disciplining a recalcitrant brother short of this extreme remedy. In the past other orders have resorted to such disciplinary measures as solitary confinement and short rations, but when Ignatius was asked how he dealt with disobedience in the ranks of the *compañía*, he simply motioned toward the door.

The rules have been relaxed somewhat since the early days, but they are strict enough to keep more than half of every seminary's entering class from completing their two-year novitiate. Many eventually find their way into other orders where life is not quite so rigorous, and others who have progressed further and completed their education still decline to take the fourth vow and choose to remain what are called "*coadjutores*," literally "associates" or "collaborators." The "*professores*," those who have made a public profession of their four vows, make up the elite of the Order. From this group the future preachers, father confessors, and instructors at the colleges will be recruited, and at one time only the *professores* were entitled to select the delegates to the General Congregation of the Order. (It is still true, however, that the Superior General is chosen by a majority vote of the *professores,* and not by the entire Order.) In case of deadlock the Order subscribes to the same admirable rule as the College of Cardinals; namely, if the electors are unable to agree on a candidate, they are put on a diet of nothing but bread and water until discord and factionalism are stifled and harmony once more prevails. This tactic was first adopted in 1271, when the College of Cardinals had been sitting for some thirty-one months and the long-awaited announcement *Habemus papam* ("We have a pope") was still not forthcoming. The mayor of Viterbo, where the conclave was being held, finally became exasperated and announced that the cardinals could expect nothing further from him but bread and water. Several days later the election of Tabaldo Visconti, bishop of Liège, who reigned as Pope Gregory X, was announced. (In the case of the Jesuits, however, this emergency clause has yet to be invoked.) Another peculiarity of the Order's electoral system is that no candidate who has been validly elected can refuse to serve as General—presumably this rule was inspired by Ignatius's initial reluctance to accept the unanimous decision of his colleagues in the Order's first election.

To Ask Is to Be Obeyed: The Administration of the Order

The General of the Order has his headquarters in Rome, the better, as some would say, to serve the Pope, or, as others would have it, simply to keep an eye on him. Suspicions of this latter kind can be traced back to the Counter-Reformation, when the power and vainglory of the Order was at its height. It was then that the Jesuit General was first given the nickname "Papa Nero" ("the Black Pope"), a malicious allusion not only to the contrast between the Jesuits' black robes and the gold-and-white vestments worn by the Holy Father, but also to the sinister forces that the General was believed to have at his command. Certainly the name was not entirely undeserved; for example, the Jesuits who were assigned to foreign missions were not permitted to carry out the orders of a papal legate until these had been explicitly confirmed by the office of their General. Since those days the General's power has been curbed considerably by a series of organizational reforms, which were intended to make sure that the entire burden of the office would not fall on one man's shoulders (and, to be sure, that all the power of the office would not be concentrated in one man's hands). Today many of the responsibilities that were formerly undertaken by the General alone have been parceled out among four General Assistants and many more regional assistants; a "region" in Jesuit parlance is composed of several provinces, of which there are now all of seventy-seven around the world. In addition, there is an official called the "admonitor," a kind of one-man Supreme Court, whose only function is to make sure that the General is always in compliance with the rules of the Order. In any case, the General is only liable to impeachment by the General Congregation in the event that he has committed any one of five extremely grave transgressions, which are also quite specifically defined in the rules of the Order; the most serious of these, of course, is apostasy from the Roman Catholic faith. The General was not even permitted to resign his office voluntarily until 1965 (the story of what happened when General Arrupe attempted to invoke this privilege can be found on page 298). In theory a General can be removed from office by a decision of the General Congregation, though this has never actually happened so far. (General Aquaviva set up a special commission to investigate himself in 1593 as a way of responding to charges that he had been living above his station. The commission obligingly rummaged through his cupboards and read his private correspondence; he was discovered to have accepted a gift of some preserves from his rich Neapolitan relatives, who included a cardinal and several bishops among them, and was duly censured for accepting an unauthorized gratuity.)*

*As this story suggests, Aquaviva was among the most enterprising of the Jesuit Generals. He was elected when he was only thirty-seven, and in response to the obvious objection

Only the General is elected for life; a provincial serves out his term of office and then steps quietly back into the ranks to serve his successor. Every three years each of the provinces sends a delegate to Rome to report to the General and then to meet with the delegates from the other provinces to determine whether the situation warrants the convocation of a General Congregation of the entire Order. There have only been thirty-three in all since 1558; and most of them were called simply to elect a new General. Both the frequency and duration of these extraordinary sessions have been increasing throughout this century, which can be read as a kind of fever chart of the Order's collective sense of crisis and malaise. There have been four of these nonelectoral sessions since the First World War; the Thirty-first Congregation lasted for six months and the Thirty-second (1974–75) for four, which is far longer than the average.

The delegates are guided in their deliberations by Loyola's *Constitutions,* which were formally adopted at the first General Congregation in 1558. The *Constitutions* were not actually published until 1757, however, when two fat folio volumes appeared under the title *Institutum Societatis Jesu, auctoritate Congregationis Generalis XVIII*; we will examine their contents in greater detail in a later chapter.

PILING UP TREASURE ON EARTH—THE FINANCES OF THE ORDER

This is a subject on which no outsider can really claim to speak with any authority, since the Jesuits are just as reticent about their financial affairs as is the Vatican itself. But this kind of discreet, lofty silence has never put an end to speculation in either case; though the Jesuits are not technically a mendicant order, they are also not in the business of accumulating great wealth. As usual, estimates vary: Those on the low side insist that the Jesuits, individually and collectively, are no richer than Christ,

---

that he was too young to assume so much responsibility, he replied, "This is a fault that I promise to strive constantly to correct, even in my sleep." He is best remembered as the Jesuits' great lawgiver, since many of the statutes and regulations of the Order were adopted during his thirty-four-year tenure in office. The nineteenth-century historian Leopold von Ranke even went so far as to assert that the golden age of the Order came to an end with Aquaviva's death.

St. Francis, or Loyola. On the high side they are reputed to own a piece of every major multinational corporation, with the possible exception of Playboy International and the Moscow Narodny Bank. Pedro Arrupe, who served as Superior General until 1981 and had the reputation of being much more candid and unguarded in discussing the internal affairs of the Order than any of his predecessors, was still not very informative when he was asked to address himself to this question: "One hears from time to time that the Jesuits are very rich. Naturally we do have a great many schools and houses for our apostolic work. But one does not get rich from owning school buildings, and let me emphasize once again that our schools are supposed to be open to all and are not solely for the benefit of one particular group." (I would have been a lot happier with this last sentence if the words *supposed to be* had been left out.) In fact, at one time at least, the Jesuit colleges must have been a financial bonanza for the Order, so much so that in 1664 the Polish king Jan Sobieski, otherwise quite well disposed toward the Jesuits, wrote to General Oliva: "I implore Your Reverence to preserve the Jesuits in Poland from the scourges of cupidity and the love of luxury with which the Order is notoriously afflicted elsewhere. The rectors think of nothing but enriching their colleges by every means at their disposal, and that is the only thing that concerns them." We do not even know how rich the Order was then, though they were clearly rich enough to have all Europe vying for their favor. The various provinces were trafficking very lucratively in foreign currencies, and credit facilities and bills of exchange drawn on the treasury of the Order were routinely made available to friendly governments. A later Polish king, the spendthrift Augustus the Strong, and the Portuguese merchant colony in China are both known to have made use of the Order's diversified international banking network.

General Oliva's predecessor, a German aptly named Goswin Nickel, had already sent out a circular letter to the provinces exhorting them to return to the path of Christian poverty and simplicity, and with good reason, since the interest rate charged by the Jesuit lending officers had risen to a scandalous 30 percent during his tenure as General. The Spanish proverb *"Don Dinero es muy Católico"* ("Don Dinero is a good Catholic") was clearly inspired, at least in part, by the financial practices of the Society of Jesus.

Although we have no way of compiling anything like a balance sheet for the Society of Jesus during these prosperous years, the circumstances under which the Order was temporarily dissolved (and its property confiscated) in all the Catholic countries of Europe during the late eighteenth century suggest that the Jesuits had allowed themselves to get very rich indeed. Certainly there were other reasons for this, but confiscation was a remedy that was always available and must have tempted many a hard-pressed minister of state and monarch who was tired of living on credit. The precedent had been set some four hundred years earlier, when the king of France, Philip the Fair, laid hands on the substantial treasure of the crusading order of the Knights Templar after he had had the leading Templars executed on trumped-up charges of heresy and witchcraft.

In the case of the Jesuits we do know that the proceeds of the confiscations were considerable. In 1772, for example, the Austrian government realized the sum of fifteen million gulden from the assets and property of the Order; the assets of the Jesuit college of Ingolstadt in South Germany were valued at some three million gulden. By comparison, Mozart's funeral in Vienna cost all of 60 gulden; his entire estate was only valued at 592 gulden (and 3 kreuzer). True, Mozart was not exactly rich, as composers go, but it seems equally clear that the Jesuits were not exactly poor. The Order has changed in many ways since then, but apparently it has kept a hand in the investment game and is still not above using money to make money. At least this was one of many accusations lodged against the Church in general in Rolf Hochhuth's play *The Deputy*. In the fourth act of *The Deputy*—which provoked a storm of controversy when it was first produced in the early sixties—a Vatican official explains in passing that the Jesuits had cornered the world market in cinnabar, the ore from which mercury is extracted, during the thirties and forties. This meant that during the war the United States Army was obliged to buy its mercury from a Jesuit-owned concern in Texas; the Germans and the Italians got theirs from mines in Tuscany and the Russians from mines in the Almadén district of Spain; the Jesuits held a controlling interest in all of them. About all that can be said in support of such a claim is that a writer, particularly a writer like Hochhuth, is unlikely to have concocted such a story out of thin air. Several Jesuits who read this chapter in manuscript pointed out that the sources on which Hochhuth based his accusations seemed to be somewhat obscure, but surely a certain amount of obscurity is only to be expected in a case like this. Hochhuth might well have replied that it was the Jesuits who had muddied the waters so thoroughly in the first place; like the other Catholic orders, they do not even permit their financial records to be examined by officials of the papal Curia, let alone the world at large.

In contrast to these covert operations in the world of capitalism, the Jesuits are not nearly so reticent about their personal finances, which are organized according to the principles of pure communism. All of the income that flows into the treasury of a particular house is doled out to the individual brothers purely on the basis of need; the Jesuit father who has written an international best seller gets just enough to enable him to carry on, as does the brother who has to bicycle fifteen miles every day to get to his one-room back-country schoolhouse. (And both, of course, are assured that the Order will continue to provide for them, in sickness and in old age, even when they are not bringing in any income at all.) The Order has no central treasury as such; each house keeps its own accounts and sends a fixed contribution to the offices of the provincial, which in turn sends on a purely voluntary contribution to the directorate in Rome.

These are the essential facts about the organization, structure, and finances of the Jesuit Order, which dominated Europe for a time and did much to bring the New World into the cultural (and economic) orbit of the Old. The Order has endured more stormy passages than peaceful interludes, and this has been in large part the fault of the Jesuits themselves, though certainly more often through arrogance and hubris than through ignorance or stupidity.

The Pope's Fifth Column

Apart from the more or less visible means of support that we have already described, the Order is also sometimes said to benefit from the patronage of a host of "invisible Jesuits" or "affiliates," by which is meant Catholic laymen who have been educated in Jesuit colleges and remain dedicated to the preservation of the Order's supremacy in worldly affairs. These "Jesuits in short coats," to give them their original name, do not take vows but go on to insinuate themselves into the professions and various useful niches in civilian life, from which they continue to pass on any stray intelligence that might prove helpful to

Rome, and to spread rumors and propaganda to demoralize and under-mine the opposition. By now the legend of the "invisible Jesuits" has become an indispensable part of the mythology that surrounds the Order and the inspiration of countless lesser rumors that would be almost as difficult to eradicate as they are to prove. For example, Otto von Bis-marck informed the Reichstag in 1874 that it was the intrigues of the Jesuits that had brought about the Franco-Prussian War (and not, as most people supposed, the intrigues of Otto von Bismarck); he added, "I am entirely prepared to produce proof of this," but perhaps the Iron Chan-cellor felt that this statement was sufficiently compelling in itself, since whatever proof he had in mind was never forthcoming. Similarly, the German High Command issued an informational bulletin dated August 14, 1941, and designated "for officers only," that described how a team of Jesuits dressed in mufti as "cattle dealers, engineers, etc." had been infiltrated into Russia as early as 1916, with a view, as the bulle-tin explained, "to introduce as many priests as possible into the [German-]occupied territories of Russia in order to lay the groundwork for a far-reaching political offensive that the Vatican was preparing against Russia." And even today in Rome, in the shadow of the Superior General's offices at Borgo San Spirito, Number 5, the usual informed sources in the cafés will tell you that the Jesuits are meeting in sym-posiums with the atheists to discuss their common interests or that (at the same time) Jesuit fathers equipped with false passports and para-chutes are being dropped "behind the Curtain" to help reclaim these vast lost territories for the Church.

What have the Jesuits done to deserve all this? Probably nothing lately, but they are still burdened with the reputation they won for them-selves three centuries ago as the commandos of the Counter-Reforma-tion. Until the sealed archives of the Order are finally opened for our inspection and the truth, if any, that underlies these durable legends can be brought to light, it is probably best to consign the legions of "invisible Jesuits" to that shadowy world of myth that is already littered with poi-son rings, iron masks, and secret panels, and where every black robe conceals the black heart of a Machiavelli or a Richelieu.

In the real world, however, the Order has never lacked for sympa-thizers, and throughout the centuries the most devoted of these have been women. Even today the charming, tweedy gentleman in the Ro-man collar who can discourse so spiritually on worldly matters and still be so worldly about the things of the spirit continues to exercise a certain fascination for intelligent, well-educated women. For me this attitude was perfectly summed up for all time by a remark a female colleague of mine at the Berlin NWDR radio network once made to a highly personable Jesuit acquaintance of ours. She looked him over, sadly but appreciatively, and said, "What a pity, Father, that you've decided to shirk your biological responsibilities." And in fact the Jesuits might also be accused of shirking their spiritual responsibilities as well, since one of the rules of the Order explicitly forbids them to serve as chaplains or confessors to women, "since they take up too much time." (This includes nuns as well. Jesuits are not allowed to serve as their confessors ordinarily, though this ban may be relaxed "in recognition of special circumstances." In practice, however, this ruling, like most things connected with the Jesuits, has proved to be very elastic, so that on one occasion, for instance, the Jesuits were actually entrusted with the reorganization and reform of a number of convents.)

Ignatius spoke from bitter experience when he advised his brothers, "We must keep ourselves under control at all times and we should not allow ourselves to become involved with the conversion of women. . . ." Apparently a number of his youthful encounters with the Inquisition had come about because of the indiscretions of his more enthusiastic female followers. He did, of course, provide the usual Jesuitical escape clause by adding ". . . unless they be of gentle birth." Certainly this in itself was no guarantee against temptation or further indiscretion (quite the reverse, if anything), but Ignatius was perfectly well aware that there was no better way of gaining a measure of influence over a great man than by winning the confidence of his wife or his mistress.

One of the first of these noble ladies to have a Jesuit as a confessor was Juana of Castile, daughter of Ferdinand of Aragon and Isabella of Castile and the mother of Charles V, who was commonly known as "*Juana la Loca.*" Juana was a figurehead ruler who was passed over in the Hapsburg succession because of her extreme emotional instability; instead she devoted herself entirely to religious matters, so that her court "seemed more like a cloister." She used her influence to secure all the most important chairs in the universities of Castile for Jesuit scholars, and in return Ignatius is said to have secretly made her a member of the Society of Jesus. (Apparently such things were far from being unheard of in the early days.) In fact, the force of the Jesuit example was so compelling that entire orders of nuns adopted the Jesuit Rule, without the consent or cooperation of the Jesuit Order. Our indispensable *Staats-*

Zeitungs-und Conversations-Lexicon defines "Jesuitesses" (*Jesuitinnen*) as "an order of nuns founded in the sixteenth century by a gentlewoman of the name of Elizabeth Rosella who sought to model themselves on the Jesuits in all things. However, the order was so beset by all manner of dissension that it was dissolved by Pope Urban VIII himself, even though communities of such are still to be found in Holland and in the neighborhood of Cologne." A later experiment on similar lines, which may have been directly inspired by the "Jesuitesses," resulted in the so-called Demoiselles Anglaises, "English Maidens," an order that was founded at Saint-Omer in 1609 by an English nun from Yorkshire called Mary Ward. The Demoiselles flourished under the Jesuit Rule (though there was never any formal, organizational contact initiated between them and the Society of Jesus itself), and by 1620 they had established their own colleges in London, Rome, Naples, Perugia, Cologne, Vienna, Munich, Augsburg, and Prague, which were generally considered to be every bit as good as the Jesuit colleges themselves. Mary Ward seems to have been a courageous woman and remarkably independent-minded for her day, which turned out to be the undoing of the Demoiselles Anglaises. She finally petitioned the Pope to allow her sisters to live outside the seclusion of the cloister, as the Jesuits did; the response was a papal bull issued in 1631 that called for the dissolution of the order. Mary Ward was sent to a convent in Munich to reflect on her impertinence and, apart from the mysterious remnants mentioned by the *Lexicon,* that was the end of the Jesuit nuns.

PART ❧ III

Loyola transformed mankind's ancient dream of a worthy and righteous life, which has remained virtually unchanged from Plato to Marx, from the object of our prayers into a military objective.

—Ludwig Marcuse (1894–1971)

I would not even believe in the Gospels were the Holy Church to forbid it.

—Francis Xavier (1506–1552)

The *Constitutions;* or, Too Much of a Good Thing

No other organization, spiritual or secular, has been as successful in reconciling two contradictory goals as the Jesuits have—in this case, discipline and individuality. As strict as the discipline may be in the Order, the individual Jesuit father still enjoys more personal freedom than his counterparts in any of the other orders. The Jesuits at their best have always been ahead of their time, and in an age when the generals still saw their tactical salvation in closing ranks and forming up in squares, the knights of Christ were already experimenting with a much less rigid order of battle: "When an army is widely scattered, then the various bodies of troops must remain in close contact with one another and with their supreme commander in the field . . . so that the same spirit, the same purpose, the same sense of striving will everywhere prevail." This, as you may have guessed, is not one of the military maxims of Clausewitz or Von Moltke, but is in fact an excerpt from the eighth article of the *Constitutions* of the Society of Jesus, the most comprehensive rule of any of the Catholic orders and very probably the most fully realized system of organization of any community that has ever existed.

The *Constitutions* mentions serving God 104 times, the honor of God is mentioned 105 times as the purpose of every task, and the theme of the renunciation of the individual self can be plainly read in every line. After eight years of work and almost two decades' practical experience, Ignatius had succeeded in drawing up a kind of ten-part personal service contract in which everything that concerned the individual's personal well-being, spiritual advancement, and eventual assimilation into the community by stages is set down in detail.

In fact the Jesuit Rule would be just about perfect if it weren't for some of the fine print. For the very reason that the *Constitutions* was intended to foresee and dispose of every possible eventuality, it also leaves itself (or the Order) vulnerable to attack in a great many unexpected places. Ever since the days of Nicholas Boabdilla, hostile critics have had no difficulty getting a foothold in this great tangled thicket of verbiage; the candor and specificity of this extraordinary document, as these examples should amply demonstrate, make it possible to back up almost any accusation with an apposite passage from the *Constitutions:*

- *The Jesuit's sense of morality is harsh and bigoted; the brothers look at the world with moral blinders on:* "Nothing of an immoral character should be read in the humanist works of pagan authors. . . . Books by Christian authors should not be read if these authors have not lived like godfearing men, even if these works should have some merit in themselves" (*Constitutions,* 468–70).

- *Jesuits are not allowed to think for themselves:* "Dissenting opinions should be acknowledged neither orally, in public preaching, nor in writing, in books, which may not be printed without the prior approval of the Superior General. Any attempt to discriminate between what one should and should not do . . . should, insofar as that is possible, be avoided. . . ." (Rule 42 of the Summary of the *Constitutions*). "For our part we shall disavow all contrary opinions and intentions in the exercise of a kind of blind obedience" (Rule 35 of the Summary).

- *Jesuits are not only blindly but slavishly and fanatically obedient to their superiors—generally the first item in any bill of particulars drawn up by their critics:* "The inferior is as a cadaver in the hands of his superior." The original wording of this paragraph 2 of Rule 36 was revised under General Aquaviva to read: "All should be of the opinion that whoever is subject to obedience should permit himself to be governed and directed by Almighty Providence in the person of his superiors, just as if he were a dead body that permits itself to be trundled about here and there and then set down, or as if he were an old man's staff, that permits itself to go everywhere and to serve in any way that suits the hand that wields it."

And there you have it. The moving finger writes, and having writ, moves on—and, as a matter of fact, this passage, as amended, is unfortunately still very much a part of the *Constitutions.* I say unfortunately because to my mind to be as obedient as a corpse is to be spiritually dead, and this kind of discipline simply turns a human being into an object, an implement. This insistence on absolute, corpselike obedience should neither be trivialized nor glossed over; instead we should make an effort to understand what all this is really about. First, it is worth mentioning that the idea of absolute, unconditional obedience was adopted by other orders long before Ignatius's time; the Carmelite rule, for example, prescribes that a monk should suppress his individual will "like a lamb led to the slaughter," which is not all that different from Ignatius's "corpselike obedience." But why has there been so much of an outcry about the slavish, fanatical obedience of the Jesuits, and not a word about the Carmelites? There are three reasons, and Ignatius is entirely to blame for the first of them—the idea of a Jesuit being like a cadaver in the hands of his superiors is certainly an arresting metaphor, far more so than that of the Carmelite lamb, and certainly not an easy one to forget. After all, this infamous phrase was officially struck out of the record some three hundred years ago, yet there are still those among us who have not forgotten it.

The second reason is that if a cloistered monk wants to exchange his free will for the docility of a sheep in a shambles, then how is this going to affect anyone outside the walls of a monastery? The Jesuits, on the other hand, are constantly rubbing elbows with the rest of us; they are just as much part of our world as we are part of theirs, and we are accordingly obliged to take each other into account.

The third reason brings us back to Ignatius again and his unsettling passion for exactness. Instead of setting down his views on obedience in a phrase or two as many another had done before him, St. Francis of Assisi among them, Ignatius went so far as to write an entire psychological treatise on the subject, in the form of a letter to the Portuguese provincial that is dated March 26, 1553, and has been given the title "On the Virtue of Obedience." This was the tinder that has kept this controversy smoldering for all these years. In his essay Ignatius distinguishes three forms or phases of obedience: 1. Obedience of the deed—means simply to do what is asked of one, without any particular conviction that this is the right thing to do, without asking the reason why; 2. Obedience of the will—to do what is asked of one because one accepts the authority of one's superiors, realizing that they know that this is the right thing to do; since one shares the same goals, one keeps one's counsel and restrains one's doubts; 3. Obedience of the understanding—the absolute obedience of the Jesuit, which Ignatius defines as follows: "Whoever has made the decision to submit unconditionally to the will of God must relinquish not only his will but his understanding also. This comprises the highest degree of obedience. This means not only to *want* the same things as one's superiors but also to think the same things, or in other words, to subjugate one's own judgment to that of one's superior—insofar as a submissive spirit is capable of directing the faculty of reason."

This phase 3 goes so far as to equate perfect obedience with the kind of absolute resignation that is otherwise only required of the devotees of certain Islamic sects; however, these sentiments are very much in the mainstream as far as Ignatius's own writings are concerned, and this passage is certainly not an isolated aberration. For example, in Rule 13 of the "Rules for Conformity with the Hierarchy," which Ignatius appended to the text of his *Spiritual Exercises,* he writes: "In order to cleave to the truth in all things, we mut believe that what I take to be white is black, if the hierarchy so ordains." The Jesuit father with whom I discussed the material in this chapter pointed out that this exacting standard applies only to individual declarations of faith, but even with this qualification, Ignatius's simple rule still proved to be inflammatory enough, for example, when the Pope's encyclical on birth control, *Humanae Vitae,* was opened up to discussion.

As for what absolute obedience meant in practice, I came across one letter in the almost infinite expanse of Ignatius's correspondence that may shed some light on this question. Ignatius had written to Peter Faber, one of his original Paris comrades, providing him with detailed instructions on the conduct of a forthcoming mission to Germany. Faber eventually wrote back, "I have done just the opposite of what you commanded me to do, since I found the situation to be quite different." Ignatius had nothing but praise for Faber for showing so much flexibility and initiative. "This," he concluded, "is what I would call *true* obedience." So this cadaveric, absolute obedience begins to seem like something quite different when matters of faith and dogma are not involved—not so much the automatic execution of an order, a "request" in Jesuit parlance, as the conscious furtherance of a common good, even by different means. "The good," as Ignatius said, "can be promoted by various means," and the infamous Rule 36 of the *Constitutions* is preceded and qualified by Rule 31, which states, "The rule of obedience is only binding when that which one has been ordered to do does not constitute a sin."

As mentioned earlier, one thing that is both refreshing and occasionally disconcerting about the *Constitutions* is the candor and directness of Ignatius's language. He not only calls a spade a spade, but, to paraphrase the English clergyman, he calls it a bloody shovel if that is what it is. If he thought it was more important for the Jesuits to minister to the spiritual needs of the rich and powerful and let the poor look after themselves, then he said so: ". . . then persons of high degree should have precedence, such as princes and lords, magistrates, clerics, scholars, since if they can be comforted, then through their influence others will be drawn after them." And if there happens to be some small point somewhere in the ten volumes of the modern edition of the *Constitutions* that requires further clarification, then a Jesuit simply has to consult the *Epitomes,* a vast collection of practical commentaries on particular passages in the *Constitutions,* some of which were contributed by Ignatius himself. This includes the famous "Rules of Modesty," which he is said to have written with tears in his eyes. Certainly it is hard to see why, since these rules show us Ignatius at his fussiest and most fastidious, the half-crazed bureaucrat of the spirit who is determined to write a regulation governing every imaginable aspect of human existence:

RULE 1. As concerns conversations among ourselves, it can be said in general that in all outside activities modesty and humility, together with priestly decorum, should be displayed, and in particular the following points should be observed:

RULE 2. The head should not be turned carelessly from side to side but only for some good reason, when it is necessary to do so. If not, then the head should be held erect and then tilted a little forward, but neither to one side or the other.

RULE 3. The eyes should customarily be lowered, without darting them about excessively or glancing too much to one side or the other.

RULE 4. Especially when conversing with persons in authority, one should not look directly into their faces, rather one should look below their faces.

RULE 5. One should avoid creasing one's brow, and especially wrinkling one's nose, since one should strive to display the visible signs of an inner serenity.

RULE 6. The lips should not be compressed too severely, nor should the mouth be kept open too wide.

RULE 7. The face should express joy rather than grief or any other less lofty sentiment.

RULE 8. Vestments and other garments should be kept clean and in decent repair, as befits brothers of a religious order.

RULE 9. The hands, when not being used to hold up the skirts of one's garment, should be kept decorously still.

RULE 10. One should walk at a moderate pace, without obvious haste unless there is some pressing necessity to attend to. Even then one should maintain one's composure insofar as that is possible.

RULE 11. All of one's gestures and bodily motions should be such that they would furnish an edifying example to everyone.

RULE 12. When a great many of us go abroad, they should go out in groups of twos and threes, in the order prescribed by the superior.

RULE 13. Whenever it is necessary to speak, one should give thought both to modesty and the edification of others in the choice of one's words and in the manner of speech.

There is nothing more ludicrous than an out-of-date etiquette book, but this deserves to be taken a bit more seriously. Certainly once you accept the idea of "the visible sign of an inner serenity" then all the rest follows, and a great many novices in the seventeenth century—perhaps Ignatius was thinking of himself as a young man—may have stood in urgent need of this kind of instruction. Or, as one Jesuit father sympathetically noted in the margin of my manuscript: "They take such pains to give form and shape to the *whole* man."

SPIRITUAL EXERCISES;
OR, CALISTHENICS FOR THE SOUL

Constitutions is like the Jesuit manual of arms, which allows the individual to take his place in the orderly ranks of the Society of Jesus. The Jesuit Rule is necessarily complemented by *The Spiritual Exercises,* the great Jesuit handbook for the training of the spirit and the intellect. But like *Constitutions, The Spiritual Exercises* presents certain problems for the uninitiated; anyone who reads it straight through will probably be disappointed, and anyone who reads it carefully will certainly be confused. The title itself was doubtless chosen by Ignatius to emphasize the similarity between the purpose of these meditations and that of physical exercise. And as with any sensible exercise program the first thing that one does is to set a goal, in this case: "to restore the soul and prepare it to put away all disorderly tendencies and, having put them away, to seek out the Divine Will and to find in the regulation of one's own life the salvation of one's soul. . . ."

As you may recall, Ignatius wrote out an early version in Spanish while he was still living at Manresa, but the definitive text of *Exercitia,* one of the most badly written and most influential books in all of world literature, was based on the 1541 revision of the Latin text written in Paris, which Ignatius submitted for the approval of Pope Paul III. As we have already seen, the difference between the two books is no less than the difference between the two men, Iñigo the vagabond ascetic and Ignatius the charismatic apostle. *The Spiritual Exercises* finally received the Pope's cautious endorsement in a breve promulgated in 1548, in which it was approved for use as a devotional handbook by both men and women *but* copies of the book itself were not to be distributed "without the consent of Ignatius or his successors." Violations of this ordinance would be punished by excommunication or a fine of five hundred gold ducats "which must be donated for some charitable purpose." And so this slim volume, written in a dry, inaccessible style, was printed but not published and reserved primarily for the personal use of the Jesuits themselves, and even they are cautioned in the author's preface that "this work is naturally not for those who will merely read it but rather for those who want to act." This is certainly true enough, since *Exercises* is decidedly not to be read for pleasure, or for any other purpose unless you are looking for a taciturn but extremely agile instructor in the gymnastics of the soul.

It is only due to the exertions of Don Francisco Borgia (1510–1572) that *Exercises* was ever printed at all. Don Francisco was a great-grandson of Pope Alexander VI, but by temperament and upbringing he was more closely allied to the respectable Spanish branch of the family, and at about the same time that his Italian relations were stabbing, garroting, and poisoning their way to everlasting fame, Francisco decided to renounce his earthly dignities (he was duke of Gandia and viceroy of Catalonia) and become a Jesuit.

Ignatius acclaimed this decision as "a cannon shot that will arouse all Europe." Actually Don Francisco's decision to submit to the ascetic Jesuit regime is more likely to have provoked salvos of laughter among his acquaintances, since, like Saint Thomas Aquinas, he was so fat that he had to have a wide crescent cut out of his dinner table to accommodate his massive paunch (and to make it easier for him to reach his favorite dishes). However he managed this difficult transition, Francisco Borgia's contribution to the Order was considerable. He became the third Superior General of the Order in 1565, and apart from financing the first printing of *Exercises,* he also helped supervise the construction of Ignatius's second great legacy, the Gregorian University in Rome, and had plans drawn up for a prototype Jesuit church. He was canonized in 1671, just about a century after his death.

And now back to *The Spiritual Exercises.* As usual, Ignatius has left nothing to chance, and in his preface to the 1548 edition he gives an additional word of warning to the unwary reader: "The spiritual exercises that follow must be modified in accordance with the nature of those who wish to use them for their own instruction, i.e., according to their ages, their attainments, and their spiritual predispositions. In this way nothing will be imposed on them that they cannot easily bear and from which they cannot get some profit. Likewise everyone should have set before him, in accordance with the level that he wishes to attain, that from which he can expect to get the most profit and to make the most progress." Or, as Cicero would have said, *Suum cuique*—to each his own, as opposed to everything for everyone. Customized alterations are not only available but practically compulsory.

Next, what exactly is the point of the exercises themselves? I can think of two ways of answering this question. First, it would be easier but not altogether charitable just to say that *The Spiritual Exercises* is the self-help book of choice if you want to learn not only how to meditate but how to have an ecstatic religious experience in thirty days or less. Second, and more objectively speaking, the spiritual exercises are intended to provide the participant, who is assisted by a guide or instructor, with a technique of meditation that will enable him (or her) to have a direct experience of his or her own sinful nature as well as of the Passion and Resurrection of Jesus Christ, all through the medium of the kind of visual and mental image projection that Ignatius developed at Manresa. The optimal goal of this four-week course of instruction is a personal decision on his or her part to embark unconditionally on "the imitation of Christ," a decision that is expected to be accompanied by some sort of concrete change in the course of one's own life.

Both of these two answers coincide in one respect at least—the entire sequence of exercises takes four weeks to get through. In the course of those four weeks the following subjects for meditation are proposed:

FIRST WEEK: Sin and its eventual consequence, the torments of hell.

SECOND WEEK: The participant must now decide whether he or she wishes to follow the banner of Satan or to enlist in the company of Jesus Christ.

THIRD WEEK: The participant vicariously experiences, down to the smallest detail, the suffering and the ultimate sacrifice of Jesus Christ.

FOURTH WEEK: The participant vicariously experiences Christ's Resurrection and is given a foretaste of the Christian's eternal reward.

Clearly this is not the sort of book that lends itself very readily to being summarized in a paragraph or two, nor is it all that easy to account for its success and the enormous influence it has had over the centuries. Its contents, as outlined above, are not very original, even for 1548, and the language is dry and labored, like a textbook or a technical manual, which of course is what it is. In terms of form rather than content, one thing that redeems it from banality is Ignatius's remarkable grasp of motivational psychology. The comparison drawn earlier between *Exercises* and a twentieth-century self-help manual was not entirely frivolous; Ignatius begins, for example, by promising his readers that anyone who is prepared to work through his four-week course of instruction will find at the end of those four weeks that all his evil or sinful impulses have left him. In their absence he will have found inner serenity. (Thirty days to thinner thighs, speed reading with full comprehension, or even making a killing in real estate hardly seems worth bothering with by comparison.) Ignatius uses a number of other pedagogical aids that were borrowed or rediscovered by later writers of edifying books and should be familiar to anyone who has ever tried to improve himself by reading a book.

To prepare himself for every exercise, the participant is asked to try to visualize exactly what it is he is about to do, as an aid to concentration; only then does he kneel in prayer, which is the way that every exercise actually begins. Each exercise is repeated a number of times before the sequence is completed, just as modern authors are constantly summarizing, recapitulating, and urging their readers to "go over what you have learned in the last chapter." Sheer repetition has yet to be improved on as a pedagogical aid (and the fact that it is often helpful in padding out a rather scanty text is only incidental). Even the blank charts and tables at the back of the book that are supposed to help us keep a record of our cumulative progress were originally devised by Ignatius. For one thing, he seems to have been the kind of compulsive personality who is always fussing with charts and schedules in different-colored inks—even in his private notes to himself he invariably wrote *Jesus* in red and *Maria* in blue. As you may recall, during his long convalescence at Loyola he invented a kind of graphic notation that allowed him to record the various fluctuations of his spiritual and emotional life. This system was later elaborated on and adapted to *The Spiritual Exercises,* so that, for example, the participant can keep a running account of how often his meditations were disturbed by wicked thoughts, how often these gave way to feelings of remorse (and to what extent), and how often he simply felt too tired to continue. (Another technique that is indispensable to the professional edifier of today is of course to introduce personal examples and anecdotes drawn from everyday life into the text, especially useful for making dry material come to life or at least seem less formidable than it really is. This method seems much less suited to Ignatius's personality as a writer; he lacks the requisite light touch, as when, for example, he illustrates his discussions of the "three classes of mankind" with a story about three men who each have a certain sum of money to spend as they wish. The first salts it away, the second spends it, and the third decides to dispose of it in whatever way would be most helpful to God.)

But Ignatius outstrips any of our modern pop psychologists in one important respect. His pathway to success, or rather salvation, is not merely paved with words; he is not just trying to win hearts and minds, he wants to win over the whole human organism by stimulating all five senses—sight, hearing, taste, touch, and smell. (In other words, a program of total autosuggestion.) He begins by carefully setting the scene, or rather by regulating the environment in which all this takes place. He specifies certain postures in which some of the exercises are to be performed and gives precise instructions on the proper way of breathing while reading through them—a long time before such a thing as yoga was ever heard of in Europe. He suggests that certain exercises should be performed in a darkened room, others in bright light. In some cases he recommends that flowers should be placed on the participant's reading table, and even suggests what particular train of thought their presence should inspire.

All of the preparations may not seem excessive when we consider the stakes involved; Ignatius is proposing to tame the unruly human spirit and subject it to voluntary control. The first prerequisite is total control over the participant's imagination; the instructions for the exercise in which the terrors of hell are invoked for example, begins like this:

"The first point consists of this, that I see with the eyes of my imagination a boundless expanse of flame and souls imprisoned in bodies that are burning.

"The second point consists of this, that I hear with the ears of my imagination the weeping, howling, and crying aloud, and the blasphemies against our Lord Jesus Christ and all his saints I hear also.

"The third point consists of this, that I imagine that I can smell the smoke, the brimstone, the foul stench and the corruption of Hell.

"The fourth point consists of this, that I imagine that I can taste the bitterness, the tears, the misery, and the acrid pangs of remorse that are in Hell.

"The fifth point consists of the connection with the sense of touch in my imagination, which enables me to feel how those flames catch hold of the soul and devour it."

And that's not all. Ignatius tells his readers not only what they are to experience, in some detail, but *how* they are to experience it as well: "The fifth point is a startling outcry accompanied by a mighty shuddering in the depths of my soul." The Jesuits' critics have pointed out that portions, at least, of *Exercises* were cribbed from other sources, and that may well be. But this does not detract in the least from the originality of

Ignatius's technique of meditation. *The Spiritual Exercises* were also addressed to the individual devotee rather than to the community of believers as a whole, and this in itself represented something new. Pilgrimages, the veneration of relics, and the singing of the liturgy had always offered worshipers the security of a communal experience of the sacred. Ignatius dismissed these as the manifestations of a superficial, conventional piety, and in *Exercises* he provided the individual Christian with a way of examining his conscience from within, as it were, as an alternative to these external expressions of communal religious feeling.

One way in which these spiritual exercises of Loyola's differed from those practiced by other orders is that from the outset penitential practices were much milder, and fasting and other austerities were only recommended as an auxiliary backup system, so to speak, whereas in the other orders they have often been employed as the primary means of achieving the kind of ecstatic state that the participant is meant to experience through the spiritual exercises.

During this thirty-day period, of course, solitude and isolation from the world outside is of the essence. The participant must speak to no one except his exercise master, a Jesuit father with great experience in these matters who, true to Ignatius's instruction, arranges the program of exercises to suit the individual capacities and character of his charge. The Jesuits first established special retreat houses for this purpose during the early years of the Order, and today a number of them are still in operation (there is one each, for example, in Germany, Austria, and Switzerland), whose doors are open not just to members of the Order but to any Catholic who desires to go on retreat and work through the entire thirty-day program. (In the last few years the Benedictines have gone the Jesuits one better, in terms of public relations for the cloistered life, by opening up their monasteries—and nunneries as well—to paying guests, who need not necessarily be Roman Catholics. These much briefer monastic interludes, advertised in the brochures as "weekend retreats" and "days of silence," offer a much less exacting program of silence, meditation, discussion, and prayer, and in Germany at least they are always booked up well in advance.)

The retreat in its original form, as prescribed by Ignatius, has since been adopted by other orders as well, and during the tenure of Claudio Aquaviva as Superior General an abbreviated, eight-day version of the exercises was introduced as well; this was to be (and is) performed annually by every member of the Order. (This annual retreat was originally intended, at least in part, to provide the Order with a kind of spiritual stiffening and a renewed sense of community during an era when the brothers were becoming increasingly preoccupied with politics.) And Pope Paul VI seems to have had much the same sort of thing in mind when he presented the Order with the peculiarly backhanded testimonial: "The exercises of St. Ignatius have been one of the most effective means of bringing about the spiritual renewal of the world and its total reorientation toward God, but only with the stipulation that they must be truly Ignatian." The last five words would seem to contain at least an implied criticism of the Jesuits for having been untrue to the precepts laid down by their founder, and it was well known that there was no love lost between the Order and Pope Paul VI. Even today, though, the Jesuits loyally insist that the Holy Father simply meant to offer a timely word of criticism "about the way the exercises are practiced outside the Order."

THE JESUIT MISSION

Luckily for the old constitution [of the Church] a newly arisen order has now come to the fore, on which the dying spirit of the hierarchy seems to have disbursed its last remaining gifts: with newfound strength to restore all that was old, with wonderful clarity of outlook and steadiness of purpose, and more cleverly than ever before, this order has undertaken to revive the papal imperium and restore it to its former majesty and supremacy. There has never before in all of history been such a body of men as this, and not even the Senate of old Rome could have laid out its design for world dominion with greater certainty of success, nor has the realization of such a great idea ever been thought out with such great sagacity.

This society will furnish an eternal example to all others that feel within themselves the yearning to extend their sway and to endure forever.

Novalis (1772–1801), from his unpublished essay "Christendom in Europe"

PART ❧ IV

THE ART OF MAKING ONESELF BELOVED—
THE JESUIT AS PREACHER AND CONFESSOR

Let the beginning be as it may be, as long as the outcome is always ours.

—*Ignatius Loyola*

Always go to the Jesuits for confession; they put cushions under your knees and under your elbows too.

—*German proverb*

As You Like It; or, What You Will—
the Jesuit as Preacher

To sit by passively and wait while people find their own way into the churches would clearly be at odds with the militant character of the Society of Jesus. It was Ignatius himself who left the standing order: Seek out the lost sheep, fight for the souls wherever you find them, and by any means at your disposal. (Does this seem to imply that the end would justify the means in such a case?) Certainly the most damning accusation that Ignatius's detractors have ever framed against him has been the authorship of that unhappy phrase, which has always been taken to represent the quintessence of Jesuit amorality. Learned Jesuits have used up countless gallons of ink and reams of paper and spent the best part of three centuries in trying to clear his name, not always with any great success. In fact, the spiritual forerunner of the phrase in question can be found in the works of Niccolò Machiavelli, who himself has not always been fairly treated by posterity but who unquestionably did write (in *The Prince*): "The prince's sole purpose is to preserve his life and lordship. Every means that he employs to this end will be excused, for the common people concern themselves only with outward appearances and judge the merit of a thing in proportion to its success."

But it was not Machiavelli's cynical self-help book for despots that created such problems for the Jesuits but rather a best-selling collection of controversial pamphlets published at the end of the seventeenth century, Blaise Pascal's *Lettres Provinciales*. In particular, it was these words, which Pascal took the liberty of putting in the mouth of a fictitious Jesuit father (the "provincial" referred to in the title was of the ordinary French, and not the Jesuit variety, by the way): "We correct the fault of our methods by the purity of our ends (*Nous corrigeons le vice du moyen par la pureté de la fin*)." It is not much of a step from here to "the end justifies the means," and, the thing the Jesuits found most upsetting, it also may not have been very far from the truth, for all of that, even if no actual flesh-and-blood Jesuit had ever admitted as much.

Certainly the Jesuits felt that the purity of their intentions could sanctify the *place* where they chose to preach, which was often not from behind a pulpit. The word of God had to be brought to man, after all, and not the other way around. Another innovation of the first generation of Jesuits was to discard the conventional sermon—a long, learned disquisition on some technical problem of church dogmatics—in favor of something more popular and more stirring: "One accomplishes more among the people through the fire in one's soul and in one's eyes than through words that are aptly chosen." The Protestant Reformation owed a tremendous debt to popular preachers who were decidedly not afraid, as Luther put it, "to look the people right in the mug" (*den Leuten aufs Maul schauen*), but there were not too many Catholic precedents for this sort of activity. Savonarola, the Augustinian spellbinder who had the Medici expelled from Florence, was finally put out of business by a Borgia, Pope Alexander VI, and the second great Catholic preacher, Abraham a Santa Clara (1644–1709), was yet to come (and he only began where the Jesuits left off).

Thus Ignatius and his early disciples had the field more or less to themselves, but if they made their reputation by preaching to a new audience—the masses of the people—they really made their influence felt by developing a new kind of sermon. Francis Xavier instructed his colleagues, "Always take some pains to discover what sort of trades are practiced in every place that you visit." The Jesuits came to specialize in what might be called the topical sermon, in which the problems of specific localities or professions were addressed and the sort of pious platitudes that might have been heard from any wandering friar were scrupulously avoided.

The Jesuits have always had a certain flair for protective coloration, for taking advantage of the terrain, and a little of this brand of spiritual mimicry can still be detected in the sermons of the great Jesuit preachers of the 1950's, Father Lombardini and Father Rotondi in Italy and Father Leppich in Germany. Father Leppich spoke before a crowd of thirty-five thousand in Cologne, of forty thousand in Fulda; he preached from atop the arm of a crane on a construction site and in refreshment tents during Oktoberfest, and though he spoke to all sorts of audiences and on every imaginable subject, he never held so much as a scrap of prepared text in his hand. The archives of German radio stations still have hundreds of tapes of the early broadcasts of "the Heavenly Daredevil" (he was also called "the Black Goebbels") on file, and though they appear to be completely spontaneous outpourings, they are so artfully constructed that they have still not lost much of their impact today. (Father Leppich, sixty-five years old in 1980, abandoned the mass media for a group called Aktion 365, which sponsors meditation sessions and discussion groups in major German cities; the distinctive signs posted at the entrances of Catholic places of worship in Europe were inspired by a suggestion of his.)

Street evangelists like Lombardini and Leppich did not exactly spring up out of nowhere, like dandelions in the middle of a parking lot; there is a centuries-old Jesuit tradition of preaching impromptu sermons on everyday subjects, as this brief selection from a homily delivered by Father Jeremias Drexel over 250 years ago should make clear: "The great mischief of giving banquets is that the leftover victuals are meant to be put aside for the poor and for the servants of the house. We all know what happens then as the banquet draws to a close. Someone says, We have spent quite enough on this, it is time to pull the purse strings taut. Let us remember to save something for the servant, and that will be so much that won't go to waste. And then the hosts proceed to ram every morsel that's left down the gullets of their guests, and the servant has scarcely enough to keep his belly from grumbling aloud."

But it is in the most demanding of all priestly offices, as military chaplains, that the Jesuits have repeatedly proved their mettle, beginning as early as 1571, when they served on board the Italian and Spanish galleys at the Battle of Lepanto. At the end of the sixteenth century in Hungary, when more men were killed by sickness and neglect and casual cruelty than by Turkish bullets, a Jesuit chaplain called Georg Scherer chose this for his text: "It cannot be the Christian thing, nor the Evangelical

A Few Selections from the Homilies
of Father Leppich

There was a time when the German people sent missionaries out into the world, but that was before we had beauty contestants. . . .

• • •

Don't come to me with the excuse that a human being has to engage in some sort of sexual activity "just to stay healthy." I never met anyone who had gotten deathly ill from practicing chastity, but I've seen thousands in our hospitals and asylums who've become incurably ill from practicing promiscuity and were just lying there dying by degrees. . . .

• • •

Yesterday I got a letter from a Communist who writes: "Dear Father, You might as well just pack it in right now if all your sermons can't even put a single sack of potatoes in some poor devil's cellar. You could give out money and food packages after the show, but if you decide not to, you'll hear no more from me about it. . . . There is one thing you could do, though. A girl I know works way out in the suburbs. Why don't you send her a bicycle? The Good Lord surely won't miss it; He can't have all that far to walk. . . ."

• • •

These young men are about to pass among you to take up the collection. If you're only planning on throwing in five pfennings, then you ought to be ashamed of yourself. . . . If you're rich, then you're of no use to me, but if you're poor, come see me later and I'll have a little something for you. . . .

[Lutheran] thing, to leave the poor sick musketeer in the open field or in the street where he fell or even behind a hedge or on a dungheap like a rabid dog, to lie there, then to die and to rot."

In 1591 General Aquaviva prepared a kind of field manual for Jesuit chaplains, which, as we might have come to expect from Aquaviva, the great lawgiver of the Jesuit order, contained a good deal of blunt, commonsensical advice: "You shall not say mass for persons of princely rank with the army, for this will only result in a fearful waste of time and other disagreeable consequences."

During the Thirty Years' War, which pitted the Catholic against the Protestant states of Europe, chaplains had become part of the standard equipment of every regiment. In the days before standing armies and universal conscription, generals worked under contract and paid their troops out of their own pockets. Consequently they tended to insist on value for money in making their requisitions; as many as sixty Jesuit chaplains might be requested for a single campaign, since, as one of them wrote, "Among our people they have performed their office to the satisfaction of all concerned, and thus have come to be universally in demand among us. . . ." Perhaps it was because they gave short shrift to the princes that the Jesuits had so much time to spare for the common soldiers.

Even in later years, when the Jesuits were not always on such good terms with the secular arm, they continued to be prized by the armies that they served with for their bravery and devotion to duty. For example, some years later, in December 1916, a certain Father Rupert Mayer was awarded the Iron Cross First Class by Kaiser Wilhelm II, at the insistence of his divisional commander; the decoration had been held up in the works since August, understandably so since the Kaiser had denounced the Jesuits as "stateless persons" and "enemies of the German Reich" not too many years before.

WASH AWAY MY SINS, FATHER, BUT DON'T LET ME GET TOO WET—THE JESUIT AS CONFESSOR

In the year 1215 the Fourth Lateran Council made the first attempt in the history of the Church to introduce some order into the highly idio-syncratic rite of confession. It was decided that every Catholic should confess his sins and receive absolution at least once a year, and as a further aid to spiritual uniformity, the newly founded Dominican Order produced a comprehensive handbook in which a great many practical examples of the sort of sins that one ought to confess to a priest were furnished, sins of the flesh in particular. This provided the Catholic layman with at least a crude idea of which of his transgressions he was expected to confess, but the matter of penance was still left entirely up to the individual confessor. And no matter how lightly the poor sinner got off this time, he was always laboring under the threat of eternal damna-tion in case things should take a turn for the worse at some indefinite future date. Medieval man's attitude toward confession can perhaps be likened to the typical modern man's attitude toward preventive dentistry (with the stipulation that in the first case the torment was likely to be perpetual). Most people went to confession once a year, generally at Easter.

This remained the *status quo* for several centuries, but the Jesuits succeeded in ending this virtual boycott of the confession booth by intro-ducing three basic reforms into the system as preached by them:

First, the primary focus of the rite of confession was completely changed; the believer was not intended simply to confess his faults but to tell his troubles to his confessor, to open up his heart. Thus the confessor became more a spiritual adviser than a sentencing magistrate. Ignatius expressed it this way: "A Jesuit should not allow anyone to leave the confessional entirely without comfort."

Second, one could also choose one's confessor freely. "No one should be blamed for seeking out a great many before he finds one who is to his liking, as long as [the confessor] appears to be wise, pious, and not en-tirely wayward in his beliefs." And in general a certain amount of flex-ibility could be tolerated on both sides: "If an opinion is defensible, one should be permitted to adhere to it, even when the contrary opinion can be said to be more correct."

Third, when imposing penance and in offering religious instruction of any kind, the confessor is to temper his remarks to suit the social circum-stances and the spiritual attainments of the individual. The classical tag *"Quod licet Jovi, non licet bovi"* ("Jove is allowed to do what the ox is not") comes close to summing up the official policy of the Order toward a uniform administration of penance, and it seems easy enough to understand that, of the two, Jove was the more likely to choose a Jesuit for his confessor.

It is also not difficult to see why the world beat a path to the door of the Jesuits' confessionals, and why the Jesuits ended up with a reputation for not being overly scrupulous or rigorous in their examination of the consciences of others. An astounding example of this latter trait can be found in the *Theologia Moralis Universalis*, written by the Spanish Jesuit Antonio Escobar y Mendoza, notably: "For merchants the giving of short weight is not to be reckoned as a sin when the official price for certain goods is so low that the merchant would be ruined thereby."

Small wonder that for almost a century the Jesuits enjoyed a virtual monopoly as confessors to the Catholic monarchs of Europe—Portugal, Spain, France, Austria, Poland, and, for a shorter time, England. To give some idea of the leniency of the Jesuit regime, Louis XV was enjoined by his confessor on a strict fast day to reduce the number of courses at dinner from eight to only five, and to limit himself to three glasses of wine at a sitting. *Quod licet Jovi* . . .

In a work entitled *Imago primi saeculi* (*The Image of the First Century*), published in 1640 to commemorate the centennial of the Order, the authors look back on all these developments with great complacency: "Thanks to the Societas Jesu sins are now repented of more quickly and with greater alacrity than ever before; it is now customary to go to confession every month, or even every week. Many believers can scarcely wait to confess a sin the moment after they have committed it." In fact the Jesuit campaign to turn the gloomy rite of penitence and absolution into a kind of spiritual counseling service had been a roaring success. Confession booths in many churches were dragged out of obscure corners where they had been gathering dust for decades; carpenters and cabinetmakers who specialized in ecclesiastical furnishings were swamped with orders, and the spare and functional model, like an ancestor of the old-fashioned telephone booth, that is still to be seen in churches today was first developed during this period. By 1648 there were sixteen confessionals in the conventual church in Amsterdam, with six more standing by for the special influx of believers on feast days and holidays.

And of course there was no shortage of criticism either, primarily to the effect that the Jesuits were corrupting the simple, straightforward morality of the Bible with their sophistries and Talmudic subtleties—"casuistry," as this brand of reasoning came to be called. This charge must be conceded a certain validity at the outset, since clearly the moral edifice that could accommodate so much leniency and flexibility would have to be built not on the rock but on the shifting sands—or rather, in this case, on the basis of a canonical system of ethics that was extremely subtle and often downright obscure. This made it even simpler for their critics to take the next step and denounce all the moral teachings of the Jesuits as merely the product of an elaborate process of rationalization and philosophical sleight-of-hand.

This brings me right away to the famous Jesuit concept of *reservatio mentalis,* "mental reservation," which is the moral philosopher's equivalent of backing out of a lie with the explanation "I had my fingers crossed all along." The way it actually works is that one answers an awkward question with a statement that in itself is a lie, but then one qualifies this initial statment in such a way as to make it actually true. The catch is that the qualification is not spoken out loud. The classic example of *reservatio mentalis* (what is sometimes called a "Quaker lie" in English-speaking countries) concerns the man who is brought before a judge on a charge of breaking and entering. "Is it true," the judge asks him, "that you forced the window to gain felonious entry into these premises?" "Certainly not!" replies the accused, instantly qualifying his denial with the mental reservation, *I came in through the skylight.* This particular kind of hairsplitting may be of no great use to an actual defendant in a court of law, but in late medieval Catholicism, when the slightest transgression could often be construed as a mortal sin and the terrors of hell were as real as those of cholera or the plague, casuistry was developed as a consolation for otherwise blameless Catholics, who were generally able to get off on a technicality of one kind or another.

The companion piece to *reservatio mentalis* was called *amphibolia,* more familiarly known as "equivocation," which has to do with turning a double meaning or an ambiguity to one's own advantage. Suppose, for example, that a Jesuit wanted to eat meat on Friday, which was clearly out of the question. But after he has explained to himself that on Friday a good Catholic can only eat a creature that lives in the water, then he can feel perfectly justified in ordering a nice roast duck. (The original versions of both this and the equivocating burglar mentioned above were devised in 1645 by a German Jesuit called Hermann Busenbaum, one of the founders of Jesuit moral philosophy.)

Eventually Jesuit confessors in every country were provided with detailed handbooks that prescribed the appropriate therapy—the appropriate penance, that is—for every lapse from grace. Unlike modern therapists, however, the authors of these works did not concern themselves with underlying causes; they hoped to arrive at the truth empirically, by exhausting all possible individual cases. The result was that these handbooks finally grew to be great tomes of ten volumes each and the individual cases became more and more abstruse and remote from reality. Another consequence of this case-by-case approach was that great portions of these volumes would be considered too sexually explicit to be published in most respectable journals today; the Jesuits themselves made no attempt to define what they meant by pornography or obscenity; they assumed that anyone would simply know it when they saw it. It was not actually forbidden to read "improper" books, by the way, as long as one did not read them explicitly for the purpose of exciting one's prurient interests. But strict confessors generally agreed that no more than three pages should be read in a single day; the more lenient commentators felt that as many as six were permissible, but both schools of thought were unanimous in insisting that improper books should always be banished from the house at the end of three days. Similarly, as regards the extremely décolleté fashions of the day, it was accounted a serious sin for a woman to leave "a large part or as much as half" of her breasts uncovered; a less extensive display, "however, is a serious sin that may still be excused by the force of custom."

Despite the complete inanity of this quantitative approach to moral questions, these handbooks occasionally did come up with a piece of humane, reasonable advice. Father Gury writes, for example, that "an adultress need not confess her fault to her husband, since she runs the risk thereby of awakening great hatred in his breast and of putting her own life in jeopardy, or at the very least of involving herself in seriously harmful consequences." On an entirely different theme Father Escobar y Mendoza explains that "paying taxes is a hateful business [res odiosa]"; consequently it is not sinful to refuse to pay a particular tax that can "reasonably be considered" to be unjust. And by the same token he recommends to his fellow confessors that they show some leniency toward tax collectors who have been generous in their dealings with the public, "particularly if they have been patient in trivial matters, and more particularly toward the poor and also toward those who usually pay up like honest folk."

So far in our survey of Jesuit morality we have not encountered anything particularly subversive or inflammatory, unless you choose to count Father Escobar's suggestion that citizens might reasonably refuse to pay taxes if their property has been assessed unfairly. In fact, one of the most persistent accusations that has been leveled against the Jesuits is that they have expressly sanctioned political assassination and what we would call terrorism as a legitimate weapon of statecraft. Once again, the origins of this controversy are quite well documented. Philip II of Spain died in 1520; his son, Philip III, was barely twenty years old and totally lacking in any obvious flair for statecraft when he came to the throne. His tutor, a Jesuit called Father Juan de Mariana, had provided him with a kind of political instruction manual that he had written himself; unlike Machiavelli's *Prince,* this is primarily a treatise on defensive tactics for a weak and unambitious monarch. One passage reads as follows:

> For it is a salutary thought that princes know that if they oppress their subjects or make themselves intolerable by their depraved habits and life, then they can be removed by means that are not only lawful but also praiseworthy and deserving of enduring fame. The prince should regulate his life accordingly. Perhaps the fear of this will restrain him from giving himself over completely to the corruptions of pleasure-seeking and sycophancy, and impel him to cultivate moderation. But it is of course important that the prince should never doubt that the great might of the state is of greater consequence than his own power. These opinions of ours are inspired by a frank and upright heart, but like any man, I may be deceiving myself and I would be grateful to him who would show me to be in error.

This is the text on the basis of which the Jesuits' adversaries have made them out to be a kind of latter-day cult of the Assassins or a KGB before its time. Father Mariana leaves no doubt that a subject is only justified, under the most extraordinary circumstances, "in killing a tyrant like a common murderer or a highwayman." (You may have already noticed that this last phrase does not occur in Mariana's text; in fact, it is a quotation from Martin Luther.) And in fact, a much more extreme version of this doctrine had already been adopted by the Roman Curia in December 1580. An English Catholic had written to the papal nuncio in Madrid inquiring whether an attempt to assassinate Queen Elizabeth of

England (who had been excommunicated ten years earlier) would be morally justified. The reply was, to say the least, unequivocal:

> Since this culpable woman rules over two noble Christian kingdoms and has caused so many wrongs to be done to the Catholic faith and has been the source of so much distress for so many millions of souls, then there can be no doubt what-soever that whoever dispatches her out of this world, with the pious intention of rendering a service to God, has not only committed no sin but rather has acquired great merit.

The idea that not only tyrannicide but out-and-out assassination of one's political enemies could be morally justified was totally in harmony with the spirit of the age, not just some mere sophistry cooked up by the Jesuits. And Father Mariana's manuscript, like thousands of other earnest treatises on similar themes, would have sunk quickly into oblivion if the Parlement of Paris had not suddenly taken it into their heads to make the Jesuits the scapegoat after their king, the supremely tolerant Henry IV, was mortally wounded by a deranged young man named François Ravaillac on May 14, 1610. Henry III had also been assassinated, by a Dominican as it happened, and though Ravaillac had no connection with any religious order—he was simply a free-lance fanatic—Parlement decided to use Mariana's manuscript to indict the Jesuits as the real authors of this black conspiracy. (As it happens, a number of French Jesuits *had* written polemics against both Henrys that not only mentioned them by name but also suggested very strongly that, as indifferent Catholics and conspicuous sinners, they would be far better put out of this world. But in the unaccountable way of all deliberative bodies the Paris Parlement chose to make an issue of Father Mariana's book instead, which, especially by comparison, was both inoffensive and irrelevant.) The upshot was that Mariana's book was burned by the public hangman, and General Aquaviva immediately disavowed all connection between Mariana's unfortunate remarks and the official doctrine of the Society of Jesus—both of which probably did a great deal to convince the general public that the Jesuits actually had murdered the king of France.

PART ❧ V

<hr>

The Council of Trent—
the Jesuits Step into the Limelight

The Counter-Reformation received the final stamp of its identity from Ignatius Loyola and the Council of Trent, which he spiritually dominated.

—Oswald Spengler (1880–1936)

I should not be concerned with my own free time nor should I hurry because time is short, that is, during our discussions I should give no thought to my own comfort and convenience.

—Ignatius Loyola, addressing the Jesuit representatives at the Council of Trent

PRELUDE: "AS SOON AS THE COIN IN THE COFFER RINGS..."

At about the same time that Squire Iñigo de Loyola must have decided to give up his place at court for a more adventurous career with the duke's life guards, an Augustinian monk, Dr. Martin Luther, in distant Upper Saxony, sent a petition to his superior, the prince-bishop of Mainz and Magdeburg, in which he drew the prince-bishop's attention to certain abuses within the Church and respectfully suggested how these might be remedied. The petition was dispatched through regular ecclesiastical channels, on October 31, 1517, All Hallows' Eve, and although Luther eventually made his ninety-five theses public, he never nailed them to the Wittenburg church door, as you may have heard—or, to adapt Kaiser Wilhelm's poetical account of the event, "his hammer *did not* ring out like a tocsin over Germany's meadows and fields."

At the time Luther was thirty-three years old, and the principal abuse that concerned him involved the sale of papal indulgences—the practice, several centuries old by now, of remitting time in purgatory in return for a simple cash donation. The theoretical basis of this traffic in indulgences, which for obvious reasons had always been very controversial among theologians, was the belief that the blessed saints and martyrs had acquired so much more merit in their lifetimes than was necessary for their own salvation that the Pope was able to draw on the accumulated surplus, "the treasury of merit," as a reward for good works performed on behalf of the Church. The Pope was thought to have the power not only to excuse repentant sinners from doing penance or from undergoing other punishments imposed by the Church (which was the original idea) but in purgatory as well (which was a later refinement intended to give the product a wider demographic base).

The most successful trafficker in indulgences on the far side of the Alps was a Dominican called Johann Tetzel, who was closely associated with one of the earliest recorded advertising jingles—"As soon as the coin in the coffer rings/The soul from purgatory springs"—and who also had raised the very respectable sum of thirty thousand ducats in an eight-year period. (A single ducat would be worth about fifty dollars at the current price of gold.) Tetzel went fearlessly from town to town, since he was under the protection of the Inquisition, set up his stall, and made his pitch. At least there was no unseemly haggling, since he operated on a *prix fixe* basis, according to the gravity of the sin:

> Sodomy: 12 ducats
> Robbing a church: 9 ducats
> Sorcery: 6 ducats
> Patricide: 4 ducats

(Perhaps the lower-priced sins were merely discounted since they were not quite as common as the others.) On the other hand, sinners who looked or merely acted as though they could easily afford it were liable to a surcharge of a ducat or two; there was also an active trade in indulgence futures, or at any rate one could pay now for a remission of punishment for a sin one merely intended to commit in the future. Fifty percent of the proceeds went to Rome—"the great tithe barn of the world" as the satirist Ulrich von Hütten called it—the rest to the local authorities—in this case the prince-bishop of Mainz and Magdeburg—or to the Emperor.

In his petition Luther only intended to strike out at the spiritual (and social) aberrations that were produced by the sale of indulgences, not at the authority of the Church hierarchy itself. But the Church—notably the Roman Curia and of course the Dominicans—reacted with such uncomprehending vehemence and severity to his relatively mild criticisms that he felt obliged to pick up the gauntlet and prepare himself for a fight in which no quarter would be given. When he was told that the sale of indulgences had been sanctioned by the Pope and various Church councils (which were regarded by many, since the Council of Constance in 1414–18, as an even higher authority), Luther replied that neither the Pope nor the councils were necessarily infallible. When he was told that indulgences were authorized by canon law as well, he denied the validity of canon law, and before long of virtually everything that could not be justified by the authority of Holy Writ. This meant, among other things, that:

- Instead of seven sacraments he counted only two—baptism and Holy Communion (now renamed the Lord's Supper). The others (confirmation, absolution, ordination, marriage, and extreme unction) were demoted to simple ceremonies—"rites of the Church"—or done away with altogether.
- The same held true for monastic vows. Monks and nuns were encouraged to leave the monastery and, as Luther did, to marry if they were so inclined.
- He denounced pilgrimages and the veneration of relics as meaningless superstition.
- First and foremost, and this is the one point that very few Lutherans are aware of, he insisted that man could only escape the consequences of his sins by the grace of God. Thus his teachings can be reduced to a kind of theological rule of three—by grace alone, by faith alone, by Holy Writ alone. Luther and other Protestant theologians went on then to assert that Adam's sin had resulted in everlasting damnation as the common fate of all mankind, and as sinners we could only hope for salvation through the intercession of Divine Grace. In other words, man can do what he likes in this world, but he can never convince God to save him from damnation if it has already been otherwise ordained.

But as far as the Curia was concerned, all of Luther's theology could be distilled into a single word, *heresy,* and he was finally excommunicated by a papal bull of Leo X on January 3, 1521. The bull of excommunication referred to Luther as a "wild boar" who was trampling the vineyards of the Lord, and that set the tone for the exchange of insults that followed. Catholic pamphleteers referred to Luther as "that whoreson ox" and "the fatted swine from the drove of Epicurus"; Luther, who had a pronounced scatological bent, wrote that cardinals were not of women born but "shat out by the Pope." In those days, of course, Lutherans and Catholics naturally thought of each other as dangerous heretics who were undermining the foundations of the one true Church and deluded followers of the Antichrist (respectively). In the intervening 450 years the spiritual climate has cooled off considerably, and these fiery passions have had plenty of time to dissipate. Nevertheless, Luther has still been getting mixed notices from the Catholic press, at least in Germany; for example, a pamphlet entitled *Catholics, You Should Know This!*, published in 1967, originally contained the sentence "Luther was incapable of controlling his passions," which was later replaced, apparently on orders from above, with the bland observation that Luther had "world-historical significance as well as decided traits of human greatness." In the same year the maverick theologian Hans Küng and a group of his colleagues called for a formal revocation of Pope Leo's original ban, since, as the American Jesuit Father Richard McSorley pointed out, "If this Augustinian monk had remained a Catholic, then he would probably have been one of our greatest saints." However, a more recent work entitled *A Short History of the Church in German,* published in 1980 to coincide with the papal visit to West Germany, exhibits none of these ecumenical tendencies. Luther himself is described as "a heretic and a rabble-rouser," and his marriage to Katherine von Bora, a former nun, "was tainted with lechery and the betrayal of sacred vows and stained with the blood of so many murdered thousands" (this presumably means that Luther had the bad taste to get married during a period of violent social upheaval; the Peasant War was still raging in 1525). In spite of the indignant protests of the German Council of Protestant Churches (EKD), *The Short History of the Church* was neither revised nor withdrawn from publication, and of course Luther still languishes under the papal ban of excommunication.*

Putting spiritual matters entirely to one side for the moment, it turned out to be a grave tactical error to have excommunicated Luther, one

---

*In November 1983, the five hundredth anniversary of Martin Luther's birth, his misdeeds had apparently been forgotten, if not explicitly forgiven, by the Church. Pope John Paul II cordially echoed the wish expressed by prominent Lutherans that "the year dedicated to Luther be marked by a genuine ecumenical spirit and by a discussion of Luther that favors the unity of Christianity." On November 10, Luther's birthday, the Pope preached a sermon on the same theme (delivered in German) to the congregation of the Lutheran church in Rome.

whose consequences were obviously not foreseen by either the Pope or the Emperor. Eight years later, in 1529, Charles V was forced to appeal to the Imperial Diet to enforce the Edict of Worms, also adopted in 1521, which had proclaimed that only the rites of the Catholic Church would be practiced throughout the Empire. An unexpectedly large number of princes and the delegates of fourteen Imperial cities joined in the resulting protest (which is why the adherents of the reformed religions came to be called Protestants). In 1530 the theologian Philipp Melancthon, one of Luther's closest associates, presented the Emperor and the Diet with a document called the Augsburg Confession, which was originally intended as a compromise formula that both sides could accept but was eventually adopted, with certain modifications, as the fundamental statement of the Lutheran articles of faith. In order to keep religious war from breaking out among the three hundred different princely states and free cities that made up the Empire, Charles had been promising the Imperial Diet all along that he would appeal to the Pope to convene a new ecumenical council that would straighten all this out. Leo X, Hadrian VI, and Clement VII all managed to procrastinate successfully, but Paul III, the patron of the Jesuits, was well disposed toward such a plan. At first it was not even possible to agree on where the council would take place. The Curia suggested a number of Italian cities, the northerners held out for a German city, but on this point at least it was still possible to compromise; the small cathedral city of Trent in the South Tyrol was finally chosen, which was a part of the Empire and whose population, though mostly Italian, included a large German-speaking minority. Only one obstacle still presented itself—Charles V had taken advantage of this lull in the proceedings to declare war on the German league of Protestant princes; an armistice was signed in November 1545, and the delegates finally began to assemble at Trent on December 13.

THE MAIN EVENT—THE JESUITS MAKE THEIR ENTRANCE

After so long a delay it seems only fitting that when the council finally was convened, it was almost another twenty years before the last delegates went home. Things began briskly enough with a two-year-long session (until March 1547) during which a panel of three cardinals and twenty-five bishops (only one of whom was not Italian) occupied themselves with procedural matters and the systematic condemnation of a series of propositions that had been advanced by the Protestants. The first intermission lasted for four more years, followed by another yearlong session, then another adjournment in April 1552. Charles V's armies had been beaten by the French, and representatives of the Imperial Diet were obliged to return home and attend to developments in their own territories beyond the Alps. The third and final session of the council was not convened until January 1562, almost ten years later.

The Jesuits appeared on the scene almost immediately and from the very first moment they did what they could to avoid being overlooked, even when they had no great role to play in the proceedings. The two youngest members of Ignatius's inner circle, Diego Lainez, thirty-four, and Alfonso Salmeron, thirty-one, arrived in May 1546, accompanied by a French Jesuit, Claude LeJay, who was also thirty-one. Pope Paul had requested Ignatius to send a delegation, and these young men, clever, industrious, and uncorrupted, were perfect for the juvenile leads of the production, which in many ways they became. Certainly at the outset they had nothing to lose and everything to gain, but Ignatius was concerned that they might seem too intent on making an impression. He advised them, above all else, to cultivate discretion and reserve, and the copious written instructions that Ignatius sent them off with show how cautious and conservative the wild hermit of Manresa had finally become. Here is a typical Ignatian order of the day, written in the first person (i.e., from the point of view of the delegates) and headed "To go into effect five days after your arrival."

> I shall try to make precious use of my time by attending quietly . . . all the better to answer when it behooves me to speak, or all the better to be silent. . . . When the matter that is being debated seems so manifestly just and right that I can no longer keep silent, then I should speak my mind with the greatest composure and conclude what I have said with the words "subject of course to the judgment of a wiser head than mine." If the leaders of the opposing party should try to befriend me, I must cultivate these men, who have influence over the heretics and lukewarm Catholics, and try to win them away from their errors with holy wisdom and love.

TRENT, TRENTO, TRIDENTUM

The capital and diocesan city of Trent, Trento, Tridentum is situated amidst mountains on the river Etsch, which is spanned there by a wooden bridge. Its inhabitants speak both Italian and German, the former more than the latter, and it lies three days' journey, or twenty-one leagues, from Venice. The city measures an Italian league all around, is in large part fortified, and has an episcopal palace, with walls and ramparts, outside the city. . . .

In the year 1545 the world-famous Concilium of Trent was held here, at which the doctrines of the Catholic Church were promulgated *bis dato pro norma symbolica.*

Reales Staats-Zeitungs- und Conversations-Lexicon, 1759

And in fact if there was any sure way for the Jesuits to distinguish themselves in this assemblage, it was by the modesty and simplicity of their deportment, something that became clear right away even insofar as such routine matters as food and lodgings were concerned. Trent was much too small to accommodate all the delegates in the style to which they were accustomed—especially since some of these worthy princes of the Church were accustomed to go everywhere with an entourage of 150 people and apparently could not make do with less (even in front of the Lutherans). Also the merchants and innkeepers of Trent, correctly judging this to be the opportunity of a lifetime, immediately raised their prices for everything to unconscionable levels, which set the stage for the Jesuits' first propaganda coup. They set up housekeeping in a "narrow, smoke-blackened baker's oven" and their cassocks were so heavily patched and greasy that the representatives of the other religious orders were ashamed to be seen with them. This was the work of Diego Lainez, who had a genuine flair for the austerer forms of publicity as well as the indefatigable industry of a true son of Ignatius (he wrote some 2,379 letters, all of them concerned with official business, while the council was in session). Lainez always traveled on muleback, with a bundle of straw tied to the mule's crupper that he used as a kind of sleeping bag; even in later years, after he had succeeded Ignatius as General of the Order, he assured everyone that it was quite as comfortable as he needed it to be. He was also the author of a celebrated diatribe against perfume, cosmetics, and elaborate hairdos, which he condemned not so much as vanities or as blandishments of Satan as because such things absorbed a great deal of money that might otherwise have been distributed as alms.

A fourth Jesuit turned up at the end of 1546, a twenty-six-year-old Dutchman born in Nijmegen as Pieter de Houndt, who had Latinized his name, after the fashion of the day, to Petrus Canisius. At Trent, Father Canisius tended to remain more in the shadows than his three colleagues, and he was ostensibly engaged as a translator by Lainez, to avoid giving the impression that the Jesuits were calling on reinforcements. This arrangement worked out very well, since Canisius had the happy gift of translating suspect Protestant texts in such a way that the heretical passages were always readily apparent.

In the ten-year intermission before the second and third sessions of the council, Catholics and Lutherans struggled to gain the advantage, first on the battlefield and then by more subtle means, and if the momentum of the struggle seemed to have gone back to the Catholics, then this is largely thanks to the efforts of the Jesuits, who were quick to exploit the opportunities that the situation presented. The Germanicum, a special institute for the training of German-speaking Jesuits, was founded in Rome in 1552.

In 1555 the Peace of Augsburg established the principle that the rulers of the individual German states would decide whether their subjects would henceforth be Catholics or Lutherans. (Bishops were assumed to have already made their choice, and the subjects themselves were only allowed the option of selling their possessions and emigrating to a more congenial part of the Empire if they disagreed with their prince's ruling.) This settlement was embodied in a crisp Latin formula—*cuius regio, eius religio,* literally "whose the region, his the religion"—by legal commentators of a later generation; this way of doing things may seem oppressive and arbitrary by twentieth-century standards, but it was certainly preferable to the disastrous religious wars that preceded it (and followed it, fifty years later, when the settlement broke down).

It also provided the Jesuits with an ideal proving ground for the elitist, intensive strategy developed by their General; rather than trying to re-convert all the heretics in an entire province, they could make their approaches directly to the prince himself.

First, Germany was divided into two provinces in 1556, called Upper and Lower Germany, to provide two different headquarters for the campaign that was about to be launched and to make it easier to coordinate the siege of particular princes in accordance with local conditions. Ignatius also advised, as he wrote to Lainez and the others, that "our fathers . . . would do best to promote the greater glory of God by preaching, hearing confessions, instructing children, and visiting the poor folk in the hospitals. Above all else, they should inspire their fellows, by exhortation and the force of their example, to pray for the council and for the Church."

The campaign was a masterly success, and by 1560 virtually all of South Germany and Austria, including Bavaria, Franconia, the Rhineland, and the Tyrol, had been reclaimed for the Church. And since the balance had shifted so dramatically in favor of Rome, at the third session of the council all pretense of compromise and reconciliation was more or less abandoned, and the remainder of the council was devoted to a reaffirmation of the differences between the two faiths. In retrospect the entire production seems to have been a mixed success; the script was weak, the ensemble work mediocre, but the Jesuits had each given a bravura performance. Lainez delivered a number of brilliant orations that lasted up to three hours, and in the course of one of them he refuted the arguments being advanced by one of the cardinals so decisively that his remarks were incorporated verbatim into the resolution that was finally adopted. Salmeron proved to be master of the brilliant riposte rather than the extended oration, Canisius, of course, an artful interpreter, and LeJay distinguished himself most by his conspicuous works of charity outside the council chamber, as if to remind the delegates that there was another side to the Jesuits that they had scarcely witnessed yet.

EPILOGUE—THE AFTERMATH OF THE COUNCIL OF TRENT

The final session of the council was adjourned on December 4, 1563. The victory of Catholic orthodoxy was conclusive and uncontested; the separation between the Catholic and Lutheran churches was complete. The resolution adopted by the council—like the communiqués issued by our summit conferences—made very impressive reading but scarcely had much impact on the way these questions took shape in men's minds, at least not at first. (In France no one got around to publishing the proceedings of the council before 1615, a good fifty years later.)

As for the larger significance of all this, that seems to be primarily a matter of perspective. Protestant historians also tend to interpret the Council of Trent as a victory for the idea that the Pope, as God's representative on earth, was personally infallible, thus reversing the verdict of the Council of Constance (1414–18), which held that the Pope's authority was subordinate to its own, or to any other ecumenical council's. Catholic historians maintain that just the opposite was the case—the relationship between Pope and council was not resolved at all and the whole question of papal infallibility was left hanging until the nineteenth century. Still, it would be hard to find much ambiguity in sonorous phrases like these:

> . . . let no one rely on his own reason contrary to the interpretation that is embraced by Holy Mother Church, whose sole concern it is to judge the true meaning and import of Holy Scripture, nor shall anyone dare to interpret Holy Scripture in a manner contrary to the unanimous opinion of the Fathers of the Church. . . .

> Whosoever says that the rituals, vestments, and all outward signs of which the Catholic Church makes use in the celebration of the Mass are conducive to godlessness rather than godliness, he shall be damned. . . .

In the original document these two very basic assertions are preceded by a long string of more specific rulings on particular doctrinal points. The "efficacy" of papal indulgences and the legitimacy of the doctrines of purgatory, priestly celibacy, and the monastic vows were also upheld. It was further decided that the motifs and symbols used in religious pictures and images should be reviewed and standardized by the Church in order to weed out any pictures "inspired by an erroneous dogma through which simple folk might be lured into error or seduced from the path of true faith" or that were merely tainted with "unchastity and incitements to lewdness." (This was the era in which thick painted loin-cloths were provided for the nudes on Michelangelo's Sistine ceiling.)

There was at least one concession to modernity, in the form of a warning to avoid the superstitious pitfalls associated with the veneration of relics and the cult of the saints. The Index of Prohibited Books was officially introduced at Trent, and henceforth Catholic writers on doctrinal matters were expected to submit their manuscripts for inspection before they could receive the *Nihil obstat* (literally, "Nothing stands against it") and *Imprimatur* ("Let it be printed") of the Church.

The Jesuits received belated recognition in a kind of addendum to the closing statement of the council, in which it was recommended that Jesuits should be given pride of place over members of other orders as preachers and professors, particularly in theological seminaries. This itself was a Pyrrhic victory for the Order, since it contradicted one of Ignatius's principles, that the Society of Jesus—thirty-six-hundred strong by now—was to be a company of *mobile* warriors for Christ, with no fixed abode and no routine duties that would tie them down to any particular place. Now it was clear that the Jesuits were more highly prized by the hierarchy of the Church for their doctrinal stability and solidity than for their physical mobility. They lost no time in seeing that this directive was carried out, since they were perfectly willing to believe that no one was as qualified as they were to impart to others the teachings of the Catholic Church.

PART ❧ VI

MANY FOES TO BE FOUGHT, MUCH HONOR TO BE GOT—
THE JESUITS IN GERMANY

O saecula! O scientia! *What a pleasure to be alive!* . . . *The schools are coming into their own, the human spirit is opening up like a flower—but you, Barbarism, you can put the halter around your neck and prepare to meet your doom!*

—Ulrich von Hütten (1488–1523)

Action is worth more than reflection.

—Pope Innocent III (1119–1180)

FATHER FABER'S RECONNAISSANCE

In the age of the Reformation, Germany was a motley political patchwork from the Baltic to the Alps, a strange assemblage of free cities, tiny principalities, and miscellaneous local authorities that was soon to be further subdivided along religious lines. The rulers of great states like France and England were barely able to keep the religious differences among their subjects from destroying the fabric of the nation, but once conformity was imposed, these rulers learned to exploit the state religion as an instrument of foreign policy. For the German princes, the introduction of still another potentially divisive force just made them even more helpless individually and collectively than they were to begin with. By 1540 all of the states of northwest Germany, and nine tenths of the entire population, had gone over to the reformed religion. Only the ancient Bavarian ruling house of Wittelsbach had not, as they put it, "compromised their honor by siding with the so-called Reformation." Across the Austrian border, in the crown province of Graz, the Archduke Charles was said to have been the only inhabitant who still took communion according to the Roman Catholic rite. He is also supposed to have said, "I would rather have desolation than damnation be the fate of the Empire," a remark that was ominously suggestive of another Austrian of our own time. (If the archduke actually did voice these sentiments, in all fairness, it was probably after the Jesuits had managed to get him a subsidy from Rome.)

The great Jesuit counteroffensive in Central Europe, which illogically but inevitably came to be called the Counter-Reformation, began in earnest after the Peace of Augsburg in 1555, but the initial reconnaissance work that was largely responsible for the success of the final campaign was carried out by Father Peter Faber, the oldest of Ignatius's Paris comrades, who first set foot on German soil in 1540. He accompanied a Hapsburg dignitary called the Imperial orator to a religious colloquium in the city of Worms (where Luther had been condemned nineteen years earlier). Faber was invited as a kind of guest speaker on religious matters, but he had not really come to address the colloquium. Instead he preached a sermon to the students at the university, instructed a group of them in the spiritual exercises, and generally showed the flag on behalf of the Order. Four years later he established the first Jesuit foundation in Cologne, but his work in Germany was already almost at an end; he died in Rome in 1546.

Faber's observations in Germany enabled him to formulate three basic principles that later became not only useful but essential to the overall Jesuit strategy in the spiritual reconquest of Germany. First, he was able to give a clear and undistorted account of the social causes of the Reformation, free from prejudice and polemic (which makes him virtually unique among contemporary observers). "It is not true," he wrote to Ignatius, "that the Lutherans have caused so many to apostasize from the Roman church simply by ensnaring them with their false doctrines. The greater blame for this development must fall upon our own clergy. God grant there are even two or three in this city of Worms who are not living in open concubinage or are not steeped in some other form of vice." This is hardly an exaggeration, since at least a sizable minority of priests were living openly with their mistresses, and "in the rectories of these spoiled priests you will sooner trip over a clutch of brats than books." Drunkenness, lechery, venality, and ignorance—these were all very much a part of the ordinary German's image of the typical parish priests. In more sophisticated circles the best ecclesiastical appointments were ironically called "courtesans," because their favors were reserved for the habitués of the papal court in Rome and homegrown German candidates were out of the running. The conclusions to be drawn from all this were easy enough to draw, less so to put into practice. The first step would have to be a thoroughgoing purge of the Catholic clergy before any attempt could be made to bring the Lutherans back into the fold.

Second, Faber realized that the social responsibilities with which the Church had been entrusted in the Middle Ages had far outstripped its capacity to deal with them by the traditional means. (Demographers have calculated that the population of Europe had increased from about seventeen million in 1450 to about fifty million in 1600.) St. Martin of Tours, the fourth-century centurion who sliced his cloak in half with his sword in order to share it with a beggar, all without even bothering to get down from his horse, could no longer serve as the model of the complete philanthropist. What was needed was not just alms and occasional acts of charity but constant self-sacrifice and devotion, and there were very few, in the sixteenth century, apart from the Jesuits and the Theatines, who were prepared to take up this challenge on behalf of the poor, the sick, and the unfortunate.

Third, in Germany the problem was complicated by the fact that, thanks to Gutenburg and Luther, every burger and peasant family had their own Bible and hymnbook in their own language. Anyone who tried to take these away from them was the enemy, and that was all there was to it. A sense of national pride was beginning to stir across this shattered land for the first time, and Peter Faber understood that the Jesuits would have to tread very warily to avoid provoking an unpleasant outcry from this infant spirit of German nationalism.

THE METEORIC RISE OF PETRUS CANISIUS

Petrus Canisius became a Jesuit on May 8, 1543, a date that is sure to be mentioned in every history of the Order; he was then twenty-two. At twenty-six he was summoned to the Council of Trent, and at twenty-nine (an age at which a Jesuit of today would be preparing to take his final vow) he was named rector of the Jesuit university at Ingolstadt. Six years later, in 1556, he was made provincial of Germany (both Upper and Lower, as well as Switzerland, Austria, and Hungary). He took up his work as provincial where Peter Faber had left off, beginning with the purge of the German priesthood that Faber had recommended but never carried out. In this he enjoyed the full confidence and support of his superiors, though, as this letter of 1556 makes clear (allowing for the diffident, walking-on-eggs sort of style of the good Jesuit), he was convinced that the situation had deteriorated to such a point that even the most urgent remedies might not be effective: "We are experiencing the gravest difficulties with both the higher and lower clergy in this country, but it would mean a vast improvement in the situation if at least a few who have led a blameless life and might be willing to assist us diligently through their word of instruction might come to join us. In the meanwhile they do not seem to even suspect in Rome . . . either they are simply not acquainted with the situation here or they have given it all up for lost."

Nine years later, in 1565, Canisius addressed a similar appeal for reinforcements of the highest caliber, this time to the second General Congregation of the Order and now for a rather different purpose. The campaign had entered its second phase: "Since the princes and municipal councillors have the power to do a great deal in Germany, we must scrupulously avoid any friction and ill-will toward us on the part of these worthy gentlemen. And we must be all the more diligent in preserving and promoting the good opinion of these worshipful gentlemen. This would include our sending into Germany good preachers, reputable doctors of theology, skillful writers, experienced teachers, zealous confessors, and priests who will make themselves beloved among the people. . . ." Now the Jesuit mission, as prescribed by Ignatius, was to make themselves indispensable both to the people and to the rulers of the land. The German clergy was chastened (and presumably chaste) by now, and the struggle with the Lutherans would no longer be waged in the churches and the chapels but in all the ordinary places of everyday life. Canisius was a pragmatist who was perfectly willing to take a leaf out of Luther's book and bring his religion directly to the people; he was also quick to discard any tactic or device that did not seem immediately effective, and this included, to some extent, Loyola's book, *The Spiritual Exercises*. At any rate, he did not share the uncritical enthusiasm of his predecessor, Peter Faber, who exulted that "the exercises, in which many of the Germans have taken part, are to be thanked for well nigh all the good that has since been done in Germany." Canisius was primarily an educator rather than a missionary, and in that respect he was willing to defer his goal, the reconversion of Germany, by a single generation and concentrate his efforts on the instruction of the fifteen-year-olds in the Jesuit colleges rather than on the older and smaller groups of spiritual adepts who would benefit from Ignatius's exercises.

"BEFORE THEY HAD EVEN BEGUN TO LEARN THEIR ARISTOTLE"— THE JESUIT COLLEGES IN EUROPE

The first of the Jesuit colleges was founded in Coimbra, Portugal, in 1542. Ignatius later recalled that it was Diego Lainez "who thought up the colleges," and he seized upon the idea at once, though at first he envisioned them only as preparatory schools for future seminarians, as well as a kind of pedagogical threshing floor where the grit and the chaff could be removed in the most expeditious way. All this changed during the Counter-Reformation, when the Jesuit colleges took on the role of spiritual indoctrination centers for students of all classes of society, many of whom were not destined for the priesthood—a number of them were actually Lutherans.

Critics have made these colleges out to be nothing more than obedience schools for boys, where students were indoctrinated with a narrow, superficial "learning" and were even systematically alienated from their families, leaving them with no choice but to go into the Order. They were not as bad as all that. The colleges that were run as boarding schools offered instruction in secular subjects, a thorough grounding in Catholic dogma and theology, and, like the convent schools of later centuries, they served to protect their students from the temptations of the great world at a very vulnerable age by keeping them locked up at night. This, at any rate, was the pious hope of the Jesuits or perhaps merely a disingenuous advertising claim intended solely for the school brochure. In either case, security was somewhat lax. As Montaigne* pointed out, "The pox has got hold of the hundred students [at the Jesuit college in Paris] before they had even begun their Aristotle." (Syphilis was much more virulent in those days, especially in university towns, so such outbreaks were not as exceptional as one might think, or perhaps seven-

---

*Michel Eyquem, Seigneur de Montaigne (1533–1592), French essayist and humanist, of whom a Jesuit once remarked, "Gently, as with a silken thread, he strangles the life out of all one's feelings for religion."

teenth-century parents were much more worldly and blasé—at any rate, the enrollment at the Paris college had increased from one hundred to two thousand by 1620, just thirty years later.)

In spite of their reputation as grim citadels of repression, many of the Jesuit schools had more holidays than schooldays in a typical week, to say nothing of midsummer and midwinter recesses. (In 1649 the General of the Order was forced to hand down a decree that severely limited the number of school holidays and shortened the vacation periods.) The schedule was roughly similar to that of a Jesuit seminary. Classes began at six in the morning when school was in session; there were three hours of classes in the morning and in the afternoon, and housekeeping chores for the students to attend to as well. "At the stroke of nine everyone was already in bed, except for the fathers, who had just assembled in one of the regents' rooms to share a quiet glass of wine among themselves without disturbing the rest of us"—so wrote a boarder in a letter to his parents (all such correspondence was censored, of course).

Latin was the language of instruction, as it was in the universities and even in the Protestant schools. (One exclusive Lutheran academy, Schulpforta, founded in 1543 and comparable in many ways to a Jesuit college, did not permit German to be spoken in the classrooms until 1808). One progressive feature was that students were assigned to their classes according to their activities and achievements rather than their ages, and as soon as a student had worked through the syllabus for a particular class, he could move on to the next one. (The fact that many of these classes contained as many as a hundred students can only have enhanced the progressive atmosphere.) Each class—rather than each subject—was the responsibility of a single teacher, which was something of a departure, and teachers were not permitted to administer corporal punishment, which was unheard of in an age in which soldiers, serfs, and schoolboys still thought of a good flogging as an inescapable part of life. This is not to say that the students were never beaten, however—punishment was meted out by a figure called "the Blue Man," usually one of the school porters wearing a blue mask, which was intended to convey the idea of swift, impartial justice administered by a faceless agency of the college rather than simply an exasperated schoolmaster. Another important aspect of college discipline was the comprehensive network of spies and talebearers that kept the staff informed of everything that went on behind their backs. This practice met with not only the tacit encouragement but the open approbation of the teachers, and was ritualized to such an extent that to be publicly identified as a snitch was considered a mark of special distinction. (This system of mutual surveillance was another feature of the seminary that was adopted for use in the colleges.)

As for the curriculum itself, it was naturally limited to those subjects and opinions that enjoyed the full endorsement of the Church. Intellectual curiosity and independent-mindedness, rarely at a premium in any educational system, were strongly discouraged in the colleges. A great deal was forbidden; very little was allowed. And so it was that a prize student of the Jesuits could leave his college speaking Latin and Greek fluently but without having any of the spirit of the classical authors whose writings make those languages worth learning. Some writers on the subject of Jesuit education have expressed surprise that so little time was actually devoted to religious indoctrination, but a closer look at the curriculum reveals that the religious implications of *every* subject tended to overwhelm the secular. (It would be instructive to know how this element was introduced into the study of the science of fortification, which was taught at a number of Jesuit colleges after the Thirty Years' War.) And even those portions of the curriculum that explicitly dealt with religion were forced into a cramped and confining mold. Textbooks, even those written by Jesuits, were actually forbidden for fear they might put too much stress on reason at the expense of revelation, even in the study of theology.

The remarkable rate at which Jesuit (or Jesuit-dominated) colleges began to spread across Europe has led some writers to speak of a vast educational grid system laid out according to some masterly grand design. This would be to give the Order too much credit, especially since the first five Generals only allowed new schools to be opened under the auspices of the Order when it was clear that they could be financially self-sustaining and could attract a qualified staff. Claudio Aquaviva once remarked, with some complacency, that he had turned down over 150 such applications during his twelve years as General. The usual reason was simply a shortage of teachers, since who would willingly choose "to take in one's charge, day in, year out, our willful, destructive, and (especially in these times) unmanageable young men, to endure the smells and disgusting sights, and to instruct them and chastise them with indescribable patience?" Most Jesuits preferred a more exciting apostolic career as a missionary overseas, and in 1646 General Carafa was obliged to remind them: "So many are clamoring for the prize of shedding their blood in the Indies that I hope that some will decide in the end to spare us some of their sweat for our schoolrooms instead and thus to win the crown of a much-protracted martyrdom that will not seem as worthy in the eyes of the world but will shine all the more brightly in the eyes of the angels."

Ignatius himself, in spite of his initial ban on "studies and reading aloud," was soon persuaded otherwise after the colleges had had a chance to prove themselves: "The good that the Order can do to promote the Roman cause depends less upon preaching than teaching in our colleges." In their earlier years these "reforming priests" had turned apostolic missionaries, and now the knights of Christ were being asked to become "fathers of the young," with all that that entailed. At the same time, during the second half of the sixteenth century, thirty-seven seminaries were also entrusted to the care of the Order (four in Italy, thirty-three in the Empire), as compared to about thirty Jesuit colleges altogether in Europe. More remarkably, all of these were fully endowed by princes, bishops, municipalities, and wealthy laymen; none of them cost the Order as much as a single ducat.

THE SCHOOL FOR POPES AND THE BISHOP FACTORY— THE GREGORIANA AND THE GERMANICUM

On February 22, 1551, a wooden sign appeared outside a doorway at the foot of the Capitoline Hill in Rome: "School of Grammar, Humane Letters, and Sacred Studies. GRATIS." This was the only indication that the inhabitants of this unpretentious residential neighborhood were given that the Jesuit Collegio Romano (later to become the Papal Gregorian University) had just opened up in their midst. The Gregoriana moved into its present quarters on the Piazza Pilotta in 1930, not far from the site of the original college, which is now called the Piazza Collegio Romano.

The sign alone was enough to attract a full complement of students, since the teachers in the other grammar school, who were paid a miserable salary by the Senate of Rome, also expected a weekly *baiocco*, a gratuity, from the parents of their students. The success of the Collegio naturally gave rise to some resentment on the part of teachers who couldn't afford to offer their services gratis, and the Jesuits were forced to prove their mettle in a series of rowdy public debates until finally, the story goes, they managed to back their opponents to the wall in a dispute over some point of Latin grammar, and from that moment on no more was heard about it.

Today most of the senior faculty of the Gregoriana are Jesuits, and the list of distinguished alumni over the last five centuries includes six saints, thirty *beati,* twelve popes, and hundreds of bishops and cardinals. In an address read before the student body in 1979 Pope John Paul II (not an alumnus) paid this tribute to the humanist, integrated approach to learning that the Gregoriana has always pursued:

> The history of your university shows us that theology has never been treated as an isolated discipline, but has always been a part of a complete structure of academic subjects. In this way the integration of theological learning and specula- tion into the common store of knowledge has always been assured down through the centuries. . . .

Ignatius originally saw the purpose of the Collegio Romano in much simpler, more practical terms; in a letter to Francisco Borgia he set forth his vision of the Collegio as a kind of proving ground in which various curricula, pedagogical techniques, and even new textbooks that had been devised for the entire collegiate system could be put to the test. The Collegio soon distinguished itself, in quality if not in kind, from the other Jesuit schools; here, even more than elsewhere, scientific brilliance man- aged to coexist with narrow-minded dogmatism. The Collegio Romano was the flagship for the collegiate system in the Latin world, and the original foundation at Coimbra for the colleges associated with the mis- sion overseas. The Collegium Germanicum was founded in 1552 as a kind of elite training school where the vanguard of the Counter-Revolu- tion could learn both good deportment and sound Catholic doctrine, so that—as the papal bull that established the Germanicum metaphorically expressed it—"they will be able to search out the hidden venom of heretical doctrine, to refute it, and then to replant the uprooted trunk of the tree of faith." The students at the Germanicum once dressed in distinctive bright red cassocks that earned them the nickname *gambri cotti* ("boiled crabs"), but to the chagrin of the Roman tourist guides and vacation photographers these were exchanged for more conventional attire in 1966. The Germanicum itself was also relocated in a World War II-vintage building that is sometimes less affectionately referred to as the "bishop factory," a nickname that the inmates of the Germanicum are heartily sick of by now.

The original curriculum was based on the course of study that Ignatius had mapped out for himself when he was a student at the Sorbonne—Scholastic theology for the most part, cut with a healthy admixture of Humanist learning, since, as Ignatius pointed out, without having mastered the classics it would be impossible to refute "the most seductive and pernicious opinion of the age." (Today the Germanicum is no longer primarily concerned with the extirpation of heresy—the modern curriculum is much stronger in the natural sciences.) By 1560 Greek, Maronite (Levantine Christian), and English seminaries had all been established on the model of the Germanicum, but none of them enjoyed anything like the success of the original. By the end of the century the bishoprics of Salzburg, Breslau, Olmütz, Augsburg, Trieste, Würzburg, and Passau were all occupied by "Germanicans," and the papal nuncio in Vienna was gratified to report that "the immediate cause of all our success has been the activities of the scholars who were educated in Rome." The Order was doubly fortunate in having Petrus Canisius on hand in Germany to carry out his General's "request"—"the proliferation of schools maintained by the Society of Jesus in many different regions, especially in such places where a great influx of students is to be expected, would be the best way that we might come to the aid of the Church in its currently beleaguered condition."

In so doing, Canisius was actually building on a foundation laid down by Martin Luther himself, since many of the German states had taken their inspiration from him in setting up a system of free primary schools. By the 1590's the number of staunch Protestant families who had enrolled their sons in Jesuit schools had become something of a scandal in Lutheran circles. "Yet," one pastor wrote despairingly, "how many of our own are so learned and well-instructed as the Jesuits? How many as diligent and as skilled in imparting that knowledge to the young as these emissaries of the Romish Antichrist?" As mentioned earlier, the Jesuit colleges founded by Canisius had more than a touch of the reeducation camp about them, and every college became the staging area for the reconversion of an entire district. To maintain some of the sense of solidarity among his former students after they had left college, Canisius encouraged the establishment of "Marian Congregations," religious confraternities whose members were especially dedicated to the cult of the Virgin Mary (and which may have been the origin of the myth of the "invisible Jesuits" as well).

By the time the Protestant elders realized that a whole generation of young people had been quietly but irretrievably lost to the Reformed confession, there was very little they could do about it but heap curses on the head of that "Latinized dog" Canisius and all his works—and these were constantly proliferating as well. After Vienna, Prague, Cologne, and Ingolstadt,* a college was founded in Munich in 1559. Canisius judged the city itself to be "lovely but corrupted," and the old-fashioned local clergy were still sunk in pre-Reformation depravity. From an educational standpoint, the corruption was even more advanced; the city's eighteen Protestant schoolmasters had lured away almost all of the eligible students—but by 1660 the report was that "everyone is flocking to the Jesuits." The Jesuits had endeared themselves to the people of Munich by their courage and self-sacrifice during an outbreak of the plague in 1572, and they had learned to brew a very creditable Bavarian beer (a feat that imported Italian missionaries could never have brought off) and proceeded to undersell all the other breweries in Munich, whose immoderate prices had driven them to become brewmasters in the first place.

By 1580 the Jesuit monopoly on higher education in Catholic Europe was secure. From Portugal to Poland the Order occupied the most prestigious university chairs; their colleges were considered to be, quite literally, citadels of orthodoxy and impregnable bastions against heresy. In 1578 Alexander Farnese, Philip II's viceroy in the Netherlands, wrote to his royal master: "Your Majesty has expressed the wish that I construct a fortress in Maastricht, but it has been my observation that a Jesuit college would be much apter to the defense of the inhabitants against the enemies of the altar and the throne, and thus I have caused one to be built." The major universities of South Germany, as well as Prague, Vienna, and Ingolstadt, were collectively under Jesuit control, and the universities of Würzburg and Graz, home of the unhappy Archduke Charles, were built expressly for them, as were a number of lesser

---

*Apart from the Catholic university, of which Canisius had served as rector, there was also a Jesuit college and a seminary (founded in 1578), which made Ingolstadt the prototype of the "Jesuit city."

institutions in other cities and towns from Alsace in the west up into (present-day) Poland and West Prussia. Not since the heyday of the Dominicans during the Middle Ages had a single organization of any kind so completely dominated the intellectual life of Europe. But this also meant that the same spirit of rigidity and subservience to higher authority that prevailed in the Jesuit colleges was now transferred to the universities as well, and over the long run could not possibly do anything but harm.

The consequences of this were not long in making themselves felt, however, and the Jesuits eventually discovered that they had been outstripped by their rivals in the Protestant countries and by a few outsiders who had managed to propagate their ideas without benefit of the authority of a university chair.

It is a tribute to whatever intellectual vitality still remained in the Order that the Jesuits at least did not decide to stand or fall with the old Scholastic philosophy; instead they decided to adopt a somewhat more ambiguous posture. Accordingly a document entitled *Ratio atque Institutio Studiorum Societatis Jesus* was approved by General Aquaviva in 1599; the *Ratio Studiorum* established a set of basic principles according to which all instruction in the colleges was to be conducted. Basically the Order was attempting to flirt with both Scholasticism and Humanism by embracing neither, or, to put it somewhat more appropriately, to maintain the authority of the Church while still allowing a very limited field of activity to new ideas and doctrines. (The *Ratio Studiorum* was not seriously revised until 1832.) As soon as the curriculum was reduced to a printed syllabus, the long-suppressed urge to draw up a code of written regulations for the individual colleges was allowed to run riot. Perhaps this was understandable—since the Order was determined to impose strict limitations on the life of the spirit, they hoped to do much the same where their students' external appearance was concerned. The instructions regarding haircuts for the students at the College at Mainz in Upper Saxony were issued by the Jesuit provincial of the Upper Rhine, but they have a positively Prussian ring to them:

> At the beginning of the academic year all instructors should acquaint their students with good reasons why they should not allow their hair to grow long and tangled, after the manner of Swiss mercenaries and stablehands. Hair that is allowed to grow moderately long but does not conceal the

features or fall down over the shoulders may more readily be tolerated.

(The regulation adopted by the Jesuits of Munich is somewhat more liberal and very interesting in the way that it hints at mysteries unknown to modern science—long hair was permitted to be worn by barons and "by those who are required to do so on the advice of a physician.")

It might be better to end this chapter with a word from Father Adam Contzen, author of *Der Hofleutspiegel* (*The Mirror of the Courtier*), which was published in 1630; Father Contzen clearly knew his own mind, at least, and was a strict German nationalist when it came to tidying up the old Gothic manners, "since the much-heralded French *politesse* is all very well for those who are accustomed to it, but for Germans it amounts to nothing more than bare-faced lying."

PART ❧ VII

GLORIA DEI ET GLORIA MUNDI—
THE JESUITS AND THE ARTS

Putting up a building is as good as giving alms.

—Pope Gregory XIII (1572–1585)

Men take to religion only so that they may do what they want to.

—Michel de Montaigne

PART VI

"MAKING FRIENDS OF THE HERETICS"—THE JESUITS
AND THE THEATER

An angel descends from an unseen catwalk high above the stage, his robes glimmering in the beams of multicolored light, and hovers protectively over Cenodoxus, striving mightily to save his soul. Cenodoxus (roughly translated as "Newfangled Beliefs") is the title character of a six-hour theatrical spectacle by Father Jacob Bidermann (1578–1639), one of the most talented of the many Jesuit fathers who turned playwright during this period. In his own time Father Bidermann was regarded by some as a second Shakespeare, though this description of a performance of *Cenodoxus* given in Munich in 1609 makes him sound more like a second Savonarola:

> Just as this play set the patrons to laughing so much that the very benches were in danger of cracking, so it also made such a wholesome impression on them that full fourteen of them, persons of the highest rank of the Bavarian court, retired into solitude during the days that followed, to perform the exercises and to reform their manner of living. Truly a hundred sermons would not have done so much good.

This is the kind of notice that a clerical playwright's dreams are made of, which can be explained, some historians say, by the fact that it was written by Father Bidermann himself. A modern critic might fault *Cenodoxus* for its plot contrivances and grandiose conception (Father Bidermann has tried to cram a point-by-point rebuttal of Luther's doctrine of salvation by faith alone into an old-fashioned evening at the theater with plenty of special effects). Still, we do know from other sources that such Jesuit plays were remarkably effective, and a drastically abridged version of *Cenodoxus* actually enjoyed a brief revival in 1958, though for strictly antiquarian reasons, as part of the celebration of the city of Munich's first millennium of existence.

Like many others in their time, the Jesuits drifted into the theater gradually; since a great deal of emphasis was placed on rhetoric and elocution in the Jesuit colleges, it was not too long before the students began to perform, or rather declaim, dramatic treatments of religious themes for an audience of parents and local dignitaries—a sort of combination Christmas pageant and high-school debating championship conducted entirely in Latin—and the first really public performance was given in the conventual church in Vienna, in 1555. The practice quickly spread to Ingolstadt and Munich and all along the Lower Rhine, where over five hundred such productions were staged between 1597 and 1773, and printed partbooks still exist for over two hundred different plays.

Certainly the Jesuits must have enjoyed putting on plays, especially since "there is no better means of winning over the Germans, of making friends out of the heretics and the enemies of the Church, and filling up the enrollment of the school than good high-spirited playacting," as the faculty of the Munich College explained. And even from the fabled realm of the Indies, a missionary reported back that "the Indians are great lovers of poetry and declamation, and nothing has made a more forceful impression than our play."

Molière got his start putting on Latin plays in a Jesuit school near Paris, and, whether or not the Germans could follow spoken Latin verse any better than the Indians could, even the dress rehearsals of the Jesuit plays, particularly in Munich, were always sold out. In fact, it was not so much the "poetry and declamation" that packed the house in Europe as the scenery and pageantry and theatrical effects; the plays themselves, dramatized Bible stories, were usually of the finger-wagging school of religious drama and could quite easily be ignored. Rather than as dramatists, it was really as set designers, scene painters, stage managers that the Jesuits excelled, and they learned to make the most of the scenic and dramatic possibilities of even the most sluggish and didactic Latin play. The theater in Central Europe was in a fairly primitive state in those days, and the traveling players who rode in their green-painted wagons from town to town had only one drawing card that the Jesuits could not match; female roles were acted by "real wenches," as their handbills sometimes phrased it, instead of beardless adolescents as in the Jesuit colleges. Thus the Jesuits were obliged to compensate both for an unintelligible script (or at best, merely a boring one) and the absence of real wenches with elaborately staged illusions and all sorts of wizardry— palaces crumbled into dust, real bonfires roared, "flying machines" with six actors on board soared up into the air, and the raging billows of the sea not only raged but changed color as well. The technical crew could "make a cloud come down that split into three different parts and then drew back together as it ascended into the flies." The magic lantern, perfected by the Jesuit polymath Athenasius Kircher, produced the illusion of burning cities, conflagrations, and the like by means of projections on a screen, and during one performance in 1640 a dummy representing the Protestant heresy was torn to pieces onstage by a pack of trained dogs! During another performance, in Munich, a group of actors who had been sitting quietly in the audience suddenly leaped up onto the stage and began to take part in the action of the play—a device that has been rediscovered by various modern experimental theater groups.

The lavish spirit of the baroque dictated the use of hundreds, even thousands, of extras on stage, and performances tended to become all-day affairs. Originally the curtain went up directly after lunch and the play might last two hours or so. *Cenodoxus* was not abnormally long for its time, however; other plays lasted for eight hours or more, and when persons of princely rank were in attendance, an intermission was announced as soon as the serenissimus began to get tired. And finally, when eight hours was still not enough to get the sacred message across, then "the first half plays today, but to our sorrow,/The second needs must wait until tomorrow" (*Den halben theil nembt heut verguet, den ubrigen morgan man halten tuet*), as the playbill to a two-day spectacular entitled *Constantine* announced. In 1577 an even bigger extravaganza, *Esther*, broke all previous records in Munich by stretching itself out for three days "with great pomp and magnificence." Just what was meant by this becomes clearer when one riffles through the eighteen closely printed pages of dramatis personae, which call for almost two thousand extras—a good 10 percent of the population in Munich in those days. The stage was set up on the Marienplatz, and, apart from the three hundred or so principal players, the stage directions mention demons, men with lions' heads, Neptune, an elephant, Moors, dolphins, a tiger, a wolf, a dragon (led by two young virgins), a troop of hunters, Turkish janissaries, and "a train of artillery with its master cannoneers."

As the spectacle grew ever more spectacular, the audiences grew larger (as many as three thousand spectators at one performance in theater-mad Vienna) and more enthusiastic (at Hildesheim in 1737 the police had to be called in to control the mob outside the theater). In 1747 Frederick the Great attended a performance at the Jesuit seminary in the town of Gross-Glogau and was provided with his own simultaneous interpreter, who improvised a German oration to match the classical reenactment of his famous feats of arms that was going on onstage. In general, though, as the spectacle grew more baroque, the plot (and the incomprehensible Latin dialogue) was all that much easier to ignore. In addition, the onstage ban on the vernacular was relaxed during the interludes performed between the acts. These introduced a rowdy vaudeville element into the proceedings that grew even rowdier with time, and of course the audience was thrilled when the actors spoke directly to them in German. At this point it seems that these Jesuit impresarios were pursuing the goal of pure entertainment for its own sake, since these developments could hardly be covered by the usual pretext that they were offering a kind of sugar-coated instruction in the classics or the Gospels (a fact that they were continually being reminded of in directives from various Superior Generals).

When the Order was revived after the dissolution of 1772, the grand manner of the earlier productions had been tempered by a certain academic restraint. Nevertheless, Goethe was fascinated by a performance that he attended at the Jesuit college in Regensburg, Bavaria, in 1816, as he describes in this passage from his *Journey to Italy:*

This public performance has once again convinced me of the intelligence of the Jesuits. They did not disdain to try anything that might have brought off an effect, and they well knew how to manage it, meticulously and lovingly. This is not just intelligence as we conceive of it *in abstracto,* but also that pure love of a thing for its own sake that enables us to take pleasure in the sheer doing of it and in ourselves for having done it, the pleasure that is always engendered when something is done out of love. . . . And just as their churches are distinguished by a pleasing effect of pomp and artifice, these sagacious gentlemen have also availed themselves of a kind of worldly sensuality through the agency of this perfectly respectable theater of theirs.

The sensuous appeal of these productions was enhanced by incidental music in most cases, and often a ballet interlude as well (with most of the dancers recruited from among the students of the college). The music was composed by the college's music master or by the *Kapellmeister* (music director) of the local church, and the standards of composition and performance seemed to have been remarkably high. The Germanicum in Rome became one of the great centers of musical activity in Europe during the baroque era, but the most celebrated of these music masters belonged to a slightly earlier period. This was Orlandus Lassus (died 1594), the last of the great Flemish masters of the High Renaissance, who was not a Jesuit himself but who taught in the college in Munich and served as court composer to the duke of Bavaria. Today the name Orlandus Lassus is known only to a comparative handful of early-music buffs—not true of Mozart, however, though his association with the Jesuits was confined to a commission for a single piece of incidental music for a play at the Jesuit college in Salzburg, written when he had just turned eleven. The music credit on the program, couched in pompous New Latin periods, read as follows: *Auctor operis musici nobilis dominus Wolfgangus Mozart, undecennis, filius nobilis ac strenui domini Mozart, Capellae Magistri.* (The second *"domini Mozart"* is Leopold, father of Wolfgang Amadeus, who served as *Kapellmeister* (*"capellae magister"*) to the archbishop of Salzburg.)

This was in 1770, and by this time the Jesuits' brand of theater was a stately antique, the last survival of the magnificent baroque style that had reigned supreme all over Europe fifty or a hundred years before. It had been superseded by the new drama of the Enlightenment, which was more concerned with human emotions and the delineation of character than pomp and spectacle. The Jesuits' great contribution was in the technique of stagecraft; plays like *Cenodoxus* had little or no influence on the secular stage, and the Jesuit theater itself, like most of the Order's forays into the arts, turned out to be brilliant but ephemeral, like a spectacular display of fireworks that entrances us for a moment, then fades and disappears.

FINDING THE RIGHT THUMBSCREW—THE JESUITS AND LITERATURE

The profession of literature, rather than the theater, might seem like a more appropriate outlet for the particular talents cultivated by the Jesuits. However, the Order was not very fortunate in its stable of authors, since the good writers tended to be bad Jesuits and vice versa. Consider the case of Baltasar Gracian (1601–58), the rector of the Jesuit college in Tarragona, today regarded as one of the foremost masters of Spanish baroque, though in his lifetime his superiors in the Order had little cause to commend him for any other reason. Ostensibly the problem was that he was overly preoccupied with the occult, which immediately seems like a pretext, since the same charge could have been leveled against almost every intellectual in those days. Actually the problem was that Father Gracian had had extensive firsthand experience of the moribund state of education in the colleges, which he had sharply criticized in his writings. The provincial forbade him to publish anything further, and Gracian countered with an even more graphic request—he asked to be released from his vows. (Gracian also responded to the provincial's order with a gesture that was part defiance, part Jesuitical equivocation: he had his last work, a novel called *The Critic,* published under someone else's name.) The next step was to order him confined to his cell, where he spent the rest of his life in complete isolation.

Gracian's *El Oráculo Manual* (called *The Oracle* in English) was rescued from semiobscurity by the German philosopher Arthur Schopenhauer in the nineteenth century. Schopenhauer published an excellent translation of *The Oracle* under the pseudonym Felix Trollmund ("Troll Mouth"), perhaps an allusion to the slightly sinister, even "monstrous" qualities that are not difficult to detect in Gracian's work. In his translator's preface, Trollmund recommends the book, which is actually a collection of practical maxims, to "everyone who lives in the great world, and most especially to young people who are eager to get on in life, since here they will learn lessons, once and for all, that otherwise could only be gotten through long experience of life."

Here are a few of Father Gracian's maxims, in one or two of which the well-known flexibility of "Jesuit morality" is strained past the breaking point:

- What brings you credit, look to it yourself; what brings you discredit, look to another to do it in your stead.
- Embark on another man's business to save yourself from thinking of your own.
- Trust your friends of today as if they were your enemies of tomorrow.
- Know how to sweeten your refusal, and learn to find the right thumb-screw so that no man can refuse you.
- Keep your eyes fixed on a happy outcome, since a victor need never excuse himself to anyone.

And finally the most Ignatian of all the maxims, number 251:

- Do things in a human way as if there were no godly way; do things in a godly way as though there is no human way.

At least it seems clear why Schopenhauer, the foremost of our pessimistic philosophers, found Gracian's outlook so congenial, and why his superiors in the Order saw him simply as a renegade who stood in need of some disciplinary restraint.

The biography of Friedrich Spee von Langenfeld, the leading German Jesuit writer of the Counter-Reformation and outwardly a much more respectable character than Gracian, also contains a few intriguing passages that suggest a similar pattern of conflict with authority, the details of which have never really come to light. Spee was born in 1591, attended Jesuit schools, and took his vows in 1610. He had hoped, like so many others, to be sent to the Indies as a missionary; instead he was made a kind of cathedral chaplain, whose duty it was to preach sermons and to hear the confessions of persons condemned for witchcraft before they were sent to the stake. He served as a chaplain with the Imperial forces during the Thirty Years' Wars, and he succumbed to camp fever while treating the wounded in the newly conquered city of Trier in 1635. So much for Spee's official biography. His most important literary work is a collection of lyrics with the admirable title *Spite-Nightingale, or The Grove of Spiritual-Poetical Delight, the Like of Which Has Never Before Been Seen in the German Tongue. For the uplifting of all Godly and God-fearing Souls and especially lovers of the poetic arts, by a priest of the Societas Jesu.* The author explains in the introduction, "This book was called Spite-Nightingale because it sings its sweet and lovely song to put *all* nightingales to shame. Its song is sincere and heart-felt poetry." Critics have detected in Spee's religious verses the promise of a simple and unaffected lyrical style, which seems to belie the fact that *Spite-Nightingale* was first published in 1649, some fourteen years after the poet's death. This is unlikely to have been due to lack of interest in his work, since several printings were sold out immediately, nor is it any reflection on style or content—the problem was with another work by Spee that was published during his lifetime and that got him into a certain amount of trouble with his superiors. This was a book entitled *Cautio criminalis* (roughly "Circumspection in Criminal Cases"), which describes Spee's experiences hearing the last confessions of condemned witches and was the first published criticism, ever, of the judicial procedures employed in the witch trials. *Cautio criminalis* was published anonymously by a Protestant printer in 1631, and it is not clear whether this was merely a case of literary piracy or whether Spee, like Baltasar Gracian, was simply being circumspect himself. In any case, when the secret of his authorship was disclosed, Spee was threatened with expulsion from the Order, at least until he was able to "prove" to his superiors' satisfaction that he had given the manuscript of the book to a friend who had gone off and had it published without his knowledge.

Cautio criminalis was not a direct attack on the witch-hunting craze. As far as Spee was concerned, there was no doubt that there were such things as witches, but he simply suspected that the rules of procedure in such cases should be overhauled in order to prevent so many defendants from being unjustly convicted. I came across a record of a conversation between Father Spee and Johann Philip von Schönborn, later the elector of Mainz, who asked Spee how it was that his hair had turned completely gray by the time he was forty. Spee replied, "It is regret that has turned my hair all gray, regret that I've had to accompany so many witches to the place of execution and among them I found not one who was not innocent." All told, Spee had heard the confessions of some two hundred condemned "witches"; as a result of his revelations the prince-bishops of Mainz and later of Württemburg prohibited any further such trials from taking place in their domains.

Over the years the Order has had its share of problems with the printed word. In countless instances Jesuits have left the Order because they could not resolve the conflict between their vows and their journalistic instincts, though, on the other hand, this is not to deny, as Father Spee might have put it, that Jesuits have not been unsuccessful in the literary marketplace. Petrus Canisius was impressed by the high esteem in which authors were held by the German public—"One writer counts for more in Germany," he observed, "than ten professors." In those days fully half of all the books published in Europe were printed in Germany, and Canisius's own *Shorter Catechism* was a perennial best seller until the early years of our century. Hermann Busenbaum, a Jesuit from Cologne, wrote a treatise on Christian ethics in 1650 that sold out more than two hundred printings over the next 150 years. (Father Busenbaum is also a dark-horse candidate for the authorship of the infamous phrase "the end justifies the means.") One book that some enterprising editor might consider reissuing today, with certain modifications, was first published in 1756 by a Bavarian Jesuit and professor of philology named Ignaz Weitenauer, who had devised a revolutionary new method of instruction "that enables one to learn the ancient and modern languages of the Orient, including the Hebrew, the Syriac, and the Chaldean, in one or two hours." If the Weitenauer Method could successfully be transferred to a couple of tape cassettes, and perhaps Arabic, Japanese, or Balinese could be substituted for Syriac and Chaldean, tourists and harried businessmen could throw away their useless phrase books, and the profits to be realized by the promoters would be enormous.

A SUBSTITUTE SENSUALITY—THE JESUITS AND ARCHITECTURE

During no other time in its history has the Catholic Church built so many magnificent churches as during the Counter-Reformation. This was the Church's response to the puritanism of the Reformers—architectural richness and emotional fervor rather than austerity and inner light. One of the first buildings to adopt the new style that departed so abruptly from the ideals of the Renaissance and that we call baroque was the Jesuit church of Il Gesù in Rome. Construction began in 1568 on a site that had been selected by Ignatius in 1544, near the Church of Santa

Maria della Strada. The seventy-nine-year-old Michelangelo had promised Ignatius that he would undertake to design the church himself "for the love of God," but he died before the project had even reached the planning stage. Since Il Gesù was the first concerted display of the new baroque style, interior as well as exterior, and since the ground plan of the church was forced into an elaborate flower-petal design by the proliferation of smaller chapels radiating out from the central nave, some art historians have awarded the Jesuits a kind of patent on the baroque style. In fact it was decided at the first General Congregation in 1558 that all buildings, including churches, constructed by the Order should be free from extravagance or pomposity or excessive ornamentation, and toward this end the plans for all future construction would be reviewed by the office of the Superior General. For many years there was still quite a distance between baroque exuberance and Jesuit severity, at least in principle—during the brief generalship of the Spaniard Vincenco Carafa (1646–49) all pictures were banished from the General's private office and a subscription for the purpose of decorating Ignatius's chapel was vetoed on the grounds that Carafa thought it better for the money to be given to the poor.

Though the Jesuits may not have discovered the baroque, they did know how to put it to good use. When the baroque sensibility, of its own accord, gave in to a kind of ecstatic trance or a ceaseless striving after new effects, then, the Jesuits decided, at least all this could be made to serve the greater glory of God. Like the Jesuit theater, a Jesuit church was intended first to dazzle, then to instruct—both to delight the eye of the beholder and to proclaim the unity and majesty of the Roman Catholic Church. Certainly this point was not lost on such a sophisticated connoisseur of theatrical effects as Goethe, who describes the interior of a baroque Jesuit church in *Journey to Italy:*

> The décor is all gold and silver, and precious metals and polished stone, heaped up in such lavish abundance that beggars of every station in society are dazzled by it. A slight touch of vulgarity is present here and there to soothe and to entice the human soul . . . and never have I seen this carried out so intelligently, so adroitly and consummately, as by the Jesuits. Everything conspires to make it seem that, unlike other religious orders repeating an old and outworn litany, they could

Loyola loosed the bonds between heaven and earth. He gave heaven its due in all the traditional ways—and took the governance of men into his own capable hands. Thus a kind of Christian atheism was let loose into the world. . . .

It is thanks to the General that the energies that Christianity had simply suppressed could now be harnessed to the service of an earthly ideal. . . .

Loyola transformed mankind's ancient dream of a worthy and righteous life, which has remained virtually unchanged from Plato to Marx, from the object of our prayers into a military objective.

He became the gravedigger of that old, conservative religion of salvation, which believed that the Messiah had already appeared on earth.

—Ludwig Marcuse (1894–1971),
*Ignatius of Loyola: A Soldier of
the Church* (1955)

still startle us with their pomp and pageantry, in keeping with the spirit of the age.

And though the Jesuits were inclined to give free play to the imagination in designing the interiors of their churches, they also took great pains to design the exteriors to suit the rural landscape or the urban cityscape that would serve as a backdrop to them. Despite a number of standard design prototypes, a certain amount of tinkering was generally in order, depending on the individual requirements of the site; it is to this concern with continuity and adaptability, always a Jesuit strong point, that we owe the Church of St. Michael in Munich, the Michaelskirche in Aachen, and the collegiate churches in Innsbruck, Konstanz, and Regensburg; in Belgium and North Germany the Jesuit concern with maintaining a harmonious facade touched off a minor revival of the regional "brickyard Gothic" style in the midst of the baroque. And it is worth noting that the Jesuits served not only as architects and designers for such projects, but as master masons and bricklayers, cabinetmakers, and altar- and organ-builders as well; just as a Gothic cathedral of three hundred years earlier was a representation in stone and glass of the collective pride and piety of an entire city, these Jesuit churches reflected the collective need of the Jesuit Order to serve God just a little more brilliantly than anyone else. Strangely enough, though, it was not in the arts but in the sciences and humanities that the creative spirit of the Order really came to fruition. No Jesuit poets or painters or composers were really moved by that spirit to achieve great distinction, and it was as scholars and researchers, historians, astronomers, and educators that the Jesuits finally excelled.

PART ❧ VIII

AMEN EST OMEN—THE JESUITS AND SCIENCE

But faith releases reason from all error, illuminates, invigorates, and fulfills it in a wonderful way, by which faith teaches reason to recognize those things that are God's.

> —*Pope Pius IX, in the encyclical*
> Qui pluribus *(1878)*

Philosophy is the handmaiden of theology.

> —*attributed to St. Thomas Aquinas (1225–74)*

FROM CHINA TO PERU—THE JESUITS AND GEOGRAPHY

The bitter, medicinal taste of quinine water and the quinine pills that European housewives still keep on hand as a home remedy for a persistent fever are reminders of an era, not so long ago, in which malaria—"intermittent fever"—was still endemic in many parts of Europe and North America. At that time our housewife's great-grandmother would have gone to the pharmacist for "Peruvian bark" (confusingly called "China bark" in some European countries), and *her* great-grandmother would in turn have bought "Jesuit powder" (*Jesuitenpulver*) from the apothecary. The bark actually came from the cinchona-succimba tree, the natural source of quinine, a very effective remedy against malaria that was first discovered by Peruvian Indians in the forests of the Andes and introduced to Europe by Jesuit missionaries in 1649. (The cinchona tree was later grown on plantations in India and Ceylon, hence "China bark"—"China" in this case being merely a generic term for the Far East, like "India" in India ink, which originally came from China.)

Jesuits lucky enough to travel to the realm of the Indies, and elsewhere, made a practice of searching out useful and medicinal plants of all sorts; they brought back new varieties of cinnamon, nutmeg, and cloves, as well as yerba mate, rhubarb (thought to have remarkable curative properties), and vanilla. Father Georg Kamel (died 1706) sent back a specimen of an unknown flower he had come across in the Philippines. This eventually came to the notice of the great Swedish botanist Linnaeus, who named the entire genus *Camelia,* in tribute to his discovery (which included not only the well-known flowering plants of that name but also the shrub from which we get tea). Jesuits were also on the alert for manmade artifacts and innovations that Europeans stood to benefit by—the umbrella, the seed drill, formulas for making porcelain, recipes for mixing pigments and dyestuffs. In many areas in the world the Jesuits' initial explorations did much to advance the interests of other Europeans with less disinterested motives; but geography and ethnography would also have remained in their inexact, unscientific infancies a great deal longer had not Jesuit missionaries been willing to risk their lives to bring light into these neglected corners of the world:

- Père Jacques Marquette and Louis Jolliet (himself a Jesuit seminary dropout) were the first Europeans to chart the course of the Upper Mississippi, from Wisconsin to the mouth of the Arkansas, in 1673. (Nine years later a second expedition, also led by a Jesuit, successfully reached the Gulf of Mexico.) Today Marquette and Jolliet are both commemorated in the sculpture gallery in the Rotunda of the United States Capital Building.

- Father Eusebio Kühn, who took to calling himself Kino when he reached the New World, discovered the mouth of the Rio Grande, and also corrected, by firsthand observation, the current misconception that California was an island.

- A Bohemian Jesuit, Father Samuel Fritz, crossed the Andes, entirely on his own, and set out on the first cartographical survey of the Amazon basin. For three months Father Fritz lay helpless, racked with fever, in an Indian village that was totally cut off from the outside world when the Amazon overflowed its banks: "Rats bit my feet and chewed up my [wooden] spoon and the handle of my knife." When Alexander Humboldt explored the region some fifty years later (1799–1804), he came fully equipped with all the charts that Father Fritz and other Jesuit missionaries had prepared—"an invaluable acquisition."

- The Jesuit Antonio de Andrade (died 1634) was the first European to cross the Himalayas and make his way into Tibet; he left a remarkably detailed account of his travels in that inhospitable country.

- Father Paez (died 1662) discovered the source of the Blue Nile and was one of the first Europeans ever to set foot in Ethiopia. Father Tieffentaller (died 1785), a surveyor and cartographer of great precision, is remembered as the father of scientific geography in India.

● The most adventurous of these footloose missionary fathers was Bento de Goes, a good Jesuit with a marvelous head for heights, who set out from India, negotiated the Khyber Pass and the High Pamir range and finally the Wakhir Pass (5,411 m.). From there he descended to the desert plateau of Sinkiang and Mongolia and continued across the desert as far as the Great Wall—De Goes had rediscovered the ancient overland Silk Route to China, one of the greatest individual exploits in the annals of the Age of Discovery. His ordeal finally at an end, he tersely reported back to Rome: "The journey is very long, full of difficulties and dangers. No one from the Society should ever attempt to repeat it."

Father de Goes may well have been disappointed that he came across so few human souls, heathen or otherwise, in the course of his four-year journey, since the conversion of the heathen was the real purpose of these reconnaissance expeditions and not merely a pretext for scaling the Himalayas or hacking through the impenetrable jungles to Brazil. It is not too surprising, then, that the Jesuits, never wont to do anything by halves, far outstripped their contemporaries in the field of linguistics. Collectively they mastered ninety-five different languages and drew up word lists for them, wrote the first Chinese grammar (in any language other than Chinese, of course), were the first Europeans to study Sanskrit, and in Brazil they compiled a dictionary of words that were common to various Indian languages, which became the basis of the *lingua geral* that tribal Indians still use to communicate with members of other tribes today. The Church's official policy of discouraging (which generally meant burning) vernacular translations of the Bible was relaxed somewhat, and the Jesuits were authorized to prepare new translations of the Bible to confound the heretics (in Poland, Bohemia, and Hungary) and persuade the schismatics (in Ethiopia), and brand-new translations to convert the infidels (in Persia) and idolators (in Japan).

The Black Leonardo—Father Athanasius Kircher, S.J.

Athanasius Kircher (1601–1680) was the universal genius of the Jesuit Order, the all-around Jesuit, who was always more at home in the field of action than in the scholar's study. The most dramatic illustration of this preference was provided in 1638, when Kircher decided to measure the depths of Europe's principal volcanoes, and accordingly had himself lowered into the crater of Stromboli at the end of a rope. He wrote a vivid account of his experience, but only in the very last sentence does he attempt to draw the obvious religious parallel:

> Amid frightful wailing, pillars of smoke admixed with pale tongues of flame ascended from eleven distinct spots in the crater wall and the side of the mountain. Awestruck at the sight of these works of the Almighty, I said a prayer and shuddered at the thought of the terrors of the Last Judgment.

Nicely put, but we still come away with the impression that this is not so much the moral of the story as a hastily improvised coda, intended to make it seem that this whole glorious geophysical adventure was undertaken purely for the greater glory of the Almighty and his works.

Kircher's most enduring achievement was probably the *lanterna magica*, that early ancestor of the film projector that became the mainstay of the special-effects department of the Jesuit theater. This usually rates him at least a brief mention in the first chapter of any book on the history of film, but Kircher did not actually invent the magic lantern,* as is often stated, though he did improve it considerably by introducing a convex lens to focus the image and project it more sharply on the screen.

Kircher, as is the way with geniuses, did not show much promise as a child—"limited powers of comprehension" was the verdict of an early school report—but he still progressed through the Jesuit school system (at every school he attended he made it his business to realign the sundial so it would keep better time), and by age twenty-eight he held the chair of philosophy and mathematics at the Jesuit University of Würzburg. Before long he was relieved of his teaching responsibilities so he could devote more time to original research and during the scientific revolution of the seventeenth century he received encouragement and offers of financial backing from many different quarters. He died in Rome at age seventy-nine, and his collected works filled forty-four volumes—

*Leonardo's notebooks contain sketches of a magic lantern with a convex lens, and a primitive version of the device (no lens) was actually constructed by Giovanni Battista Porta around 1589. Kircher's perfected design is described in his *Ars Magna Lucis et Umbrae,* which appeared in 1646.

certainly a rich and untroubled life for a scientist of any age, though like many other Jesuits before him, including Ignatius, he was originally denied his greatest wish in life, to be sent off as a missionary "without companions or money for the journey." General Vitelleschi, for some unknown reason, refused his request.

In 1979, the tercentenary of Kircher's death, Father Franz Lennart prepared a more complete list of his accomplishments, which appeared in *Canisius,* a German-language magazine published by the Order. Just to begin with:

- He built the world's first calculator.
- He discovered that the relative strength of a magnet can be measured with the help of a balance scale.
- He was the first to use the expansion of mercury to measure changes in temperature.
- He invented an extremely powerful megaphone, which drew a crowd of two thousand people when he gave it its first open-air trial.
- During an outbreak of the plague in 1656 he analyzed the blood of a plague victim and concluded that "the plague is carried by animalcules that are so small, so thin, and so subtle-bodied that they could only be detected by a very good microscope."

In addition, Kircher was a tireless observer of all sorts of natural phenomena (the psychological effects of different colors on human moods and behavior), and a collector of striking or merely curious facts (that sea ice yields fresh water when it melts, that the South Atlantic Equatorial Current splits in two at the Brazilian coast and that the northern branch empties into the Gulf of Mexico, and that chalk lines drawn on the ground exercise a peculiar fascination over chickens—this last fact prompted a number of precocious speculations on the nature of hypnotism and autosuggestion). And like all great speculators and theorizers, Kircher was often most original and most interesting when he was completely on the wrong track. For example, Kircher was one of the first modern scholars to take an interest in Egyptian hieroglyphs, and he published a four-volume work on the subject, with many translations of actual Egyptian inscriptions, none of which corresponds in any way to the real meaning of the originals. Kircher had started with the plausible but incorrect assumption that hieroglyphs were pure picture-writing, but this in turn suggested the more promising idea of a pictographic script that would enable the deaf to be taught to read and write.

In the related field of biblical scholarship, Kircher reveals himself as a more conventional child of his times—he believed not only in the literal truth of every word in the Bible, but also thought that a great deal could be read between the lines. For example, he drew up a plan of Noah's Ark that includes a detailed description of the sanitary arrangements provided on board for both man and beast, and he confidently asserted that construction was halted on the Tower of Babel in exactly the year 1984 (after the Creation). To us it may seem both quaint and incomprehensible that a gifted scientist like Kircher could have spent so much of his time so unprofitably, mistranslating hieroglyphs or diagraming the scuppers and bilges of Noah's Ark; the first of these may just be another instance of the Jesuits' unfortunate tendency to spread themselves a little too thin, but the second provides a serious illustration of the limitations imposed on seventeenth-century science, particularly Jesuit science, which remained the handmaiden of theology, a handmaiden who was still expected to serve, to defend, and above all never to contradict her mistress, however undignified or incongruous these services might be to perform.

The Crime of Galileo—the Jesuits and Astronomy

The Jesuits lived up to their seventeenth-century nickname, "Heaven's Grenadiers," in a variety of ways. First, they made two memorable if abortive attempts to storm the heavens directly. In 1670 Father Francesco Lanaterzi became intrigued by the experiments of the German scientist Otto von Guericke, who had demonstrated that it was possible to pump the air out of a hollow sphere to produce at least a partial vacuum. Father Lanaterzi was convinced that it should also be possible to leave the ground altogether and soar through the air with the help of one or two of Von Guericke's spheres. Though admirable in theory, this scheme was far from being practicable, and Father Lanaterzi remained earthbound. Fifty years later a Portuguese Jesuit, Father Lorenço Gusmão, rigged up a gondola beneath a hot-air balloon made out of paper and actually got it off the ground—only to be arrested by the Inquisition on a charge of sorcery when he returned to earth. It would be another fifty years before the Montgolfier brothers repeated the experiment in a more favorable social climate, and there is no evidence that they were inspired in any way by the example of Father Gusmão—who had served as a missionary and, as his diary makes clear, had merely copied the design for his balloon from one he had actually seen used by the Indians for a number of successful ascensions in Peru!

Perhaps wisely, though, the majority of Jesuit scientists preferred astronomy to aeronautics, though astronomy was often to prove as controversial and as dangerous. The Bavarian Jesuit Christoph Clavius was one of the leading mathematicians and astronomers of his time, perhaps second only to Galileo. Clavius discovered and mapped a great many lunar craters, one of the largest of which is named for him (an industrious Jesuit historian has calculated that no less than thirty-two lunar landmarks are named for their Jesuit discoverers). The idea that made it possible for seventeenth-century astronomers to sweep the skies with such encouraging results—the principle of the telescope—seems to have occurred to a number of inventors in the early years of the century, and it is not clear who was the first to arrange a series of lenses in the winning combination. A German Jesuit, Christoph Scheiner, is certainly well up among the claimants to the title—he turned out his first telescope in 1613 (only a few years after Galileo and to specifications supplied by Kepler), and, along with Galileo and several others, was among the first to make accurate observations of sunspots. Kepler himself was given his first telescope by a Jesuit instrument maker called Father Zuechi; that Kepler was a staunch Protestant who thought of Catholicism as "a tare among the upright stalks of the true apostolic doctrine" was apparently neither here nor there. Certainly Kepler received a great deal less sympathy and encouragement from his fellow Protestants, who tended to be mistrustful of his astronomical theorizing and kept intoning the same biblical passages about the sun standing still upon Gibeon that the Inquisition was later to invoke against Galileo.

Thus far, though, the theologians and the astronomers had avoided open conflict, thanks largely to the complacency of the former and the timidity of the latter. Nikolaus Copernicus had first written out an account of his new "system of the worlds" around 1510, but he was reluctant to have his theories appear in print for fear that he would be ridiculed, or worse, for daring to contradict Aristotle, Ptolemy, and the Book of Joshua by suggesting that the earth revolved around the sun, and not the other way around. Copernicus finally relented and agreed to publish when Pope Clement VII, himself something of an amateur astrologer, "most emphatically" requested him to "share his discoveries with the learned world." *De revolutionibus orbium coelestium* ("On the Revolution of the Heavenly Spheres") appeared in 1543, the year of Copernicus's death. He himself was a Catholic, canon of a Polish cathedral, but the work was edited by a Lutheran theologian, Andreas Osiander, who contributed a lengthy preface in which he was careful to explain that Copernicus's ideas were no more than mathematical constructs for the benefit of professional astronomers and were not to be taken literally. (Perhaps Osiander was simply being cautious, but Luther, Melancthon, and other leading reformers were genuinely reluctant to believe that the earth could possibly move around the sun.)

Not surprisingly, *De revolutionibus* did not have much of an impact on the learned world when it finally appeared. First, the book was packed with mystical, magical allusions that made it largely incomprehensible; and second, Osiander was quite right in saying that Copernicus's system was still no more than a theory that would have to be proved or disproved by astronomical observation. It would be sixty years or more before Galileo Galilei—who was born in Pisa in 1564, twenty-one years after Copernicus's death—would be able to demonstrate that Copernicus's system actually corresponded to the way things were.

Galileo himself had hesitated for some time before he became a convert to heliocentrism, and it was only when he discovered the moons of Jupiter with his telescope that he acknowledged his conversion publicly (in the old Ptolemaic system only the earth was allowed the distinction of having a satellite; the other planets were not supposed to have any, let alone five). At that time Galileo was already fifty years old, he enjoyed a considerable reputation in the scientific world, and he held the post of court mathematician to the duke of Tuscany. This announcement did have quite a marked effect on the learned world, and on theologians as well; Galileo's colleagues may not have been won over by the sheer force of his reputation, but they definitely had been given something to think about, and some of them actually refused to read his announcement of his discovery for fear that they would be convinced of something they were not fully prepared to believe.

At least it must have been no small consolation for Galileo that one of the leading astronomers of the day, Father Christoph Clavius, checked over his calculations and endorsed them without reservation—which is not to say, of course, that Father Clavius necessarily endorsed his conclusions as well. This distinction appears to have been lost on Galileo, however, who was delighted to discover that he had found such a formidable, if unexpected, set of allies in the Jesuit astronomers. Before long he had become an habitué of the Jesuit college in Rome, and was cordially received by Pope Paul V, who engaged him in highly technical discussions of scientific topics, and by his successor as well, Urban VIII (with whom Galileo is said to have become rather close friends).

The idea of Galileo's dropping in on the Collegio Romano and hobnobbing with the Pope does not square too well with more conventional accounts, which you probably remember from school, of Galileo languishing in the dungeons of the Inquisition, being shown the instruments of torture, and finally recanting his Copernican views while muttering a defiant *"Eppur se muove"** under his breath. For a number of years now it has been clear that this was not the way it happened at all. A group of Dominican scholars sifted through the original documents in the case—including the confidential archives of the Vatican—and as a result of several decades' work a very different picture of both Galileo and of the Jesuits has finally emerged.

- Galileo was tried twice—the first trial was concerned with the theological problems that were posed by his theories in general. The second trial, also conducted by the Inquisition, was primarily an investigation of Galileo's personal beliefs.
- Galileo was detained "at the pleasure of the Inquisition" during his trial—but not in a cell; he and servants occupied a three-room apartment that overlooked the Vatican gardens.
- *"Eppur se muove"* was never said by Galileo at all (as nearly as we can tell) but appears to have been the happy inspiration of a French Jesuit, Abbé Traith, 128 years after the fact.
- The Jesuits were not quite the reactionary villains and enemies of free inquiry they have been made out to be, or at least not all of them, since some of the Jesuits involved in Galileo's second trial testified for the defense.
- As is often the case, even with a *cause célèbre* like this one, the preliminary skirmishes and the goings-on behind the scenes were much more interesting and eventful than the trial itself.

These are the circumstances: Galileo was riding on the crest of a wave of approval. As far as he was concerned, the Copernican theory, and his own, were both as good as proven. His Jesuit friends tried to make him realize that as long as really conclusive proof was lacking, the Church

---

*Literally, "And yet it [the earth] moves [around the sun]"; colloquially, "It does *too* move!"

could only accept these theories as mathematical suppositions; Galileo was certainly no match for the Jesuits in tact or diplomacy, and he inopportunely proclaimed that everyone who declined to embrace the Copernican system was "a spiritual pygmy who scarcely deserves to be called a human being." As far as the Jesuits were concerned, Galileo had only two alternatives—to be silent (at least on this one sticky point) or be silenced. Galileo refused to accept the first alternative, and in fact he insisted that his opponents should prove to him that his theories were *not* true, which (from the Church's point of view) was both unrealistic and provocative. Galileo was certainly aware of what the Jesuits thought of all this. Cardinal Robert Bellarmine, a Jesuit and the most prominent Catholic theologian of the age, wrote to Galileo's student Foscarini on April 4, 1615, and explained the situation with remarkable candor:

> It seems to me that you and Galilei would do well to speak *ex suppositione* [hypothetically] rather than absolutely, as I believe Copernicus himself did. If there were genuine proof that the sun is located in the center of the universe and that it does not turn around the earth, but rather the earth around the sun, then in interpreting those biblical passages which appear to assert the contrary, we should have to exercise great care and we should do better to say that we did not understand them than to declare this viewpoint to be false when it has been proven to be true. For the present I am of the opinion that no such proof exists, since none has been set before me.

The judges in Galileo's first trial finally arrived at much the same formulation when they met to consider the possible dangers to the faith that were posed by Galileo's theories. (Pope John Paul II gave an address at the Gregoriana in 1979 in which he praised Bellarmine as a "farsighted genius" who "in the case of Galileo wished to avoid unnecessary tension and a destructive hardening of relations between faith and religion." A decade earlier this would have sounded like heavy irony, but it is probably an accurate appraisal of Bellarmine's real intentions.) In any case Galileo took the cardinal's advice very much to heart, though he chose to apply it in a way that was both subtle and unexpected. In his next major work on astronomy, he decided to treat both the Copernican and the rival Ptolemaic system *ex suppositione,* so that the Ptolemaic theory endorsed by the Church and the learned world for over a thousand years was demoted to a mere hypothesis. He also chose to write his book in dialogue form, so that he could play these rival theories against each other without appearing to take sides in an obvious way. The decree of the Holy Office, dated May 5, 1616, which set forth the decision in his first trial, had imposed a number of severe constraints—he was not permitted to refer to the earth as a "star" (i.e., a planet), and the Copernican theory was denounced as "false and in all points antithetical to Holy Scripture."

Perhaps he would have gotten away with this; however, he seems to have gone too far when he gave the name "Simplicius" to the character in his dialogue who defends the orthodox Ptolemaic theory with arguments that are not only simplistic but downright asinine. Envious and malicious tongues at the papal court managed to convince Pope Urban that this buffoonish figure was meant to be a caricature of himself— Galileo had had plenty of opportunity to observe his subject at close range. On April 12, 1633, Galileo was taken into custody by the Inquisition—which proves that even popes are not immune from personal vanity.

The Inquisition did not hand down formal indictments, and it was not until the seventy-year-old Galileo was actually brought before the tribunal that he learned he was being charged with heresy. His accusers— and a number of Jesuits were among them—produced as their principal piece of evidence a memorandum of a conversation between Bellarmine and Galileo in 1616, in which Galileo had allegedly been instructed "neither to profess nor to defend [the Copernican theory] in any manner whatsoever." (The incriminating document was presumably found among the cardinal's papers a dozen years after his death, which suggests either a remarkably efficient filing system or an opportune forgery; most historians suspect the latter.)

But when confronted with this accusation, Galileo broke down, promised to mend his ways, and swore an oath "that I have believed, do now believe, and with the help of God always shall believe in the future everything that is preached, professed, and otherwise transmitted by the Holy Catholic and Apostolic Roman Church." The yellowed parchment that Galileo signed with a trembling hand at the conclusion of his trial can still be seen in the Vatican archives today (they were opened up to the public in 1981), an old man's confession of helplessness in the face of an impersonal, all-powerful organization: "I am in your hands," he wrote. "Do with me what you will." Faith had triumphed over science —without having to resort to the dungeon or the rack—and Galileo had been silenced, and the stars moved once more (or rather did not move) as the Holy Office had decreed. Galileo got off with a conditional release—house arrest, we would call it today—and, in addition, as a "wholesome act of contrition" he was ordered "to repeat the seven penitential Psalms every week for the next three years."

The penance imposed on the victors was more arduous and lasted a great deal longer. The Jesuits continued to maintain observatories in fifteen different locations around the globe, their astronomers continued to chart the heavens (Father Francisco de Vigo was the first to observe the two moons of Saturn that are closest to the earth), but officially the Jesuits remained inhabitants of a static, pre-Copernican universe until 1822. Before that date all books "which treat of the mobility of the earth and the immobility of the sun in accordance with the consensus of modern astronomers" were automatically placed on the Index. And even after that date—though it was no longer forbidden to discuss Copernicus or the moons of Saturn—the boundary between permissible speculation and prohibited knowledge was not always that finely drawn.

ORIGINAL SIN AND THE CRIMES OF TEILHARD DE CHARDIN

Pierre Teilhard de Chardin (1881–1955), French Jesuit and world-famous paleontologist, was concerned with the problem of evolution—more specifically, the collective development of the natural world, including man, as a complex and growing organism. However, he found himself unable to publish his conclusions, the result of decades of field work and scholarship, since Pope Pius XII himself had decreed that Teilhard's views offended against "the traditional teachings of the Church with regard to Original Sin." In such a case, when a Jesuit natural scientist champions the view that the evolution of the cosmos can be explained, or at least described, scientifically, he might naturally expect to encounter some resistance from his Church, and if he does, then it is the Jesuit who gives way, packs up his manuscript, and puts it back in the drawer. Teilhard, a twentieth-century scientist, sought-after lecturer, already a cult figure among university students, a philosopher who spoke with the tongue of a poet, was also a dutiful Jesuit who accepted the Church's decision that his greatest work, *Le Milieu Divin,* would not receive the imprimatur. Cardinal Merry de Val, secretary of the Holy

Office,* also insisted that Teilhard explicitly renounce his unorthodox views on Original Sin in writing, which he agreed to do, knowing full well that by so doing he would only be inviting the ridicule and disdain of his scientific colleagues. Teilhard endured all this with remarkable forbearance; a remark like "I can no longer believe in the immediate and tangible value of official directives and decisions" was as close as he would come to criticizing his superiors (and even this held out the generous implication that there were long-range, intangible benefits to such things that might not yet be apparent).

Teilhard had been sent to China in 1923, where he spent more than twenty years and made his scientific reputation as one of the co-discoverers of Peking Man. In Peking and after his return to Paris he was kept under surveillance and subjected to the same sort of petty harassment that dissident writers in police states everywhere have come to be familiar with. Manuscripts are said to have disappeared from his desk and been mysteriously spirited off to Rome to be checked, line by line, for signs of a further outbreak of unorthodoxy.

The established facts of Teilhard's career reflect little enough credit on the Order, and stories like these, of a dissident thinker in the hands of an unscrupulous Orwellian bureaucracy, are tantamount to a declaration of moral bankruptcy. The Jesuit father who read through this portion of my manuscript made a marginal notation to the effect that "this is nothing but backstairs gossip"—and let us hope that this is so—and the Order has tried to excuse its treatment of Teilhard with catchphrases like "there is no place for pioneers in the Society of Jesus," which seems to make a mockery of the four-hundred-year history of the Order and to ensure the triumph of the mediocre over the exceptional.

During his lifetime Teilhard was best known as a scientist; it was only after his death—when his books were finally allowed to be published—that he earned an even greater reputation as a philosopher. A number of his former colleagues in the Order, the "pioneers" among them at any rate, resisted the Church hierarchy's effort to discredit or to repudiate his work. Cardinal Frings came to his defense at the Vatican Council, Father Henri de Lubac wrote a book defending his reputation from the posthumous slanders of his critics, and General Pedro Arrupe, barely a year

---

*The agency responsible for maintaining the Index of Prohibited Books, which was only abolished in 1966. The office itself has since been disbanded, and many of its responsibilities have been assumed by the Congregatio pro Propaganda Fidei.

The break [between Teilhard and the Church] was clean and seemed to be irreparable: the Bible and the Scholastics on one side, all of philosophy from Descartes to Henri Bergson plus the natural sciences (with Darwin as the Archfiend there) on the other. Teilhard's love for the truth was such that he could not and would not come to terms with the notion that God was only supposed to be at home in half of this world, let alone in that half that was dead set against the living reality of nature in every essential aspect. The innermost law of the material universe, whose heartbeat Teilhard, as a paleontologist, believed could be detected everywhere, was creative evolution, whereas the orthodox picture of the world propounded by the Church was strictly static.

—Albert von Schirnding, writing on the occasion of the centennial of Teilhard's birth, 1981

after his election, pronounced himself in favor of total rehabilitation: "It is conceivable that he did not foresee all of the possible ramifications and consequences of some of his views. It still needs to be emphasized that the positive elements in his work far outweigh the negative or doubtful elements. . . . It is impossible not to acknowledge the value of Teilhard's message for our time." These tributes come far too late to soften the disappointment of Teilhard's last years—he died in New York City in 1955—but perhaps not too late for the Order. Some Jesuits, at least, interpreted their General's eulogy of Teilhard as a call for the rededication of the Order and a signal to revive the spirit of the Order as it was in the beginning, a community of pioneers. (We will return in the last few chapters to see how they have fared since 1968.)

PART ❧ IX

If the members of the Society of Jesus continue in this wise, then the day will come, which God forfend, when the kings of Europe will wish to rise against them but will find that they are no longer capable of doing so.

—Melchior Cano, a Spanish Dominican, 1549

The man who asks to lay all the cards on the table usually has all the tricks in his hand.

—Graham Greene

WILHELM THE CONFESSOR—THE JESUITS IN THE EMPIRE

There are those who think that it was the Jesuits who stirred up the trouble between the Protestants in Bohemia and the Emperor in Vienna that turned into the Thirty Years' War (1618–1648), the bloodiest and most destructive of all the wars that have ever been waged in the name of religion. And, on the other hand, there are those who claim that the Capuchins and the Franciscans had much more to do with it than the Jesuits, who in this particular matter were as blameless as woolly lambs. The first of these views is certainly on oversimplification, but about all that can be said in support of the second is that the Jesuits were not nearly as numerous as the Capuchins and the Franciscans, and even then they tended to occupy positions that made their influence disproportionate to their numbers, particularly over the Imperial house and the more prominent Catholic generals. The greatest of these, Count Tilly and Wallenstein, were both educated by the Jesuits—in Tilly's case this might have accounted for the fact that his twelve heaviest field guns were named after the Twelve Apostles. The devotion of these former pupils might be called into question, not so the loyalty of their most important protégé, the Emperor Ferdinand II (1578–1637), a graduate of the Jesuit college at Ingolstadt, though the crucial factor here was the Emperor's confessor and chief adviser, Father Wilhelm Lamormaini.

Father Lamormaini was without question an extraordinary man, spartan and uncorruptible. He remained aloof from the showier side of life at court and refused to accept presents of any kind from the Emperor. He was a native of Luxembourg, then part of the Empire, and his loyalty to the throne, or perhaps his love of power, seems to have made him more solicitous of Ferdinand's political fortunes than the state of his immortal soul. General Vitelleschi was obliged to remind both Lamormaini and the Jesuit who served as confessor to Maximilian of Bavaria, Ferdinand's junior partner in the Imperial coalition, that they had been sent to advance the interests of Jesus Christ and of the Society that bore his name, not the ruling houses of Hapsburg and Wittelsbach.

Lamormaini's residence in Vienna reminded visitors more of the office of an Imperial chancellor than the bare, uncluttered cell of a Jesuit father, primarily because it was packed to the ceiling with bundles of dispatches and abstracts of official documents that dealt with every phase of the political life of the Empire. Every diplomat in Vienna knew that it was useless to approach the Emperor without first consulting Father Lamormaini, who possessed a first-rate intelligence service, a fund of temperate and reasonable advice, and, of course, a great deal of influence over his Imperial master, who was intelligent but inclined to be headstrong.

When General Vitelleschi began to receive complaints about Father Lamormaini's excessive preoccupation with temporal affairs, he was naturally confronted with something of a dilemma. The Order could not easily dispense with their man in Vienna, nor could the charges against Lamormaini simply be swept under the rug—though the General devised a Jesuitical solution to the problem that was not so very different from it. "There are complaints," he wrote, "of the great volume of correspondence you engage in, and though I can find nothing blameworthy in this, in and of itself, it appears to me that it would be more suitable if this epistolary archive of yours were to be removed from your lodgings altogether, or at least concealed behind a curtain from the eyes of visitors." Lamormaini chose the curtain, and stayed on to serve his General, his Emperor, and his Church for thirteen years. This was a time, during the early years of the seventeenth century, when the Church had need of wise councillors and adroit diplomats like Father Lamormaini to defend her against the encroachments of powerful national and dynastic interests who would hardly be inclined to pay much attention to a directive from Rome, though they might seek out advice and information from a Jesuit father confessor. Even in countries like England or Sweden, where the Church's influence was failing or nonexistent, the Jesuits managed to parlay their talent for finding friends in the highest places into an impressive, if less than permanent advantage.

FROM ST. BARTHOLOMEW TO MADAME POMPADOUR— THE JESUITS IN FRANCE

From the beginnings of their mission in France, in 1561, the Jesuits had a difficult time of it. The professors at the Sorbonne and the Parlement of Paris were not well disposed toward them, mainly as a result of the so-called Gallican controversy, the long-standing dispute between the Pope and the kings of France over which of them was to be recognized as temporal head of the French Catholic Church. (Things had reached such a pass that Charles IX refused to allow any of his bishops to attend the final session of the Council of Trent.) A much livelier religious controversy, between the Catholics and the Huguenots,* was also about to erupt into a full-scale civil war. Hostilities broke out in that same year, 1562, dragged on inconclusively for another ten, and then suddenly entered a new and horrifying phase on the morning of August 24, 1572, St. Bartholomew's Day. The bells of St. Germain l'Auxerrols sounded the call to arms, though this had originally been proclaimed a day of national reconciliation by Catherine de Medici, the queen mother and effective ruler of the country. To win the trust and goodwill of the Huguenots, she had arranged a marriage between her daughter, Marguérite de Valois, and Henry of Navarre, the nominal head of the Protestant party and the future Henry IV of France. (It was also agreed that Henry would stand first in the line of succession after Catherine's youngest son, who was also called Henry.)

The notorious blood wedding of St. Bartholomew's Day culminated in a massacre of virtually all the prominent Huguenots who had come to Paris for the celebration. (It was Catherine who had arranged the massacre, by the way, and not her older son, Charles IX, as is sometimes

*No one really knows why the French Protestants, Calvinists for the most part, came to be called Huguenots. One theory evokes a legendary King Hugo whose ghost was supposed to have stalked the streets of Tours by night, just as the Protestants did as they hurried off to their secret midnight conventicles (prayer meetings). Another possibility is that *Huguenot* is simply a corruption of the German word *Eidgenosse* ("confederate").

stated.) The orgy of killing spread from Paris to the provinces, and over ten thousand Huguenots are thought to have lost their lives. In Paris it was said that "the blood would not be confined by the doorsills of the houses but spilled over and ran through the streets so that the shoes of the assassins were drenched in it."

Evidently the French people were reluctant to think that their own rulers might have been responsible for all this bloodshed and perfectly willing to suppose that the Jesuits were capable of anything, since they were widely assumed to have been the instigators of the massacre. No evidence to support this accusation has ever been found, and in fact a number of contemporary documents speak of Jesuits who gave shelter to fugitive Huguenots and saved them from certain death. In Rome the reaction to the news of St. Bartholomew's Day was one of unmixed jubilation, as this letter, dated September 8, 1572, from Cardinal de Como to the papal nuncio in Paris makes abundantly clear:

> Since His Holiness [Gregory XIII] wished to communicate these glad tidings to the Sacred College at once, he had the letters [the nuncio's dispatches from Paris describing the massacre] read aloud to them himself. Then His Holiness addressed himself to their contents and concluded by saying that in these times that are so full of unrest one could hardly have hoped for a better or more splendid piece of news. . . . His Holiness and the entire Sacred College were highly gratified and full of rejoicing after these tidings were read out. And that same morning His Holiness and the entire College of Cardinals went straightaway to the Church of St. Mark and had a *Te Deum* sung and gave thanks to God for the gracious mercy that was vouchsafed unto his Christian people.

Pope Gregory immediately had a medal struck to commemorate this happy event, but he had already been presented with a less agreeable souvenir, which had not been produced for the edification of the Sacred College; this was the head of Admiral Coligny, the elder statesman of the Huguenots, which had been dispatched to Rome by a band of fanatics in Paris.

That admirable system by which so many of the Catholic monarchs of Europe were guided, advised, and to some extent supervised by their confessors (Jesuits for the most part) did not function so smoothly in France. Charles IX was a devout Catholic, but otherwise broody and unstable. Father Edmond Anger served as confessor to Henry III (reigned 1574–1589), a dandified homosexual who filled his court with painted *mignons* (literally, "pretty boys") and suffered from intermittent Huguenot tendencies as well. But, as mentioned earlier, the Jesuits' troubles really began with the murder of Henry III. The Jesuits' theory of justifiable tyrannicide was held to be responsible, and the fact that the assassin was actually a Dominican was indulgently overlooked. In reality the Jesuits were suspect not because of their political theories or even their unquestionably subversive preaching and pamphleteering, but simply because of their skill at the great game of power politics at court, a reputation that was certainly borne out during the reign of Henry IV. Henry turned out to be a godsend for the people of France, but, since this was his second conversion to Catholicism for reasons of political expediency, he was still regarded by the Church as a lapsed heretic and was immediately excommunicated by the Pope. A botched attempt on Henry's life gave him the opportunity to expel the Jesuits from France as persistent troublemakers, and this time the Order adopted a more farsighted policy. They sent their most persuasive diplomats, Robert Bellarmine and Antonio Possevino, to appeal to the Pope, and the ban of excommunication was lifted about a year later, in 1595.

But even after that, Henry was still cautious in his dealings with the Order. His primary concern was the reunification of his kingdom, and above all to put an end to any religious dissension among his subjects. It was not until eight years later, in 1603, that he let the Jesuits return to France, and then only on two conditions. First, they were expected to take an oath that they would do nothing to subvert the realm of France and would not conspire against Henry personally. Second, a Jesuit father would be allowed to live at court as a kind of hostage for the good behavior of the others. This, in the opinion of General Aquaviva, was more like extra penance than a dispensation, but he agreed to Henry's terms. At the time this was interpreted as a sign of weakness, but the benefits of this policy of conciliation became apparent before too long. Father Pierre Coton, the Jesuit who was sent to court, had been well chosen for this mission, and before long, in the manner of Father Lamormaini, he made himself indispensable to the king as a bountiful source of political advice and information (this inspired the wits at court to comment that "the king has Coton in his ears"). Father Coton was less in demand as a spiritual adviser, since Henry, in spite of his Calvinist (and his Catholic) convictions, lived pretty much as he pleased. The king and queen liked to amuse themselves by tucking the young dauphin up in bed with a buxom servant girl, or with one of his sisters, and overseeing his first, fumbling sexual experiments. Henry himself was famous for his lack of self-restraint where women were concerned, even by contemporary standards—contemporary standards being typified, perhaps, by the sister of one of his mistresses, Angélique d'Estée, an abbess of a convent who had borne twelve illegitimate children.

Actually Father Coton was more concerned about Henry's conduct in foreign affairs than with his lax domestic policy. He was said to be preparing to join forces with the German Protestant princes against their common enemy, the Emperor Ferdinand II, which, it was feared, might also provoke a third and final conversion, back to the Calvinist faith of his boyhood. (It was also rumored that he was eager to invade the Spanish Netherlands to recover a former mistress who had been spirited off by an uncooperative husband.)

But the danger of a Protestant anti-Hapsburg coalition was averted by the intervention of a deranged provincial lawyer named Ravaillac, who stabbed Henry to death with a dagger while he was riding through Paris in his coach ("The Lord of Hosts has guided his hand!" was the appreciative comment of Pope Paul V). This, as you may recall, was good news for Rome, not quite so good for the Jesuits; the Parlement of Paris and many others were convinced that it was they, rather than the Almighty, who had guided the assassin's hand. By this time, however, the Jesuits' position at court was so secure that Marie de Medici, now acting as regent for the ten-year-old Louis XIII, calmly deflected all the attacks against them and placed the Jesuits under her personal protection.

The situation took a sharp turn for the worse in 1624 with the rise to power of Cardinal Richelieu. Armand du Plessis de Richelieu (1585–1642) was not about to turn Protestant, but he was determined to conduct a purely French rather than a Catholic foreign policy, and it was he who finally turned Henry IV's vague schemes for an anti-Hapsburg coalition into a reality. "No French Catholic is so deluded," he once remarked, "that in matters of state he would prefer a Spaniard to a French Huguenot." When on his deathbed he was enjoined by his confessor to forgive his enemies, he replied, "I have none—save the enemies of France." And he considered the Jesuits to be among them. One of his first priorities when he took office was to curb the power of the Jesuit confessors at the French court and at the court of the French client state of Savoy, in Turin. Louis XIII's confessor, Father Caussin, was packed off to exile in the provincial city of Rennes when he tried to interfere with the cardinal's plans, and the cardinal even objected to the Jesuit colleges, not, oddly enough, because of the program of instruction or the Romanist sympathies that were inculcated into the students, but because the colleges accepted students from the lower classes, the sons of peasants and artisans, which, to the cardinal's way of thinking, was likely to disrupt the delicate balance of society. In this at least the cardinal would have agreed with the freethinker Voltaire, who felt that "the lower classes should be led, but never taught."

The Jesuits, long since accustomed to manipulating kings, queens, and bishops to suit their pleasure on the great chessboard of European diplomacy now found that they were little better than pawns themselves in the hands of an international grandmaster like Richelieu. Certainly they could not prevent him from granting handsome subsidies to Protestant princes in Germany—the cardinal would rather have them as unruly Protestants than loyal subjects of the Emperor. On the other hand, the cardinal was obviously quite willing to pursue a Catholic policy if French interests were not at stake—he was willing to see Imperial lands ceded to Protestant princes, but he insisted on inserting a clause in the treaty that would guarantee protection for any Jesuits who might be found there. The Jesuits recognized that they had been outmaneuvered and retreated into the background, probably in the hope that they would come into their own again after Richelieu's death. But things did not work out so neatly, and during the reign of Louis XIV, long after their old adversary was gone, the Jesuits seemed to be content to squander most of what they had regained by a sanctimonious insistence on their power and prerogatives at court, the sort of arrogant and obtrusive behavior of which they had rarely been guilty in the past and which actually marked the beginning of the long decline of the Order in France.

First of all, the confessors at the court of Versailles seem to have lost the Jesuits' greatest gifts of diplomacy and tact, the ability to work out compromises and make the rough places smooth. The court chaplain, Father Louis Bourdaloue, a man of formidable oratorical gifts, preached his Easter sermon for the year 1685 on the text "Fly then from that place of repose where the very air threatens to enflame the passions anew," which is not a scriptural text but, as Louis and everyone else in attendance clearly knew, a reference to the king's current mistress, Madame de Montespan. Father Bourdaloue succeeded in browbeating Louis into giving up Madame de Montespan, but her successor, Madame de Maintenon, was hardly an improvement—she was what was called a *dévot*, a fanatical Catholic with an almost Calvinist attitude toward the harmless pleasures of the court. Louis's confessor, the Jesuit Père de la Chaise, was forced to intervene to prevent her worst excesses—a total ban on all theatrical performances, for example—from going into effect.

An even more portentous tactical blunder was committed by two Jesuit confessors at the court of Louis XV, some seventy years later, at a time when Madame de Pompadour, née Jeanne Antoinette Poisson, occupied the position of *maîtresse en titre*. Though the Jesuit confessors at the French court had been accustomed to dealing with promiscuity, pederasty, transvestism, voyeurism, and all manner of sexual excesses for over 150 years, these two inexplicably embarked on a campaign to convince the usually pliable Louis to get rid of Madame de Pompadour— instead of the more usual Jesuit tactic of ingratiating themselves with Madame in order to get a securer purchase on Louis. At any rate, the Jesuits and La Pompadour soon found themselves at an impasse (through no fault of hers at all), and the end of the story—which will have to wait until a later chapter—turned out to be a major disaster for the Order.

When the Bough Breaks, the Cradle Will Fall— The Jesuits in England

One of the most puzzling of traditional English holidays, at least to the uninitiated, is Guy Fawkes Day—more familiarly known to its participants as "Gay Fox Day"—which falls on the fifth of November, when bands of children dressed in outlandish costumes run shrieking through the streets, shooting off firecrackers and chanting:

> *Remember, remember the fifth of November,*
> *Gunpowder treason and plot,*
> *We see no reason why gunpowder treason,*
> *Should ever be forgot.*

Guy (or Guido) Fawkes was an English Catholic gentleman who, with a band of co-conspirators, plotted to blow up both Houses of Parliament, along with King James I and the entire royal family, on November 5, 1605. The plot was betrayed at the last minute. The numerous barrels of gunpowder that Guy Fawkes and his colleagues had somehow managed to secrete in the cellar of the House of Parliament were trundled away again, and the conspirators, mostly drawn from the ranks of the old Catholic gentry, were sent to the scaffold.

The Gunpowder Plot was only the best known, and best remembered, of a dozen or so "Popish plots," real or imagined, that crowd the pages of English history between 1558 and 1685; the object of all of them, all of the real ones at least, was to restore the "old religion" in place of the Anglican state church established by Henry VIII and, in most cases, to put a Catholic on the English throne. Henry's older daughter, Mary Tudor (reigned 1553–58), was something like Catherine de Medici in France, a sincere Catholic but a politically inept monarch who made her religion the centerpiece of her foreign policy; her attempts to undo in five years what her father had wrought in fifteen cost the lives of three hundred or more of her subjects and won her the nickname "Bloody Mary" but had few other apparent effects. Her half-sister and successor, Elizabeth I (reigned 1558–1603), was much closer in temperament to Henry of Navarre—her religious convictions were not all that well defined and considerably less precious to her than the unity and tranquillity of her kingdom. Like Henry, she had also changed her religion to save her life, during her sister's reign, and she was prepared to extend a fair measure of tolerance to her Catholic subjects (thought to be about half the population of England).

Naturally this policy did not make her any more acceptable to Rome —she was still a heretic, and in the event of her death, her cousin Mary Stuart, the Catholic queen of Scotland, stood first in the line of succession. The English Catholics had been extremely restive in the early years of Elizabeth's reign, and the Pope's advisers on foreign affairs were convinced that a Catholic rebellion, properly supported and directed from abroad, stood a very good chance of success, and then Mary Stuart could start afresh where Mary Tudor had left off. (The fact that Mary Stuart had been a closely guarded prisoner in England since 1568 was dismissed as an unimportant detail; that the English might prefer their own home-grown religion to a Spanish or Italian import was not even taken into account.)

Queen Elizabeth was excommunicated in 1570, and the Jesuits were entrusted with the mission of arranging for her to be deposed, and assassinated if necessary. There were now several seminaries in France, in addition to the original English college in Rome, to train English Jesuits, like an elite form of commandos, who would be infiltrated back into their native country, and every Jesuit who crossed the Channel was quite aware that he was part of what a soldier of that day would have called a "forlorn hope," a suicide battalion sent out to engage a vastly superior force. Still, the Jesuits approached this task with their usual stoical detachment and their customary energy—though they were hardly prepared to carry it to a successful conclusion—and only a third Jesuit virtue, thoroughness, was lacking. The Jesuit commandos often emerged from these seminaries without any very clear idea of what was expected of them, and many of them were spirited off to England just as soon as they had completed their novitiate.*

The first wave came ashore at Dover in June 1580; their arrival was eagerly awaited, not only by the English Catholics but by Elizabeth's secret police as well. The game was afoot, and the Jesuits quickly learned to resort to guerrilla tactics to stay clear of their pursuers. They moved from one county to the next, hearing confessions, preaching defiance to Elizabeth, and proclaiming Mary Stuart to be the rightful queen of England—a couple of them, disguised as physicians, even came to give comfort to her in prison—dispensing the Blessed Sacrament, and changing their wardrobes and their hiding places every day. The special agents who were sent out after them—"poursuivants" they were called—were so demoralized by all this that they took to carrying hammers and axes to flush out Jesuits from concealed "priest holes." "They not only ripped out the walls," a Jesuit reported back to his superiors in Rome, "but the floorboards as well, even of the outbuildings and cowsheds. They thrust their swords through the cornricks and the standing shocks of grain, and dug up the unpaved parts of the garden and the courtyard with iron-shod staves."

Anyone who reads through this clandestine correspondence—which includes recipes for invisible ink, tips on wigs and disguises, ingenious ways of keeping one's voice from being recognized—cannot help but get the feeling that the great game between the "papists" and the poursuivants had become an end in itself, even though in reality it was likely to end for the Jesuits on the rack and then on the scaffold. Out of 182 Catholics who died for their faith or were executed for high treason (which amounted to much the same thing after 1571) during the reign of Elizabeth, eleven of them were Jesuits. Eight seminarians were all re-

---

*The Jesuit father who read through this portion of the manuscript was quick to point out that some of the missionaries involved in this enterprise were also idealistic and intelligent men, steadfast in their faith, and not just bewildered novices. I agree completely (as the next paragraph should make clear), which is why I wrote "many of them" rather than "most" or "all of them."

ceived into the Order while they were already under sentence of death—a comforting and not entirely symbolic gesture for these young men who, even on the threshold of eternity, were eager to be enrolled in the corps d'élite of the army of blessed martyrs. The Jesuit campaign continued into the 1590's, but the issue had already been decided on February 18, 1587, when Elizabeth reluctantly signed the death warrant for her cousin Mary Stuart; in the following year the threat of the Armada and a Spanish invasion made militant Catholicism seem too much like treason for all but a very small minority of Englishmen.

In the years that followed, the Catholics fixed their hopes on James VI of Scotland, Mary Stuart's son, who ascended the English throne (as James I) in 1603. In this respect, as in many others, James proved to be a disappointment. He had actually promised to reintroduce Catholicism as the state religion before he came to the throne; the "wisest fool in Christendom"—as Henry IV had once called him—possessed a vast store of knowledge but a very poor memory, apparently. No more was heard from him about restoring the old religion, though he did produce a number of learned works on witchcraft and tobacco (which he was opposed to) and on the divine right of kings (which he was in favor of). In fact King James was one of the originators of the theory that kings are by God appointed and cannot be lawfully deposed by their subjects (as his mother had been in Scotland) or even by the Pope (as Elizabeth had been, at least in theory). Catholics were not encouraged by this; some of them—Guy Fawkes and his friends—were driven to desperate measures to get rid of King James. But Guy Fawkes notwithstanding, the rest of the Stuart kings remained at least sympathetic to Catholicism—until the last of them, James II, set sail across the Channel in a fishing smack for a life of comfortable exile in France.

James II (reigned 1685–1688) was a king after the Jesuits' own heart, and Catholics, including many Jesuits, filled most of the important positions at court and in the government during his reign. His only real shortcoming, in their eyes at least, was that he lacked a male Catholic heir to succeed him; his daughters by his first marriage, Mary and Anne, had both been brought up as Protestants and were married to Protestant princes. James's Jesuit advisers entertained a number of fantastic schemes for evading the laws of dynastic succession; they even proposed that the throne could be offered to Louis XIV of France, on the theory that "it would be better for Catholic Englishmen to be vassals of the king of France than enslaved by the devil." As it happened, both of these unpalatable alternatives seemed to be ruled out when James was unexpectedly presented by his second wife with a son, a Catholic Prince of Wales.

The Jesuits exulted, the Protestants sulked and gradually managed to convince themselves, by a process that is easy enough to follow, that the infant prince was no prince at all, that the queen was not his mother and the king was not his father. Finally the rumor began to appear in print— in broadsheets and pamphlets, the yellow press of the day—that the Jesuits had impregnated a nun, with exactly this purpose in mind, and that the changeling was smuggled into the queen's bedchamber in an outsize warming pan. (The nursery rhyme "Rockabye, Baby" is thought by some to have originally been a derisive reference to this infant Prince of Wales and his subsequent misfortunes.) The story of the "warming-pan baby" was really not so much a cause of James's downfall as an indication that the English people had had enough of their king and his Jesuit councillors and were ready to believe almost anything to his discredit. The Calvinist Prince William of Orange, who was Princess Mary's husband, had promised to do away with all this "papistical chaos"; he landed in England at the head of an army, James fled to France, and Parliament declared him deposed—on the grounds that he had sought to subvert the constitution of the realm "on the advice of Jesuits and other persons"—and offered his vacant throne to William and Mary. James II was the last Catholic king of England; the Jesuits had helped him to win a few of his battles against his people, and finally had helped him to lose the war.

Northern Approaches—The Jesuits in Sweden

In 1523 the kingdom of Sweden and the canton of Zürich became the first independent states in Europe to embrace the Protestant religion— Zürich, the home of rock-ribbed reformer Ulrich Zwingli, was prudently given up for lost, but the Jesuits made a number of concerted and surprisingly successful attempts to entice the Swedes back into the fold. The first of these occurred during the reign of John III (1568–92), a broody and introspective monarch with a pronounced theological bent; the Jesuits seem to have originally gotten one foot in the door because John had married a Polish princess, Katarina Jagellona, who had brought her confessor with her to Stockholm. (Most historians seem to think he was a Jesuit—they were great favorites with the Polish ruling classes—but Ludwig Pastor, in his magisterial history of the papacy, says not [ix,686].) But even if not, perhaps he should have been, since he prevailed upon the king to restore the Catholic forms of worship in his private chapel.

Then, in 1574, a second emissary of the old religion appeared in Stockholm—this one definitely a Jesuit, though he was dressed as a gentleman of the Polish court—and was closeted with the king for a number of confidential discussions. Two months later the Catholic liturgy was reinstated in all the churches of Sweden. Before the Lutheran clergy had had time to recover from the shock, King John managed to disarm their protests by announcing that a famous scholar would be summoned by royal command from Norway to give the inaugural series of lectures on the works of Martin Luther at the new theological seminary in Stockholm. The visiting Lutheran scholar, Laurits Neilsen, was a bravura performer who had no difficulty in filling a hall; the king himself attended his lectures regularly. The seminarians were struck by the judicious evenhandedness of Professor Neilsen's approach. He was careful to present the arguments on both sides of every question, and as the seminar drew on, the possible objections to Luther's teachings began to proliferate alarmingly; the king himself was finally compelled to intercede in Luther's behalf. But King John, strictly an amateur theologian, was no match for the professor and was forced to concede defeat. The audience was at first delighted by this unexpectedly theatrical turn of events, at least until they realized that the professor had not only stood Luther on his head but had done so by citing the detestable doctrines of the Church of Rome. (What was not made clear, at least for some time, was that this was strictly a put-up job, and that the professor, though he really was a Norwegian called Laurits Neilsen, was actually a Catholic himself, and a Jesuit to boot.)

After Father Neilsen had successfully sowed doubt and confusion among the Lutheran clergy, he was recalled, and the second phase of the campaign began. His replacement was a courtier rather than a scholar—Antonio Possevino, who had served as secretary to General Mercurian, was considered to be the Order's chief negotiator and consummate diplomat. Possevino was a flamboyant figure with a well-known penchant for sniffing out state secrets, particularly of the backstairs or bedroom variety. Traveling under diplomatic cover and plausibly disguised *"in habito secolare con spada e cappa"* (in civilian dress with sword and cape), he presented his (bogus) credentials as an envoy of the German emperor at the Swedish court. Possevino's mission was simply to take things one step further, to convince King John, who had already re-introduced the Catholic liturgy, to renounce Lutheranism altogether and restore the state church to communion with Rome. Possevino's bargaining position was based on the traditional carrot-and-stick approach—in this case, the carrot was a promised subsidy of two hundred thousand ducats from Philip II of Spain (ostensibly as compensation for the expenses King John might incur in returning the altarpieces and devotional images to the spare, whitewashed Lutheran churches of Sweden). The stick was the prospect of the torments that would await a heretic in the fires of hell, or a monarch lax enough to permit heresy to flourish in his domains. Father Possevino was the kind of speaker who could make the torments of hell seem as real and as imminent as a bribe of two hundred thousand ducats, but King John was only half-persuaded. He agreed to turn Catholic himself, but insisted that his subjects could only be received back into the Church if twelve specific conditions were fulfilled. These included all the standard points of contention between Rome and the Reformers, but, surprisingly, seven of the king's conditions were agreed to, though the Holy Father could still not countenance such radical measures as

- having the mass sung in Swedish;
- administering communion in both kinds (i.e., both bread and wine) to the congregation, which was the Lutheran practice;
- abolishing priestly celibacy, the use of holy water, and the saying of prayers for the dead.

Father Possevino, who had dropped his cover by now and openly proclaimed himself as a Jesuit, shuttled back and forth between Stockholm and Rome and spared no effort to persuade the king to drop his remaining five demands. However, the king refused to budge any further; the bishops and the royal family—particularly the king's second wife, a woman as blunt and uncompromising as her name, Gundula Blicke—had worked their will on him. He renounced Catholicism, and Sweden seemed destined to remain a Protestant nation.

For the next forty years or so, the Jesuits did not have an easy time of it in Sweden. Banished from court for the duration of King John's reign, they went underground, tramping from one farmhouse to the next (reportedly in the guise of Italian ratcatchers) to pursue their clandestine missionary work. John's son Sigismund, a former Jesuit pupil who had also inherited the Polish throne from his mother, Katarina Jagellona, brought them back to his court as military advisers, but Sigismund was only king of Sweden for a comparatively short time; he was deposed by one of his Lutheran relatives in 1599. Gustavus Adolphus (reigned 1611–32), "the Lion of the North," made Sweden into the leading Protestant power in Europe and was an implacable enemy of the Pope, the Emperor, and his hapless Polish cousin. "There are three L's I would like to see hanging," he is once supposed to have said, "the Jesuit Lamormaini, the Jesuit Laymann, and the Jesuit Laurentius Forer." When Gustavus was killed in battle in 1632, he was succeeded by his seven-year-old daughter, Christina, who grew up to be a remarkable young woman who was ardently courted by the Jesuits in their second major campaign for the conversion of the Swedes. Christina struck up a friendship with Father Antonio Macedo, confessor to the Portuguese ambassador; then, at Christina's invitation, General Nickel dispatched two Jesuits from Rome, who arrived in Stockholm disguised as merchants and provided with the usual false papers; they were to take charge of Christina's religious instruction.

Finally, on November 6, 1655, the daughter of the redoubtable Gustavus Adolphus was received into the Roman Catholic Church amid much pomp and solemnity in Innsbrück—the ceremony was held on Imperial territory because Christina had found it necessary to renounce her throne in order to become a Catholic. (Thus Christina's defection was a great prestige success for the Vatican and for the Order, but not quite the triumph they had hoped for.) Queen Christina was a formidably intelligent woman—"the first European bluestocking," she has been called—which perhaps explains her affinity for the Jesuits; she spoke eight languages well, she was the first European ruler to outlaw witch burnings in her domain, and she also enticed the philosopher Descartes to visit her court in Stockholm (where he promptly caught cold and died). Though her compatriots Greta Garbo and Liv Ullman have both starred in film versions of her life, she was sharp-featured and on the stocky side, not really a beauty either by the standards of the seventeenth century or of our own. Among her other accomplishments—she had a great gift for political intrigue, she was an expert fencer, and she invariably led the field when she rode out with the hunt. (On one occasion, after she had taken a fall, she deliberately neglected to pick herself up and simply remained where she had fallen, with her skirts hiked up around her waist until her courtiers came hurrying to her rescue; this was her way of combating a persistent rumor that she was a hermaphrodite, or a man dressed in woman's clothing.) Christina lived the rest of her life in exile at various Catholic courts in Europe; she died in Rome in 1689.

THE CASE OF THE FALSE DMITRI—THE JESUITS IN RUSSIA

After scoring a tantalizing near-miss with King John III of Sweden, in 1580 Father Antonio Possevino was given the even more daunting diplomatic assignment of paying a courtesy call on the self-proclaimed "Tsar by the Grace of God and Autocrat of All the Russias." This was Ivan IV (1530–1584), better known as Ivan the Terrible, a manic-depressive despot who in his time had desolated whole provinces, murdered a number of his friends with his own hands, and beaten his beloved eldest son to death with a cudgel. Possevino had actually been sent in as a third-party mediator to help put an end to a war in which Poland and Russia had fought each other to a standstill. Ivan was unexpectedly cordial, but it turned out that he was only hoping to enjoy the benefits of an indefinite armistice without actually going so far as to commit himself to a peace settlement. The story of Father Possevino's mission to Moscow should make instructive reading for any prospective diplomat who is planning on an Eastern posting. First he discovered that every time some small concession had been wrung out of the Russian negotiators, they would subsequently disappear for days, ostensibly to consult with the tsar. Finally they would return, profusely apologetic, to deliver the tsar's reply—which was always a string of meaningless diplomatic courtesies. Finally Possevino decided to resort to the Jesuit tactic of total accommodation—if the Russians had all the time in the world, then he had all of eternity. He found the Russian obsession with protocol was an excellent way of making the hours flow like days, and if they could never mention the tsar without pausing to list all his titles, then he could do the same for the Pope—"our Holy Father, Pope Gregory XIII, Pastor of the Universal Church, Vicar of Jesus Christ on Earth, Successor of St. Peter, Servant of the Servants of God, Prince of Princes, Supreme Pontiff, Ruler of Many States and Provinces . . ." followed by an exhaustive catalogue of the pontiff's temporal possessions.

The real purpose of Possevino's mission was to sound out the Russians on the possibility of bringing the Eastern Orthodox Church back into communion with Rome—a less conspicuous but nevertheless important preoccupation of the Counter-Reformation Church. The original split had occurred over five hundred years earlier, and there had been a series of fairly serious negotiations along these lines during the previous century. (Such a church actually was established a few years later among the Orthodox subjects of the king of Poland.) Ivan was very encouraging at first, and when he decided that he was finally ready to make peace with Stephen Bathory, the Polish king, he did Father Possevino the signal honor of proposing him as the mediator who would oversee the actual negotiations between the two powers. At this point, however, Ivan seems to have forgotten about the even more fundamental accord that was supposed to be brewing between the Pope and the Orthodox Patriarch of Moscow. Father Possevino had once again acquitted himself brilliantly—and done a good turn for the Poles and the Russians as well—without really accomplishing anything on behalf of the Order or the Church. He has always been rated highly by historians as the Order's most successful diplomat, and far be it for us to begrudge him his posthumous reputation, but it is also worth noting that General Aquaviva subsequently "requested" him to retire from diplomatic service. He finished up his career as a teacher in Padua.

The Jesuits were presented with a spectacular opportunity for bringing off a rapprochement between Rome and the Russians some twenty years later—in the person of a young Orthodox monk named Grishka Otrepyev, who turned up in Kiev (then part of Poland) in 1603. When he fell sick and his cowl was removed, he was discovered to be wearing a diamond-studded gold cross that was recognized as having belonged to the Tsarevich Dmitri, grandson of Ivan the Terrible, who was thought to have been murdered a dozen years earlier by Boris Godunov, who had subsequently had himself crowned tsar in his place. (The official story put out by Boris Godunov was that Dmitri had had an epileptic seizure and stabbed himself to death while engaging in his favorite pastime of practicing juggling with a dagger.) Brother Grishka readily admitted to being the rightful Tsar of All the Russias, and his cause was quickly taken up by the Jesuits, King Sigismund of Poland, and eventually the Russians themselves, after Boris Godunov dropped dead of an apoplectic stroke while holding court in the Kremlin.

This was universally regarded as a judgment, and Dmitri—accompanied by his Polish retainers and a squadron of Jesuit councillors—was welcomed into Moscow by the Russian boyars and princes, who had never much cared for the usurper Boris Godunov. One of Dmitri's first official acts was to provide for the establishment of a number of Jesuit colleges and Catholic churches in Moscow, which was not well received by the boyars, who were fickle in their political leanings but staunchly Orthodox to a man.

Dmitri only managed to hang on to his throne for a year. In May 1606 he was assassinated; his corpse was torn to pieces (and, according to one story, fired out of a cannon whose muzzle was pointed toward Poland). Not long after he began his reign, most of his subjects seem to have decided that this young man who claimed to be Dmitri was merely deluded, and a willing dupe of the Jesuits and the king of Poland besides. Several other False Dmitris turned up in the course of the next few years, but this was definitely the end of the Jesuits' hopes for a Catholic Russia and a reunification of the two great churches of the East and West.

In surveying the overall record of Jesuit diplomacy—particularly this episode of the False Dmitri—it seems clear that the diplomats themselves were never lacking in energy, courage, or imagination. They scored astonishing tactical successes, but in pursuing their great goal of reuniting Christendom, as it was before the Reformation, they invariably met with failure. There are basically two reasons for this. First, all appearances to the contrary, there was no real unanimity of purpose in the day-to-day conduct of Jesuit diplomacy. General Vitelleschi did try to impose a kind of formal unity, but this gave rise to such bureaucratic complications that further efforts at reform had to be abandoned.

Second, the Jesuits were even more seriously hampered by their obedience to the fourth vow, which subjected them to the authority of an ill-informed, arbitrary, and despotic papal bureaucracy, which meant in turn that the political assumptions on which their diplomatic objectives were based were generally false and their goals unattainable. They achieved their greatest successes in reclaiming lost territories for the Church—in Germany, Poland, and Bohemia—in their original role as educators and missionaries, not as diplomats, though it might be said that their greatest successes were scored not in Europe at all but in the mysterious realm of the Indies and the newly discovered lands beyond the seas.

PART ❧ X

A Beggar from an Unknown Land—the Jesuit Missions Overseas

It is one thing to sit by oneself in a warm parlor and come to the conclusion that one wishes to endure all manner of suffering for the love of God and one's neighbor; it is another thing to do it when it needs must be done.

> —Father Koffler, fl. c. 1642, a missionary in the East Indies

Let us have a Jesuit for breakfast.

> —Voltaire, Candide

THE LIGHT OF THE WORLD—THE JESUIT AS MISSIONARY

The notion that Jesuits make the best missionaries has persisted for several hundred years, which implies that there might actually be something to it, or, alternatively, that all the evidence that might tend to suggest the contrary has been carefully swept out of sight. In fact, both of these are correct. As to the first point, during the sixteenth century no other Europeans with the educational background of the Jesuits were willing to devote (and possibly sacrifice) their lives to a career as a missionary in remote regions of the earth that until recently had been thought to be populated exclusively by dragons and men with the heads of dogs. The Jesuits were not the first Christian missionaries to set foot on these exotic shores, where the Franciscans and Dominicans had often preceded them, and during the early years at least they received no special training for their task; the main advantage they enjoyed over their colleagues from other orders was their willingness to endure hardship, and their extraordinary capacity for self-sacrifice. (While these qualities were no less in evidence in later years, a formal training program was also inaugurated by General Aquaviva, who organized the intensive Jesuit missionary efforts in China, Paraguay, and Canada.)

The conversion of the heathen had been the one great goal of Igna-tius's life—consider his pilgrimage to Jerusalem, the Montmartre oath, and the emphasis on conversion in the original charter of the Order (the first Jesuit missionaries set out from Rome in 1541, on the day before the charter was officially approved by Pope Paul III). Conversion was also one of the great motivating forces of the age that we have come to call the Age of Discovery, in which the possibilities for commercial exploita-tion, the advancement of knowledge, and the propagation of the faith that were offered by the discovery of the New World and the new sea route to the Orient were all mingled—or muddled—together in a single great adventure. Baptism, for example, was not necessarily the preroga-tive of a Catholic priest—Columbus baptized the first Indians he en-countered in the Caribbean—and one of the great trials that a priest would have to endure in the New World was to witness the cruelties that were visited on the pagan souls that he had come to win for Christ by the soldiers and sailors of his ship's company.

At the beginning of the sixteenth century the Spanish and Portuguese appealed to Pope Alexander VI to divide the world between them; he obliged by drawing a line around the globe from pole to pole, about a hundred nautical miles next to the Azores. The Spanish claimed every-thing to the west, the Portuguese everything to the east, which gave them exclusive rights over the Spice Islands, India, and the Orient (at least as far as the Spaniards were concerned). In 1540 King John III of Portugal requested Pope Paul III to send out a group of Jesuits to his Indian trading stations—the Jesuits had already gained an international reputation before they had been formally recognized as an order—not so much to convert the local population as to help "the Portuguese settlers to lead an upright and Christian life." (In the face of some opposition, the Jesuits refused to confine themselves to looking after the spiritual welfare of the Portuguese colonists, which is greatly to their credit and is also the main reason why Goa and the other former Portuguese territories in India have remained largely Catholic to this day.) Apart from their mis-sionary activities among the heathen of the New World and the "idol-ators" of the Orient, the Jesuits' reports of their brilliant successes in the field also served as an advertisement for the advancing power of Chris-tendom around the world—which is reflected in the frescoes in many baroque churches that depict Asia, Africa, and America as Christian lands. In a fresco in the Jesuit church of Il Gesù a beam of light streams down from God Almighty to Jesus Christ to Ignatius Loyola, where it is refracted into four separate rays to the continents of Europe, Asia, Africa, and America.

Fortunately the Jesuit missionaries were diligent correspondents, since their dispatches from the field, even when heavily censored, still provide us with a unique record of the first European contacts with many of the world's peoples. It is no less fortunate that the Jesuits were ingenious enough to make sure that their letters would actually reach their destinations, a problem that is not a trivial one for us today and in the seventeenth century was almost insurmountable. A letter from India might take three years to reach Rome, if all went well, and the writer might often have to wait seven years in all to receive an answer. Clearly this meant that the correspondence between Goa and Rome was not cluttered with inessentials, and the missionaries only troubled their superiors with questions when it was really essential for them to know the answers. Many of their letters were serious literary efforts, several copies of which would be entrusted to the captains of various ships returning to Europe by various routes, in the hope that at least one copy might escape the ordinary hazards of pirates, storms at sea, overturned coaches, and stolen mailbags and finally arrive in Rome. Such letters that did arrive, of course, were greatly prized and soon circulated in multiple copies— which did not necessarily correspond at every point to the wording of the original. King John of Portugal was so impressed with Francis Xavier's letters that he ordered them to be read aloud from every pulpit in his kingdom. In this letter of January 1545, which was later approved for publication, he gives an enthusiastic account of his missionary activities in India:

> I can report that in the kingdom of Travancore [on the southwest coast] . . . in the space of a few months I have baptized more than ten thousand men, women, and children. . . . I went from village to village and made Christians of them. And everywhere I went I left behind a copy of our prayers and commandments in the native language.

Not much is made of the monsoons and the epidemics and the other natural perils that a missionary might encounter, and this letter does have something of the tone of a report from a supersalesman who has an inexhaustible supply of what everyone wants to buy. Before long half the students in Europe, "falling to their knees and pouring forth hot tears," were clamoring to go to India and convert the heathen. The idea that it might take more than a couple of holy-water sprinklers and a satchelful of tracts to convert an entire kingdom does not seem to have occurred to many at the time. A Jesuit called Father Nicolas Lancilloto was among the few to preserve a praiseworthy skepticism in the midst of the missionary craze. As he reported back to Rome:

> Most of those who are baptized have some ulterior motive. The slaves of the Arabs [i.e., Muslims] and Hindus hope to gain their freedom by it or gain protection from an oppressive master or simply to get a new robe or a turban. Many do so to escape some punishment. . . . Any who are driven by their own convictions to seek salvation in our teachings are regarded as madmen. Many apostasize and return to their former pagan practices not long after being baptized. . . .

Of course, there cannot have been many Jesuit fathers who were unaware of all this, but they were simply not about to give up in any case, if only for the sake of the few who really did regard being baptized as the beginning of a new life for themselves. The Jesuits, being Jesuits, were not all that likely to be too unrealistic in their expectations, and, moreover, they could take heart from the example of the first and the greatest among them, Ignatius's Basque compatriot Francis Xavier, who had started from even less promising beginnings and by the time of his premature death had presided over flourishing communities of hundreds of thousands of Christian souls.

WHEN THE BLACK ROBE RINGS THE LITTLE BELL— THE JESUITS IN INDIA

Francis Xavier, the patron saint of all Catholic missions overseas, has been called "the most important Christian evangelist since Paul," which is high praise indeed. It is certainly fair to say that his travels took him farther, among more different peoples, than any other missionary since Paul. Like the other Jesuits of the first generation, he received no special training or preparation for what was to become his life's work; he simply set out from Lisbon Harbor on April 7, 1541, on board a Portuguese caravel that was bound for India. Nicolas Boabdilla had originally been intended to go to Portugal in answer to King John's request for steadfast priests to help his merchants in Goa to resist the temptations of life in the tropics. Boabdilla fell ill, though whether his illness was organic or diplomatic in origin we shall never know. (It seems clear enough that if the irascible Boabdilla had been sent to Goa instead of Xavier, the Jesuit mission in India would have withered and died within a few months' time.) But Francis Xavier happened, providentially, to be with Ignatius in Rome at the time, and Ignatius, who had not yet been elected General of the Order but was simply the first among equals, sent Xavier and three companions to Lisbon to await King John's instructions. (I suspect, judging by the evidence of his later life, that the thirty-one-year-old Francis Xavier was so badly smitten with the urge to travel that he would have moved heaven and earth to secure the appointment for himself.)

So Francis Xavier set out "with nothing more than the clothes he stood up in, a breviary, and a few provisions for the journey," or so we are told in a number of books. In fact, this picture of holy poverty and helplessness is somewhat altered by the fact that, apart from his three companions, Xavier was also bringing with him a papal breve that entitled him to the power and privileges of a papal legate, so that he could expect to command the obedience of every Catholic cleric in Asia, as well as any Portuguese officials he might encounter, since he also had been provided with a "general order" to that effect signed by King John. When he finally reached Goa, however, Xavier made use of these powers very cleverly, which is to say not at all. He realized that Lisbon was far away, and that brandishing a parchment with the royal seal stamped on it under people's noses was not the way to get along in a remote colonial outpost like this one. He took a cell in the Goa hospital for himself, and probably lived more simply than any other priest in the city.

Francis Xavier arrived in Goa on May 6, 1542, a little more than a year after he set out from Lisbon. The voyage around the Cape of Good Hope was particularly harrowing; the Portuguese captains generally signed on a double crew at home, so they would still have enough men to work the sails when they reached the Indian Ocean—the mortality rate was generally no less than 50 percent. The storms were only the most dramatic of the hazards and privations of the voyage; the caravels themselves were scarcely seaworthy, eaten up with shipworm, the crews were weak with scurvy, "the bread was hard as stone, unsalted, the meat was stinking and had been sitting in casks for over a year, all out of the captain's notions of economy, for which he was punished straight-away by a just God with a pestilence, whereof the cattle all sickened and had to be thrown overboard. There is stench and corruption everywhere, our clothes are all in rags"—so runs an account of an otherwise routine sea voyage in 1691.

The city of Goa, on the right bank of the Mandavi River, was the largest Portuguese settlement in India. The city had been under Por-tuguese rule since 1510, and Xavier was delighted to find that it was like a miniature Lisbon, with Dominicans and Franciscans to look after the spiritual needs of the inhabitants, for, as he wrote back enthusiastically to Ignatius in Rome, "Goa is entirely populated by Christians. . . . We must be very thankful to the Lord our God that the name of Christ has reached these distant shores and has prospered so splendidly among these hordes of infidels." This, as it turned out, was a serious misconception—Xavier had rashly assumed that the word *Krishna,* which he observed as con-stantly on the lips of the Goanese, was nothing more than a local corrup-tion of *Christus,* the first of many such misunderstandings that were to crop up in the course of his missionary career.

Xavier grew restless before he had been in Goa for more than six months, and decided to make his way toward the country of the Paravas, far to the south. They made their living primarily as pearl divers, and some years earlier they had sent emissaries to the Portuguese in Goa, asking to be delivered from the hands of the Muslim pirates who were plundering their coast. The Portuguese sent out a punitive expedition to chase away the pirates, and the Paravas were required in return to send two boatloads of pearls to Goa every year as tribute. In addition, they had all consented to be baptized. (The mass baptism of the Paravas was even more perfunctory than usual—a priest asked them in Latin if they were ready to be received into the Catholic faith, they replied in Tamil, the principal language of South India, that they were, each of them received a slip of paper with his new Christian name written on it, and twenty thousand new Catholics were launched into the world.) The tribute of pearls had arrived punctually every year, but it had been some time since the Paravas had seen a priest—the first to penetrate as far south as Cape Comorin, the southern tip of India, and then beyond to the east was Francis Xavier.

To prevent the recurrence of anything like his earlier contretemps with *Krishna* and *Christus,* Xavier had a number of prayers and sermons translated into Tamil, which he painstakingly committed to memory; nevertheless, some misunderstandings did arise from the fact that his interpreters had for some reason translated the Catholic *missa* ("mass") as *misei* in Tamil, which means "mustache." A great deal has been written about Xavier's missionary activities, more of it negative or actually derisive than positive. Superficially at least there does appear to be something more than a little ridiculous in the image of a black-robed priest walking along a blazing tropical beach and ringing a little hand bell to attract the local children, then preaching one of his carefully memorized Tamil homilies and teaching them to repeat a prayer in singsong unison. This does sound exactly like the standard twentieth-century caricature of the overdressed, ineffectual Christian missionary in the tropics, the outlandish intruder in Paradise, but these were Francis Xavier's methods exactly, and they seem to have been remarkably successful. (Unfortunately Xavier's own tendencies to gauge his success in purely numerical terms leaves him even more vulnerable to criticism, or derision, in much the same way: ". . . my arm is often tired out with baptizing," he once wrote to Ignatius, "since in this last month I have administered this blessed sacrament of regeneration to more than ten thousand.") Still, it seems wrong to condemn a pioneer like Xavier for his naiveté or his excesses of zeal; his real failing, a much more serious one it seems to me, was his lack of patience, a Christian virtue in which the Apostle to the Indies was almost totally deficient. He shared in the restless, turbulent spirit of his age, and he had more the temperament of a conquistador than an apostle. He never put down roots, and he never remained long enough in any one place to make a good end of anything he had begun. In 1549, when he realized that the Christianization of India was not proceeding quite as rapidly as he would have liked, he wrote these bitter and reproachful lines to King John of Portugal: "I have had to recognize that Your Majesty does not dispose of sufficient might to propagate our Christian faith in India . . . and since this is the case, I am taking myself off to Japan so that no more time shall be lost." This last phrase is typical of this impatient, driven character; equally typical is the fact that Japan had first been visited by Europeans only six years before, which meant that Xavier would be the first missionary to set foot in that island kingdom at the edge of the known world that even Marco Polo only knew by hearsay. Xavier spent two years in Japan—in which he laid the foundation for a Christian community that would number over a hundred thousand by the end of the century—and then decided that China was the richer prize and moved on again.

During his years in India, Xavier wrote out a list of practical maxims or instructions for his fellow missionaries that really seem to have nothing to do with India at all and simply reflect the sixteenth-century ideal of the Jesuit as man of the world and sophisticated and sympathetic confessor:

> When the merchants and moneylenders realize that you are as well informed as they are as regards the affairs of daily life, then they will admire and confide in you. Otherwise the admonitions of a priest are only greeted with laughter.

> When talking to a sinner about his transgressions, do so in strictest confidence. Always speak with a smiling face, and without too much severity, in a friendly and loving tone. The character of the man will tell you whether to embrace him or humble yourself before him. . . .

FROM ONE OF XAVIER'S LETTERS TO IGNATIUS LOYOLA:

If the Lord our God has separated us by these vast distances, we are still united by our awareness of the strong bonds that unite us in a single spirit and a common love, since, if I have judged aright, neither physical separation, nor estrangement, nor forgetfulness can have any meaning for those who love one another in the Lord. For it seems to me that we shall always sustain each other as we were ever wont to do before.

Unfortunately Ignatius's famous injunction, "Be all things to all men," failed to take into account the peculiarities of the Indian caste system, and a high-caste Brahmin could probably have thought of few things more repugnant than being embraced (or even approached) by a meat-eating, wine-drinking foreigner, and a known associate of low-caste persons—like the Paravas—and even Untouchables. Still, the problem of making contact with the Brahmins, the priestly caste and scholarly élite of Hindu society, seemed calculated to appeal to the Jesuit temperament, and Father Roberto de Nobili arrived in India in 1605 and patiently set about solving it. He began by teaching himself Sanskrit and absorbing both the letter and the spirit of the Hindu scriptures: He scrupulously observed the prescribed Brahminic rites, learned to live and to think like a Brahmin, and even to dress like one in flowing saffron robes; he shaved his head, traced a caste mark on his forehead, and took to wearing heavy brass earrings. He cut himself off completely from other Europeans, and the only vestige of his Christian past that he allowed himself was the small cross he wore on a chain around his neck. (He made converts among the Untouchables, but he had to give communion to them in secret and in a highly unchristian manner—he passed out the hosts to them at the end of a cleft stick—otherwise his higher-caste converts would never have forgiven him.)

Nobili was the first Jesuit missionary to stretch the Jesuit principle of accommodation to include such wholehearted acceptance of the tenets of another faith. This is something that the Jesuits have repeatedly been criticized for, but without these Trojan horse tactics, it is doubtful that even the most dedicated missionaries could have penetrated the citadel of these far eastern religions, which in many ways were as exclusive and intolerant as their own. It is certainly true that the Jesuits who pursued this particular course must have felt some spontaneous affinity for the religious doctrines they encountered in India, China, and Japan; some of them, however, seem not to have been able to distinguish between accepting the tenets of another religion—on a strictly tactical or provisional basis—and abandoning Christianity altogether.

Nobili was also the first to get into difficulties with Rome on this score; in 1623 he was censured by the Superior General for conducting himself more like a shaven-headed pundit than a Catholic priest. This judgment was reversed on appeal by Pope Gregory XV, though in most cases it was the other way around—such practices were usually sanctioned by the General and censured by the Pope. Nobili was peculiarly fortunate in being the nephew of the influential Cardinal Bellarmine.

From the standpoint of character, Francis Xavier and Roberto de Nobili were diametrical opposites—Xavier was restless and impulsive, Nobili was introverted, painstaking, and circumspect. Both, however, were exclusively concerned with the things of the spirit; there was also a group of Jesuit missionaries who were active in India at about the same time who favored the diplomatic approach—several instances of which we have already met with in the last chapter—and decided that the Great Mogul, the Indian emperor Akbar (1542–1605), was just as much in need of wise council and urbane, polished conversation as Henry IV of France or Ferdinand of Austria. A miniature from the year 1605 depicts two Jesuits kneeling at the feet of Emperor Akbar, in the ornate, almost perspectiveless style that is typical of Mogul painting. The text explains that the Jesuits have just put a remarkable proposition before the emperor: They propose to leap into a roaring bonfire, each carrying his Bible, if the emperor will do the same immediately afterward while carrying his Koran. (The emperor and his court were Muslims, though most of his subjects were Hindus.) As it happened, the emperor had a reputation as something of a freethinker in religious matters—hence unlikely to trust to either scripture to carry him through the flames unscathed—so the Jesuits were perfectly safe in making such an offer; their real reason for making it, to create a sensation at court, seems to have been achieved, at least insofar as the Indians took the trouble of memorializing it in this way.

Emperor Akbar—who had done far more than most to deserve his sobriquet "the Great," which is what *Akbar* actually means—had already shown more than a polite interest in Christianity, and the possibility that he might convert to Catholicism was certainly worth exploring. Akbar himself grew so accustomed to the society of his Jesuit courtiers that he even took them along on his military campaigns, and he seems to have let on to them that he would be even more favorably disposed toward Christianity if they could get hold of some heavy artillery for him. (There is no indication that the Jesuits ever followed through on this suggestion.) In any case, it turned out that the Jesuits had misread the emperor's intentions; Akbar died, unbaptized, in 1605, and Islam crept in, on soft, sandal-shod feet, to take back most of the beachheads that the Jesuits had won for the Church in India. (Catholicism fared best in some of the Portuguese enclaves, especially where Francis Xavier had made his presence felt.) Worse than that, the Indians stuck with their sacred cows in the end; Hinduism outlasted both the Jesuits and the Moguls, and today seems to be exporting its surplus divinities to the Christian West. The Krishna cult has offered itself as a refuge for the spiritual outcasts of our own society, and today one is just as likely to hear the praises of Krishna—rather than Christus—resound through the streets of our cities.

WHAT ARE SOULS MADE OF?—THE JESUITS IN JAPAN

From the beginning of the Japanese mission in 1549 until the present day, the Jesuits have had a special, and mainly tragic, relationship with the people of Japan. The city of Nagasaki, for example, was founded as a Jesuit settlement in 1579, and the instructors at the Jesuit college there (along with the German Jesuit fathers at Hiroshima) were among the more than two hundred thousand casualties of the atomic bomb. General Pedro Arrupe spent over two decades as a missionary in Japan, from 1939 to 1965, and since the sixteenth century the words *Jesuit* and *Christian* have been virtually synonymous in Japan.

But when Pope John Paul II visited Japan during his far eastern trip in 1981 and officiated at the first beatification ceremony ever held outside Rome, the sixteen Japanese martyrs (fourteen men and two women) so honored were not Jesuits, but Dominicans. In spite of appearances this was not another deliberate slighting of the Jesuits on the part of John Paul II, since their own saints and blessed martyrs had long since been recognized by the Church—thirty-six of them in all. The Jesuits were also the first to arrive in Japan, of course; Francis Xavier and three companions landed at Kagashima on the island of Kyushu on April 15, 1549, and immediately set out on a series of reconnaissance sorties around the main islands to get a clearer picture of the land and the people and—most important for a Jesuit—the balance of power. Most of what Xavier had learned from Marco Polo's book—about all that was previously known about Japan—was almost centuries out of date and usually wrong in the first place. Japan was an empire, insofar as the nominal ruler was called the emperor—*Tenno Nara*—but, as in the Holy Roman Empire, the real rulers of the land were the petty princes, or warlords, who were called *daimyos*. The emperor might dine off a special service of porcelain that was thrown away after it had only been used once, but these eggshell-thin bowls were filled with scanty portions of poor man's food—the emperor was poor; he had no revenues of his own, and poverty in Japan, even more than elsewhere, was the same thing as powerlessness.

Xavier took note of this, and when he was granted an audience by the powerful *daimyo* of Yamaguchi, he made a point of appearing in his priestly vestments rather than his usual black soutane; only thus could he count on being treated at least as deferentially as the Buddhist and Shinto priests, whose robes were made of the finest silk. The audience was a complete success, not so much because of the papal letter of greetings that Xavier passed on to the prince as because of the splendid assortment of presents that he had brought with him. The court chronicler was so entranced with the latter that he made out an itemized list on a scroll, including "a clock that strikes twelve times each day as well as twelve times each night, a musical instrument that emits the most wonderful sounds without anyone touching it [i.e., a music box], glasses for the eyes that permit an old man to see as clearly as a young one. . . ."

When the *daimyo* politely inquired what he could possibly offer Xavier in return for such largesse, he was no doubt puzzled, and probably greatly relieved as well, by Xavier's request that he and his fellow *bateru* (the Japanese version of *patres*, "fathers") should be allowed to preach their religion in public and to baptize any of the *daimyo's* subjects who felt so inclined. The *daimyo* promptly assented to this request, primarily because Xavier seems to have given him the impression that this Christianity that he intended to preach was simply another variant form of Buddhism (of which dozens were already in existence). This was said more out of conviction than any deliberate attempt to deceive, but once again—as in the case of Krishna-Christus in Goa—Xavier seems to have been tempted to draw premature comparisons between two rather different religions, based on casual similarities—in this case the entirely fortuitous similarity between Catholic rosary beads and Buddhist prayer beads. Even Xavier was forced to recognize that Christianity and Buddhism were fundamentally opposed on more important points of dogma (such as the fact that the Buddhist seeks total annihilation in Nirvana rather than eternal life).

Although some of his earlier intelligence work may have been faulty, Xavier had at least realized that Christian humility had no place in Japan—the black robe and the handbell were permanently retired, Xavier learned to outfit himself in costly garments and to survey the world like a haughty mandarin, from "behind the mask of pride," as he put it. Next, Xavier had to convince the Japanese that he was not only a man of substance but of education as well: "Only when they had satisfied themselves that we were men of learning were they truly ready to listen to our speeches on the subject of religion." The Japanese may have held themselves aloof from the world outside, but they were far from indifferent to it. "The Japanese are so curious," one of Xavier's companions reported back to Rome, "that not a day has gone by since our arrival here that was not taken up from morning until evening with *bonzes* [Buddhist monks] and lay persons who had come to ask us all manner of questions." And when the subject of Christianity was finally broached, Xavier, as the chief of these foreign scholars, was expected to cope with the most exacting questions (fortunately he had studied dialectics at the Sorbonne): What are souls made of? for example. What does God look like? And—the favorite of doubters and village atheists everywhere— why did this good God Almighty of yours create evil in the first place? Xavier reported back to Rome that he was able to answer these questions to the satisfaction of the Japanese (unfortunately for us his answers are not recorded), but we are in no position to doubt his word; the *bateru* were overwhelmed with converts. By 1577 (many years after Xavier's departure from the islands) more than one hundred thousand Japanese had accepted baptism; there are said to have been as many as three hundred thousand by 1589. In 1585 a decree of Pope Gregory XIII awarded a kind of exclusive patent on missionary work in Japan to the Society of Jesus in recognition of their extraordinary success. In view of all this—plus the fact that the entire population of Japan was no more than a few million at the time—how does it happen that only 0.3 percent of all Japanese are Roman Catholics today?

The history behind this question usually given in the textbooks is simple enough—a shogun of the Tokugawa clan (the shogun of *Shogun* fame, in fact) came to power and established a strong centralized authority in 1603. Japan turned its back on the outside world once more, culturally, economically, politically—spiritually as well, in 1614, when the missionaries were proscribed as enemies of the state and the emperor decreed that Christianity would no longer be tolerated in his dominions.

All this is true enough, but there seems to have been a bit more to it than that. There are two versions of what actually happened: According to the first account, a new emperor came to the throne, who, though favorably disposed toward Christianity at first, became enraged and ordered the persecution to begin when a number of Japanese virgins he had chosen to be his concubines refused to cooperate because they had been baptized. According to the second account, it was envy and economic rivalry that brought about the persecutions rather than unrequited lust: Dutch traders had finally found their way to Japan, and the most effective way they could think of to undercut their Portuguese rivals was to plant the story that the Jesuits were not really priests at all but agents of the king of Portugal, the fifth column of an impending Portuguese invasion of Japan. The emperor was a xenophobe of the old school, mistrustful of foreigners on principle—though not nearly enough, in the case of the Dutch—and it is true that the Jesuits had been all too willing to make the Portuguese cause their own. The result of this commercial intrigue was the greatest persecution of Christians the world had seen in well over a thousand years. Converts who refused to renounce the new religion were crucified by the tens of thousands—no doubt this was intended as a ghoulish parody of the outlandish beliefs of the foreigners—whereas more elaborate horrors were reserved for the missionaries themselves, who were burned or roasted alive, dismembered, thrown into pits full of venomous snakes, plunged naked into vats of ice water until they froze to death, or even asphyxiated by being hung head downward over natural fissures in the earth that emitted great clouds of sulfurous vapors (which was perhaps also intended as a travesty of the Christians' idea of the afterlife).

The Jesuits endured these torments silently and stoically, but the idea that the Jesuits were incapable of doing anything that was not calculated to advance the Roman cause has become so ingrained that some historians have assumed that the courage and stoicism of the Jesuit martyrs was all part of a carefully staged performance; as recently as 1977 the English historian Christopher Hollis wrote, evidently with some disappointment: "In general the Christian cause did not profit as much as one might have expected from the sufferings the Christians were willing to endure for the sake of their convictions." Ignoring the facile cynicism of such a remark, it is interesting to note that it is simply not true—at the end of the eighteenth century, when Christian missionaries were finally permitted to return to Japan, they discovered that a number of secret Christian communities were still in existence whose great-great-great-grandparents had borne witness to the courage and serenity of the first Jesuit missionaries in the face of death and had been inspired by their example to remain steadfast in their Christian faith.

But all this was to take place more than fifty years after Xavier had left Japan, in 1552. He had become convinced that "China must be won over as the Roman Empire once was," since his conversation with educated Japanese had taught him that the Japanese had become so accustomed to borrowing their culture and religion ready-made from the Chinese that a religion that the Chinese themselves had never heard of could never expect to find favor with the more discerning element in Japan. (Xavier and his Japanese informants had no way of knowing that there had been a flourishing Christian community in China as early as the year 781—Xavier himself had come across a Nestorian Christian sect in India that had been there even longer, but the first evidence of the Chinese Christians—who had long since died out—was only discovered in 1623 by a French Jesuit called Father Trigault. When the foundation was being dug for a new building in the northwestern city of Sian, a stone tablet was unearthed with inscriptions in Chinese and Syriac [the liturgical language of the Nestorians] that spoke of a Christian congregation that had been flourishing during the Tang dynasty. Father Trigault sent word of his discovery to Rome, but the idea of Chinese Christians seemed so inherently preposterous that Father Trigault was suspected of having perpetrated a hoax.)

Francis Xavier died at the age of forty-six, on the island of Shangch'uan Shan in the Gulf of Canton, within sight of the Chinese mainland. He had given a handsome bribe—twenty sacks of pepper—to the captain of a Chinese junk, who was supposed to ferry him across the straits in secret, but the captain had apparently decided that the risk was too great. The junk never appeared, and Xavier's body was hastily buried in the sand by Portuguese traders, later recovered and taken to Goa, where it was laid out in great state and supposedly remained unchanged and uncorrupted for many hundreds of years. In fact there was more symbolism in the real circumstances of his death than in any of the legends or the pious tracts that are handed out in churches—he died as a homeless wanderer, caught between arrival and departure, in transit between two worlds.

Dr. Li Meets the Son of Heaven—the Jesuits in China

Five years after Xavier's death, in 1557, a Dominican missionary called Caspar de la Cruz appeared before the walls of Canton, a city whose gates were hung with placards that warned, in gold characters, that "bearded round-eyes" would not be admitted. Father de la Cruz was accordingly sent straight back to Macao, where the Portuguese had just been awarded a trading concession in return for their material help in suppressing a fleet of pirate junks in the South China Sea (and which is still occasionally useful for making East-West personnel exchanges of a similar kind). A Jesuit college was established in 1562, and some thirty years later three Jesuits were selected (out of a staff of thirty-six) to receive an intensive one-year course of instruction that would enable them, if all went well, to talk their way past the gates of Canton.

For the first time the Jesuits were confronted with a culture that was not only older and more sophisticated than their own but also had a long tradition of being totally impervious to all foreign influences, short of outright conquest. Training and preparation were more important here than they had been elsewhere; the initial course lasted for a year, and the first lesson the three trainees learned was that the Chinese held the Portuguese beneath contempt, which is why they would be wearing saffron robes like Buddhist monks and would be careful to disavow any connection with those uncouth barbarians from the southern ocean.

Next they faced the intricacies of spoken and written Chinese, with its five tones and thousands of characters, followed by a crash course in Chinese history, customs, and law, at the end of which they knew about as much about China as any other living Europeans—which was not all that much after all, since the first Portuguese caravel had sailed into a Chinese harbor as recently as 1513 to take on a cargo of gold, silks, and rhubarb (which was greatly esteemed in Europe for its laxative properties). With so many potentially embarrassing gaps in their knowledge and so many opportunities for putting their collective foot in it in China, the Jesuit missionaries of this first wave were fortunate that one of their number turned out to be a remarkably suave and persuasive diplomat, a kind of intellectual Francis Xavier in fact.

This was Matteo Ricci, subsequently known as Li Ma-tu or simply "Dr. Li" to his many Chinese admirers. Ricci was born in Macerta, Italy, in 1552; his father was an apothecary. He was trained as a lawyer at first; then, after he entered the Order, he studied mathematics and astronomy with the celebrated Christoph Clavius. After a year at the seminary in Coimbra, Portugal—a kind of training college for missionaries—he served for two years as a teacher in Goa before coming to Macao. Ricci was active as a scholar and missionary in China for sixteen years, and his collected works include over twenty translations of books on scientific and technical subjects (as well as the catechism) into Chinese, plus a Latin translation of the *Analects* of Confucius. (It was Ricci who gave the philosopher Kung Fu-tzu the Latin name by which he is known in the West; in Ricci's translation his name is always preceded by the Chinese honorific *shang* ["lofty"], which roughly corresponds to "Saint Confucius.")

When Father Ricci first appeared for an audience at the Imperial Palace in Peking, the court chamberlains who kept the register of foreign visitors made the following entry: "A beggar of uncertain origin; the name of his country does not appear in the imperial register," concluding with the brusque recommendation, "Let him be sent back to his own country." But Ricci was not sent back, primarily because he brought with him an assortment of presents for the emperor, just as Xavier had done for the *daimyo* of Yamaguchi, including such technological marvels as a telescope, several music boxes, various scientific instruments, and a clock with a spring mechanism. The emperor—the Emperor Wan-Li of the Ming dynasty, to be precise—was delighted with Ricci's tribute up to this point, but unfortunately the final item—a costly reliquary containing the bones of a number of saints—which was intended as the *pièce de résistance,* turned out to be a total loss. "The foreigner also produced a box," as one chronicler noted, "which is alleged to contain the bones of several immortals—as if the immortals would leave their bones behind when they ascended into heaven. . . ."

Ricci was quick to realize that, as far as Christianity was concerned, the Chinese could "only be brought around by the exercise of cunning." He devised a three-phase plan to that effect. The first phase was simply to convince the Chinese that there could be another civilization besides their own, on the other side of the world—which had certainly never occurred to them, any more than it might have occurred to Father Ricci that there could be any other civilization besides his own and the Chinese. Ricci had brought a map of the world along with him that reflected all the latest European discoveries and was certainly less parochial in its view of the world than the Chinese maps, which showed their own Middle Kingdom occupying about three quarters of the land area of the earth, surrounded by a few insignificant dependencies and barbaric outlands.

It would be some years, however, before Ricci could report back to Rome "that everything that I have to tell about our nations and peoples, and our learned men above all, has slowly come to seem entirely normal to them." The crowning success of this first phase of Ricci's operation was a commission from the emperor to prepare a map of China using Western cartographical techniques. This provided Ricci with an excellent transition to the next phase, which was to convince the Chinese that there was much in the learning of Western scholars that they themselves might profit from. He began by pointing out a number of errors in the standard Chinese geometry texts—he had not studied with the great Clavius for nothing—and his prestige soared among the Chinese intelligentsia, who began to refer to him as "Dr. Li, one of the greatest and wisest of teachers." He went on to supply further corrections for the Chinese mathematics textbooks and astronomical tables (mathematics and the sciences had been in a state of complete paralysis in China for the last few dynasties), and phase two was successfully completed.

And all this was simply a prologue to the third phase of the operation, to persuade the mandarins and scholars who made up China's intellectual elite to embrace Christianity. This, as Ricci knew very well, was not a task to be accomplished in a single lifetime—after all, it had taken him seven years simply to make his way from Macao to Peking in order to present himself at court. He realized that he was not going to enjoy the fruition of all the cultivation he had done so far, as he confided to one of his Jesuit companions shortly before his death: "I shall leave you in front of an open door." Ricci had spent nine years at the Chinese court, and when he died in Peking on May 11, 1610, he was given a state funeral by order of the Wan-li emperor—and the bells of three hundred Christian churches across China tolled his death knell.

The more permanent effects of Ricci's mission were felt in Europe rather than China, however, where the reports of Jesuit missionaries and Dutch and Portuguese merchants touched off an artistic and intellectual craze for *chinoiserie* that lasted well into the eighteenth century. In France, for example, two hundred "descriptions of China" were published in the space of forty years; the English philosopher Francis Bacon (1561–1626) made a serious effort to devise a universal language inspired by Chinese characters (since the way in which a character is read is symbolic rather than phonetic). At the height of the craze Louis XIV sent geographers and mathematicians, painters and landscape architects, to complete their studies in China, and Voltaire, as usual, had the last word by observing that it would make better sense for the Chinese to send missionaries to Europe to bring the gospel of reason and enlightenment to the people of that dark continent.

In China, on the other hand, it seemed that Ricci had left nothing behind him. The three hundred church bells were stilled within a year of his death, which was not his fault but for which he was still somehow held to be accountable in Rome—and still is, at least in certain quarters. For example, in his book *The Jesuits* the historian Heinrich Boehmer observes that the reverses suffered by the Chinese mission after Ricci's death "furnish striking proof of the fact that Ricci had failed to find the correct answer to the difficult question of how to establish a mission among a people with their own distinct culture." Or in other words— since all peoples have "their own distinct culture"—Ricci was a failure because his mission was not a success, which does not seem like a very satisfactory explanation. Nevertheless, the Church clearly agrees with Boehmer that nothing succeeds like success—Xavier was canonized because his mission flourished (for a time at least), Ricci was slighted because his mission was suppressed.

The charge has also been leveled against Ricci and his successor, Father Johann Adam Schall von Bell, that they were far better mathematicians than missionaries—particularly against Schall, since he was presumably in a position to begin to harvest what Ricci had sown and cultivated. This, however, was really not the case. The Wan-li emperor died the following year, in 1611, and his successor forbade all further missionary activity in China and sent the Jesuits back to Macao. He was forced to relent slightly in 1620, but only because he needed military aid from the Portuguese to stave off the Manchu invaders on his northern border. Still, the emperor made no secret of his hostility to Christianity, and although the Jesuits were allowed to return, their congregations had been dispersed and an imperial edict was circulated throughout China which began with the words, "The men from the West are expounding a dangerous doctrine. . . ." And certainly the major flaw in Ricci's plan was that the teachings of Christ did not seem to have much appeal for the

Chinese scholar-elite, who had been brought up on the ethical subtleties of the *Analects* and the paradoxes of Lao Tzu; to them the injunction to love our enemies must have just seemed like an absurd misquotation of Confucius, "For good return good, for evil return justice." The Jesuits' answer to this, of course, was to make concessions, to try to throw a bridge across this doctrinal abyss, rather than to expect the Chinese to leap over it themselves as the Franciscans and Dominicans expected. The Jesuits were criticized for compromising with "idolatry," the Franciscans and Dominicans continued to preach hellfire and damnation at the Chinese, who would have preferred to endure the fires of hell in the company of their ancestors than eternal bliss with a lot of long-nose Western barbarians. By 1664 there were said to be 324,000 Catholic converts in China, but this figure was only arrived at by means of a number of creative accounting tricks—infants who had been abandoned by their parents during famines and hastily baptized before dying of hunger were included in the total, for example. (In any case, China had more than two hundred million inhabitants at the time.)

But in spite of these disheartening developments, Father Schall made quite a career for himself at court; under the name of T'ang Jo-wang he became a trusted imperial councillor, a mandarin of the highest grade in 1629, and in 1644 he was appointed astronomer royal, director of the Peking observatory, and president of the Mathematical Council—in which capacity he was responsible for regulating the official (lunar) calendar, fixing the dates of ceremonies and public holidays, and casting the official horoscope for the imperial family. (Devotees of the occult might be interested to know that the modern ephemeris tables used by Chinese astrologers, with their strangely prosaic constellations—the Rat, the Pig, the Snake, and so on—were based on observations provided by a German Jesuit.) Some years later, the Kang-hsi emperor was so impressed by Father Schall's description of the splendor and magnificence of the court of the Holy Father in Rome that he devised a plan to unite their two great realms by taking the niece of Pope Clement IX as his wife (one of many, in fact). The original letter in which the emperor outlines his proposal to Pope Clement was part of a collection of "interesting" documents that was filched from the Vatican archives by Napoleon in 1809 and remained for many years in the possession of the French Foreign Ministry. The text appears below; unfortunately Pope Clement's reply has not been preserved:

To you, Clement, most blessed among Popes, most sanctified and puissant Emperor of all Popes and Christian churches, Lord of the Kings of Europe and Friend of God.

The mightiest of the mighty on Earth, he who is greater than the greatest under the Sun and Moon, he who sits upon the Emerald Throne of the Empire of Chin, which is mounted upon the topmost of a hundred golden steps, the better to proclaim the Word of God, he who holds the power of life and death over one hundred and fifteen kingdoms and one hundred and seventy islands, writes to you this letter with the most virginal of ostrich quills.

Greetings and long life!

The time has come that the bloom of our royal youth should advance the fruit of our old age to ripeness, whereby the wish of our loyal subjects might be fulfilled that they should be afforded the shelter and security of an heir to our imperial throne. Consequently we have decided on a maiden of noble birth and great beauty who has fed on the milk of both a doughty lioness and a gentle doe. Since your Roman kinsmen have always been accounted to be the sires of the bravest, purest, and most incomparable women, we therefore wish to reach out our mighty hand and take one of these women to wife. We hope that she might be one of your nieces, or of some other great priest on whom God looks down with his right eye. . . .

We wish that she might have the eyes of a dove that surveys the heaven and the earth, the lips of a mussel that has fed on the gold of sunrise. Her age should not exceed two hundred months; she should be no taller than a stalk of standing grain, and no thicker around the waist than a handful of parched corn. . . .

Inasmuch as you, Father and Friend, should accomplish our wishes, you shall be forging an alliance and a bond of eternal amity between your kingdoms and our mighty realm. Our laws will be united as the mistletoe is wedded to the oak. We ourselves shall propagate our royal blood throughout many provinces, and we shall be warming the beds of your princes with certain of our daughters as well, of which the

mandarins we have sent to you as envoy will furnish likenesses. . . .

In the meantime we arise from our throne to embrace you.
We declare to you that this letter has been sealed with the
Imperial Seal in this our capital city of the world on the third
day of the eighth month of our reign.

It is difficult to see how Pope Clement could have resisted such an
appeal, but somehow the marriage never took place.

During this period—the middle decades of the seventeenth century—
the Jesuits in China were encouraged to show off all their talents (as long
as these were strictly secular). They built fountains and mechanical toys,
laid out ornamental gardens; "it suddenly began to seem," writes the
historian René Fülöp-Miller, "as if the Society of Jesus was a guild of
painters and architects, and Christianity merely an esoteric branch of
landscape gardening." This is not too far from the truth, since the Superior General had been encouraged by the early reports from Macao to
send no one to China who was not trained as an architect, an engineer,
or an artist. There is a painting in the Hamburg art museum entitled
Court Ladies Playing Chess, done on silk rather than canvas in the Chinese style, which depicts three Chinese ladies of fashion in European
dress (and which must have had much the same impact at the time,
about 1720, as the press photographs that began to appear a couple of
years ago of former Red Guards in Peking disco-dancing in designer
jeans). The artist was an Italian Jesuit, Giuseppe Castiglione, who first
arrived in China in 1715 and evolved a remarkable hybrid style that is
half Ch'ing dynasty and half rococo—he signed his work either as Castiglione or Lang Shih-ning, depending on which element was predom-
inant.

Fifty years earlier, in the last days of the Ming dynasty, the Jesuits had
shown that they were equally accomplished at the arts of war. When the
emperor was hard-pressed by the incursions of the Manchus, Father
Schall and his younger colleague Father Ferdinand Verbiest set up a
model cannon foundry and—since the Jesuits never did anything by
half-measures—personally trained a troop of artillerymen to man the
guns they cast. But this was still not enough to keep the last Ming emperor from being dislodged from the Emerald Throne by the Manchus,
though the Jesuits weathered the transition from Ming to Ching (as the

Manchu dynasty came to be called) without any particular difficulty—in fact it was the first Ching emperor who gave Father Schall his second big promotion to the presidency of the Mathematical Council. The irony of all this was that while the Jesuits were getting along so famously with the Chinese—who spoke deferentially of Christianity as "the religion of the great Schall"—they were continually being harassed and vilified by their fellow Christians; Schall, for instance, was accused of having married a young woman from an influential Chinese family (with the connivance of the Order) as well as keeping a stable of concubines, of allowing Chinese converts to worship idols and wear heathen amulets instead of crucifixes (also that he had neglected to inform them that Christ died on the Cross). The Jesuits were also accused of saying mass in Chinese instead of Latin—which in those days, much closer in time to the Council of Trent than Vatican II, was no less scandalous than concubinage and idolatry. These slanders were of course earmarked for Rome; the Chinese were simply told the same old story, that the Jesuits were the advance guard of an invading barbarian army.

Father Schall eventually fell victim to a court intrigue (hatched by jealous courtiers and not by fellow missionaries); he was condemned to death on a charge of high treason, but an unfavorable omen (an earthquake) on the day set for his execution brought about his release. He was posthumously cleared of all charges by the emperor, but the Pope was less forgiving where the Jesuits were concerned. The clanking machinery of a full-scale bureaucratic investigation was set in motion at the Curia; a papal legate, Cardinal Tournon, was instructed to go to China and look into the matter personally. Fortunately for the Jesuits, a diplomatic crisis intervened before the cardinal had even left Rome that they were able to turn to their advantage (and the cardinal's mission was indefinitely postponed).

The crisis involved Peter I of Russia, not yet the Great, who had just deposed his domineering sister—it was 1689 by now—and seemed to be bent on celebrating his accession with a full-scale war with China. The tsar's Cossacks had already provoked several border clashes with the Manchus—and this was back in the days before such incidents had become part of the normal routine. A boundary commission was dispatched to a Russian frontier settlement, accompanied by a number of Jesuit interpreters, who helped in negotiating a treaty that successfully stabilized the frontier for a great many years to come. (This was the first time the Chinese had deigned to sign a treaty with a European power.)

In return for their help in dickering with the Russians, the Jesuits were rewarded with an imperial edict that authorized the practice of the Christian religion throughout the Middle Kingdom—the edict specifically mentions that "no one shall be prevented from burning a pinch of incense in the temple of the Heavenly Lord," probably one of the few Catholic rituals that was comprehensible to the Chinese. Unfortunately, though, this is not quite the end of the story—the papal investigation into the Jesuits' alleged bad habits was still pending; a papal legate (the first of two such envoys) finally arrived in 1703 to determine whether the so-called "Chinese rites" that the Jesuits permitted their converts to practice could actually be sanctioned by the Church.

This marked the beginning of a lengthy wrangle between the Jesuits and the papal legates, in which the emperor of China was the only participant who really acquitted himself terribly well. He sided with the Jesuits in the rites controversy, of course, since, as he explained, the veneration of one's ancestors was an ancient and edifying practice that had absolutely no religious significance whatsoever (which was far from being the truth). The emperor further remarked—being an emperor, he had never had much occasion for tact or diplomacy—that he himself would never presume to set himself up as a censor of rites and customs he was not personally acquainted with. The papal legate ruled against the Jesuits; the emperor promptly expelled him from the country and he died in Macao shortly afterward (the Jesuits took the blame for at least the first of these occurrences).

Finally in 1742 a papal bull, *Ex quo singulari*, definitely forbade the practice of ancestor worship to all Chinese Christians; Christianity was outlawed in China once more, and the missionaries were expelled— except, of course, for the Jesuits, who were encouraged to remain at court in their alternate capacities as painters, technicians, and astronomers. The Jesuit mission in China was not entirely at an end—there were still 120 Jesuits in China in 1880—but it was not destined to progress any further than Ricci's phase two, which had finally become an end in itself—the Jesuits had been so eager to dazzle the Chinese with their technical wizardry that they had forgotten that they had been sent to China to serve God. The Roman Curia had made their usual mistake of clinging to the old way on the assumption that it was the only way. It seems only fitting that in later years the China mission came to be regarded by the hierarchy as a kind of Siberian exile for rebellious or recalcitrant Jesuits, like Teilhard de Chardin or Father Michel, whom we shall be meeting before long.

The Holy Experiment—the Jesuits in South America

The Jesuit missions in the Americas were not associated with any great names like Francis Xavier and Father Ricci. The history of the mission in North America was, even more than usual, a story of gallant failure that can be told quickly enough, with many lesser-known heroes—like Father Marquette, who had traveled farther into the unknown lands beyond the Great Lakes than the hardiest voyager—and martyrs, of course, like Father Jean de Brébeuf, whose unflinching courage under torture so impressed his Iroquois captors that they tore the living heart out of his body and ate it in the hope of acquiring some of his courage. The Indians that the Jesuits had been sent out to convert were being driven to the edge of extinction by trade whiskey, smallpox, and intertribal warfare (usually encouraged and abetted by the English and the French). The Iroquois killed Father de Brébeuf because they were allied with the English against the French, not because they were particularly hostile to Christianity; in 1699 the governor of Massachusetts offered the tribal chiefs a bounty "in money or costlier presents for any Jesuits residing among them that they will deliver to me alive." And, as had happened elsewhere, the fate of the Jesuit mission was closely linked with the fortunes of the colonial power that stood sponsor to their activities. When the St. Lawrence basin became a bloody battleground, and when the French and their Huron allies began to get the worst of it, then the failure of the mission became a foregone conclusion.

The South American mission, on the other hand, while not an unqualified success, was at least the most ambitious and most unorthodox enterprise that the Order was ever involved with and, though perhaps not too well known in Europe and North America, has still attracted more than its share of legends, misapprehensions, misconceptions, and recriminations. The story begins in the usual way, with a request from the king of Portugal for missionaries for his overseas dominions in the

"New Indies"—Brazil, in other words. Ignatius himself supervised the initial phases of the mission in order to avoid some of the problems that had plagued the few earlier expeditions of this kind. In 1553 a new province was added to the Jesuit overseas network, and at the same time the city of São Paulo—now a megalopolis of some ten million souls— was founded as a settlement by and for a team of six Jesuit missionaries.

In North America, Jesuit missionaries would customarily set out with a pack of trade goods—fishhooks, magnifying glasses (for lighting tinder), and metal traps—for the Indians' hunting grounds, like a nomad following his flocks. In South America it was considered more prudent to operate from a permanent base. For one thing, the Indians that had been encountered so far—the Caribs and the coastal tribes of Brazil—were fiercely cannibalistic for the most part, "wild, naked, ferocious maneaters" in the words of Hans Staden, a German castaway who had lived among them and survived to publish a book of his reminiscences in 1557. (He complained that the only useful work they ever did was to fatten up their womenfolk for the slaughter.)

The second reason for this was that in Brazil the Jesuits were also charged with the spiritual oversight of the Portuguese planters and settlers, who needed "a good dose of decency with a few drops of religion," as one missionary put it, even more desperately than the Portuguese traders and adventurers in Goa. They were a pretty rude lot, all in all, who not infrequently used their rosary beads to count the number of lashes they had just given one of their slaves, vied with one another to see who could support the largest harem of Indian girls, and when taken to task for this by the Jesuits simply had them all baptized "so the sin would not be great."

Since there clearly was not much that could be done for these unregenerate characters, the Jesuits decided to do what they could to improve the lot of the settlers' Indian slaves. (This is by no means to imply that the Jesuits tried to abolish slavery, or even that they disapproved of it particularly—they had plenty of slaves of their own on their own plantations, all of whom were branded for purposes of identification, as was the custom in those days.) But the Jesuits did what they could to expedite the current trend to replace Indian slaves with imported African blacks; a Spanish Jesuit called Father Pedro Claver interceded with the governor of New Granada (now Colombia), who decreed that every slave who arrived at the slave market in Cartagena should be instructed in the Christian faith for an "adequate" period of time (namely, until they had recovered from the horrors of the passage and were ready to mount the auction block).

In some areas the Jesuits managed to compel the planters to allow their slaves a few hours off every week for religious instruction, which seems like little enough to us (as it probably did to the slaves as well), but this edict was greeted by the slaveowners with howls of indignation— much the way our own industrial magnates reacted to the passage of the first child labor laws in the early years of this century. It seemed as if open conflict was about to break out between the planters and the padres, particularly since the colonial authorities tended to side with the planters.

The Jesuits sent a delegation to the Spanish court, but not simply to plead for, or to demand, redress (depending on whether or not you subscribe to the conspiratorial theory of the Order as an all but omnipotent secret society that commanded the cadaverlike obedience of popes, emperors, and statesmen, as well as of their own). Instead they had come up with a novel proposal—that Indians and whites should be physically separated, since "the Spaniards are addicted to a great many vices of which our simple-hearted Indian folk know nothing but which they would doubtless soon acquire as a result of their association." Specifically what the Jesuits had in mind was a system of Indian reservations, a scheme that was immediately approved by the Spanish authorities not so much because it was foresighted and progressive in itself—two qualities of which the Spanish authorities were particularly wary—but because the Jesuits had also suggested that the inhabitants of these reservations would pay an annual poll tax directly to the Spanish crown. This would make the Christianizing and sanitizing of the Indians a going proposition, and Philip II of Spain offered the unexpected concession that no white man except the viceroy should be allowed to set foot on these Jesuit reserves without their permission.

The Jesuits graciously responded by promoting the whole scheme as if it had been entirely Philip's idea from the outset: "But it was a very bad thing for the newly converted Indians to associate with the Spaniards, since they not only oppressed them with hard labor but also put them in grave danger of perdition through the unbridled viciousness of their conduct, so that his Catholic Majesty has strictly forbidden his Spanish subjects any sort of traffic or intercourse with these Christian people, to whom he has given their freedom under the governance of our priests" (from a Jesuit account published in 1609).

The reserves were to be located in the unexplored wilderness beyond the Brazilian backlands, which became the site of a kind of theocratic socialistic commune on the high plateau of South America that has been variously called "the Holy Experiment"—the title of a play by the dramatist Friedrich Hochwälder—and, somewhat more cynically, "the Jesuit state." The Jesuits began by replacing the old plantation economy with a system of economic autarchy—total self-sufficiency, in other words—in which both the lash and the labor gang were abolished, crops were consumed locally rather than exported, and barter was the only form of exchange; there was no money, and virtually none of the problems that money can buy, as long as the outside world could be kept at bay.

The "Jesuit state," which did manage to last for a good 150 years, was not really a state, since it consisted of a string of isolated settlements called *reducciones* (from the Spanish *reducir,* "to bring together," "coalesce") instead of a contiguous territory, and it always remained at least nominally under the authority of the Spanish viceroy. There is a legend about the founding of the first of these settlements that is referred to in several missionary sources and was picked up by the French Romantic author François Chateaubriand (1768–1848) in his book *The Genius of Christianity* (though it has not necessarily been authenticated in any of the standard works on the subject). It seems that the first missionaries to penetrate into the interior were making their way down the Upper Paraná River, but all the Indians they encountered had instantly fled into the forest, no doubt taking them for an advance party of slavehunters. To relieve the tedium of the journey, and perhaps the anxiety of floating through the primeval forest on a flimsy homemade raft as well, the padres began to sing hymns. Then, as Chateaubriand takes up the story, "The Indians were caught in this tender trap. They came down from the mountains and stood on the riverbank the better to hear these entrancing sounds. Many threw themselves into the river and began to swim after the enchanted boat. Bow and arrows slipped insensibly from the hands of the savages. They felt in their very souls the presentiment of a nobler form of life, the first sweetness of contact with mankind's higher aspirations."

Whether or not this affecting scene actually took place as described, it is true that later, when the settlements had already been established, the Jesuits did select missionaries who had a talent for music as well as some technical skill for service in South America, and the padres soon had the

Guaraní Indians in their charge tootling and sawing away on European instruments. It seems to have taken them less time to absorb the principles of harmony and counterpoint than the Jesuit work ethic, however, and it often happened that the leisure-loving Guaraní had to be lured out into the fields by the seductive strains of the municipal chamber orchestra.

When the *reducción* system was at its peak of organization, there were about a hundred thousand Guaraní living in thirty-one different settlements on the central highlands of South America, roughly in the area where Brazil, Argentina, and Paraguay come together (the Guaraní still make up the majority of the population of Paraguay) and westward toward Bolivia. Every settlement was laid out according to the same basic plan; the adobe mission church stood on the central market square, the plaza, and was topped off by a handsome baroque belltower. As many as four thousand Indians might live in a single community, usually with two Jesuits in residence, one of whom served as parish priest, the other as district administrative officer—a well-ordered, peaceable kingdom in which even the architecture of the churches was partly Indian, partly European in its inspiration. (For the past fifteen years the ruins of these settlements have been investigated by scholars with the help of UNESCO funding, the sculptures and other devotional artworks catalogued and restored, and by the end of our century a whole new chapter in the history of Latin American art will have been rescued from the white ants and the lianas.)

During the 1920's, when a kind of drawing-room Leninism was in fashion in Europe, the *reducción* system was being celebrated as "the unique instance of a communist state that actually functioned in the realm of praxis and was only destroyed from without rather than torn apart from within." However, just from what we have already seen, it appears that the "Jesuit state" would have to be disqualified, first on the grounds that it was not really a state at all, second because, however progressive it may have been as an economic unit, politically—like many more recent entities that might make the same claim—it was still a despotism (benevolent in this case) however much it may have seemed like a workers' paradise from the outside. If this system was to have a name, it might be best to call it a patriarchal autarchy—a phrase that is not going to send anyone rushing to the barricades in a hurry—and leave it at that, though the same idea was expressed much more eloquently by Montesquieu when he observed, "The Jesuits have succeeded in working a kind of miracle, since they have made the Indians happy and made them work as well."

Father Florian Pauke, a missionary who served in the *reducciones,* gives a wry illustration of how this miracle was actually accomplished: "I took hold of the plow and began to till the soil, letting my Indians stand off to one side until they had had a chance to observe how the thing was done. I managed the job very badly and could not succeed in plowing a straight furrow that did not somehow look like the track left by a snake. Come here now, I said to them, and see how you fellows get on with it. To this they replied straightaway, Keep working, Father, you are doing ever so well."

The Guaraní, as this anecdote makes clear, were nobody's fools, and they made the transition from Stone Age hunting and gathering to baroque handicrafts and concertizing with hardly any difficulty at all (and without the usual consequences of such rapid leaps into the future— alcoholism, syphilis, social instability, and mass extinction). "Apart from Christianity," wrote another Jesuit, "we have taught these people to bake bread and stitch clothing, to cook and to paint, to cast churchbells, to play upon the organ, the cornetto, the hautboy, and the trumpet. . . ." The Jesuit settlements had the best of everything—the finest looms, the most efficient sugar mills, the first candlemakers and glassblowers, the sturdiest carpenters and the steadiest pack mules, all provided by the Guaraní once the Jesuits had supplied the model.

One of the padres' few accomplishments that is still in evidence is the standard Guarani language, a synthesis of many divergent tribal dialects that became the trade language of the settlements and is still, along with Spanish, the colloquial and official language of Paraguay. In other respects the paternalist rule of the Jesuits may have been a mixed blessing for the Guarani. They discouraged polygamy by offering handsome bribes to men who contented themselves with only one wife, but promiscuous women were simply locked up in the "widows' lodge" (where the normal period of mourning was spent in complete seclusion) without being offered any material inducement to change their ways. Children were left in their mothers' care, for the most part, though the padres did encourage the juvenile espionage system that was so prominent a feature of the Jesuit colleges in Europe. The story was told, for example, of a boy who had reported to the padre that his father had been practicing sorcery on the sly; his father got wind of this and beat him bloody, but "the young fellow endured the pain for the love of God."

Such methods of social control were not considered oppressive or abnormal by seventeenth-century standards, but the Jesuits were criticized, and not without good cause, by missionaries from other orders who were concerned with the danger that the Jesuits might be converting the Guaraní into materialistic "rice Christians," whose only notion of Christ was of a kind of vague symbol of where their next meal was coming from. Another plausible complaint was that the settlements' wholesome barter economy was all very well, but that the Jesuits were really playing at self-sufficiency to preserve their own political autonomy, and that they were neglecting their priestly duty to the Christian souls in their charge in order to attend to the massive responsibilities of running a secular state on the side. The Spanish and Portuguese settlers in the adjoining territories (as soon as there *were* any adjoining territories) were opposed to the Jesuit state for more practical reasons, as quickly became apparent. The proximity of the Jesuit settlements had made contract laborers—slaves, in other words—scarce, and had driven up the price of free labor as well. They decided to remedy this imbalance by recruiting a group of local desperadoes called *mamelucos* to raid the settlements for slaves. The *mamelucos* were the half-breed offspring of Indian women and Portuguese settlers, so called because their reputed cruelty and ferocity reminded someone, at least, of the fighting Mamelukes of Egypt—and before this they had made their living as bandits on the frontier, so the planters were actually solving two different problems with a single bold stroke.

The Jesuits accepted the raids of the *mameluco* slave-catchers as simply another trial sent from God, but they did take the precaution of moving some of their settlements farther up the Paraná, rebuilding them closer together, and surrounding them with palisades. When the *mamelucos* followed them upriver, they responded with a step that proved to be fatal to the future of the *reducción* system. The Jesuits decided to raise their own army, as described, not without some complacency, in a contemporary report: "If any danger should present itself, we can put thirty thousand mounted Indians in the field at once, and they well know how to fire a musket, and swing a saber, and form up in squadrons and execute all the prescribed evolutions. Our fathers have recruited them and trained them all." Here the famous Jesuit versatility was put to the ultimate test, since the difference between leading a confirmation class and a cavalry charge is not a trivial one. (Any Jesuit father who felt a little self-conscious while putting his Indian irregulars through their paces must have consoled himself with the thought that Ignatius himself began his career as a fire-eating ensign in the viceroy's foot guard.)

The Spanish crown encouraged these martial escapades; there was certainly no cheaper way they could have raised a force of thirty thousand troopers who could live off the country to guard their frontier with Brazil. Philip V of Spain praised the Jesuit army as "the foremost bastion of our Spanish defenses," and, as any old soldier knows, that is the sort of talk that generally costs lives. When war did break out between His Most Catholic Majesty of Spain and His Most Christian cousin of Portugal, the Guaraní lost six hundred men (plus a German Jesuit adviser) on the field of battle. "One of our musketeers fired off a round," wrote a Jesuit who took part in the campaign, "and the blessed Saint Francis Xavier guided the path of the ball so that it struck one of the Portuguese and shattered his thighbone." The Jesuit state had flourished many years in splendid isolation, but this sort of thing could not go unnoticed for long. Voltaire, who hated generals and Jesuits about equally, is usually acknowledged to have had the last word on the subject in *Candide:* "'And where is the Reverend Father Provincial?' asked Camacho. 'He went on parade just as soon as he sang mass,' the sergeant replied. 'You won't have a chance to kiss his spurs for another three hours now.'"

Now that they had mounted their first, inconclusive military campaign, the Jesuits decided to start conducting their own foreign policy as well. In 1750 the Spanish and Portuguese governments signed a treaty that would have settled the Brazilian boundary dispute at the expense of the Jesuit reserve—eighteen settlements to the east of the Uruguay River (which at this point is closer to Paraguay) were to be handed over to the Portuguese and their inhabitants relocated farther west. The Jesuits were in no mood for starting afresh at this late date, and they threatened to defend the eastern settlements by force of arms if necessary. In 1751 the powers finally relented and the frontier was redrawn to accommodate the Jesuits, but this turned out to be something of a Pyrrhic victory. Some years earlier the Jesuits in South America had acquired another enemy against whom neither powder and shot nor the power of prayer could prevail; this was Pope Benedict XIV. The bull *Immensa pastores,* handed down in 1741, was a scathing denunciation of the Jesuits as slaveholders and "missionary tricksters," but the moral indignation of the Holy Father only helped in the end to furnish a pretext for the dismantling of the *reducción* system. A more compelling reason for those involved was the rumor that the Jesuits had accumulated a vast hoard of hidden treasure somewhere in or beneath their settlements—a rumor of great age and respectability, since it had first appeared in connection with the suppression of the Templars in 1312. Nevertheless, the feeling was that such things are always worth investigating, if only on the off chance, and royal commissions of inquiry were duly convened for that purpose. When the decision was finally reached to disband the missions in 1766, never before had orders from Madrid and Lisbon been obeyed with such encouraging thoroughness and alacrity. Troops were sent out to the settlements—this time the Jesuits did not offer any resistance— every hut was ransacked from top to bottom, the Jesuits were arrested and sent back to Europe in disgrace, and the Guaraní fled into the bush. The treasure itself never materialized, or rather—according to certain books of the "stranger than science" variety—it is still waiting to be found by the enterprising treasure-seeker, somewhere in the jungle up above Iguazu Falls.

FATHER LaVALETTE'S LETTERS OF CREDIT— A JESUIT *CAUSE CÉLÈBRE*

The island of Martinique is one of the Lesser Antilles, a tiny speck on the edge of the Atlantic (only four hundred or so square miles) that has belonged to France since 1658 and seems just as unlikely a setting as the jungles of Paraguay for the denouement of the story of the Jesuit enterprise overseas. The word *enterprise* is used advisedly here, since this final episode began in 1746, when a shrewd French Jesuit called Père LaValette took over the administration of the debt-ridden mission on the island. Père LaValette decided to go for double or nothing and accordingly borrowed still more money and bought several plantations on Martinique, hoping to end up with enough to pay his debts and cover his expenses by the time his cargo of sugar and coffee had been sold in Europe. Certainly this is the kind of strategy that has been the beginning of many large fortunes—and the losing of many small ones, too, of course.

Predictably the other planters and traders on Martinique were concerned that Père LaValette's activities would be cutting into their profits, and they raised such a fuss that LaValette was finally recalled to Rome by General Ignatius Visconti, but this Ignatius was only a shadow of his great namesake, and internal discipline in the Order had totally broken down. Père LaValette refused to go to Rome, and the four inquisitors who were dispatched to investigate the complaints against him never turned up on Martinique.

Père LaValette might eventually have paid off his creditors and even turned a profit, but unfortunately the French merchant vessel that was carrying his first year's crop to market was captured off Bordeaux by an English privateer. LaValette's pyramid scheme had collapsed, and his creditors began clamoring for payment. Some of them applied directly to the Office of the Superior General, which naturally declined to give satisfaction. The creditors sued the Order in the French courts and won.

At this point the Jesuit hierarchy made what soon turned out to be a colossal blunder. They lodged an appeal with the Paris Parlement, which in spite of its name was more of a Supreme Court than a legislature; the Parlement was also rabidly anticlerical, and in particular it had been spoiling to get at the Jesuits for some time. The attorneys for the Order led off with the argument that since the *Constitutions* forbade its members to engage in any kind of trade, then the Order was clearly not responsible for Père LaValette's renegade commercial ventures. This failed to have a pacifying effect on the court, especially since it had long been common knowledge that the Jesuit missions in India, Mexico, and Brazil had carried on a lucrative trade in spices, chocolate, tea, and other tropical specialty items, the proceeds of which were eventually used to finance the Japanese mission (but only after the original funds had been invested in Chinese silk, which was sold in Japan at an excellent rate of return). The members of the court would have had no difficulty in exposing the Jesuits' claim as the flimsiest legal fiction, but at this point they were more interested in the *Constitutions*. They demanded that the Jesuits furnish written evidence of their claim—remember that the *Constitutions* had so far never been made public—and when the volumes were produced, the attorneys for the government fell on these choice morsels like hyenas on a carcass. The most aggressive of them, a Breton lawyer called LaChatolais, claimed to have discovered in the *Constitutions* a handbook of "every known form of heresy, idolatry, and superstition, [which] provides tutelage in suicide, legicide, blasphemy, and every kind of impurity, usury, sorcery, murder, cruelty, hatred, vendetta, insurrection, and treason." This was exactly the sort of "evidence" that Parlement had been looking for, in short—not only to dismiss the case but also to proceed against the Order in a matter of far greater importance.

Père LaValette was not entirely forgotten in the midst of all this. He confessed his fault and was expelled from the Order; he spent the rest of his life in England, as a private citizen. It was the English who came out best in the end, since not only had they made off with LaValette's original cargo, but they also took over the Jesuit plantations when they occupied the island of Martinique during the Seven Years' War and sold them, slaves and all, at an advantageous price, which would have been more than enough to pay off LaValette's outstanding debts.

In 1540 the Jesuits launched their first missionary campaign, which consisted of Francis Xavier and two companions, at a time when the Order was still an informal association of "reforming priests" living in a rented house in Rome. During these first two centuries the Jesuits had made their presence felt almost everywhere in the world, even in areas where they were not conspicuously successful—in 1860, for example, the Scottish missionary David Livingstone came across entire tribes in Portuguese East Africa who had learned to read and write from the Jesuit fathers. It may be that the original spirit of the Order died the hardest in these neglected corners of the world, since when the Order was finally dissolved in 1773, most of the three thousand Jesuits who were serving with overseas missions preferred to remain at their posts rather than return to Europe.

It would be useless to try to draw up a geographical balance sheet for the Order's first two centuries of missionary activity. As we have seen, the failure of a mission was almost invariably the result of unfavorable political developments within the region (as in Japan) or of some sort of political rivalry between the colonial powers (Canada) or between factions within the Church itself (China). Still, there are a number of points worth mentioning that might be considered the collective legacy of all the Jesuit missionaries from the days of Francis Xavier to the dissolution of the Order. First of all, the Catholic Church is beginning to acknowledge that there is still some truth and beauty to be found outside of Catholicism, which of course was exactly the position that was adopted by the Jesuits during the rites controversy (and even then they were far less diffident about expressing it). The idea that a missionary's first duty was the spiritual and social well-being of his flock, rather than the fulfillment of some sort of baptismal quota of uninstructed and uncomprehending "converts," was another Jesuit innovation that was no less unpopular when it was first put into practice. And, finally, the objection that the Jesuits' real achievements were far outstripped by their expectations is really not very relevant—who has a better right than a missionary to let his reach exceed his grasp?—and not always even accurate, since the longevity of the Jesuit utopia in Paraguay, for example, and the extent of Xavier's initial successes in India and Japan certainly far exceeded all "reasonable" expectations for these ventures at the time.

Missionary work in itself is successful by definition insofar as its real effect is to translate the idea that all men are equal in the sight of God from a Sunday school motto into a demonstration of practical Christianity. There are still six thousand Jesuit missionaries scattered around the world today, and their work is no longer carried out exclusively among the "heathen" and the "idolators" in faraway lands. With the advent of the North Sea oil boom, when the godforsaken Shetland Islands became the final staging area for helicopters full of oil roughnecks from all over Europe, two Jesuit fathers accompanied the first crews who went out to man the steel drilling rigs in the middle of the North Sea. This was not so much an anomaly—like Father de Nobili in his Brahmin robes—but a matter of official policy, as enunciated by General Arrupe in an address in Trier in 1970: "Our missionary work is sure to require a great deal more attention and adaptability from us in the future. We let the opportunity slip through our fingers once; we should not let it get away a second time."

PART ❧ XI

THE HOLY FATHER DISOWNS HIS CHILDREN—
THE DISSOLUTION OF THE ORDER

We came in like lambs and ruled like wolves; we were driven out like dogs, but we shall rise up like eagles.

> —*Francisco Borgia, third General of the Order (1565–72)*

Your Eminence knows as well as anyone that the fall of the Order was engineered in Rome, and that it has more formidable enemies there than are to be found in Madrid.

> —*Severoli, papal nuncio in Vienna, to Cardinal Pacca, 1804*

The Butcher with the Ax—the Jesuits Are Expelled from Portugal

Every tourist who comes to Lisbon has seen the statue of the Marquês do Pombal that gazes down the broad Avenida da Liberdade toward the Baixa, the lower city. Sebastião José de Carvalho e Mello, Marquês do Pombal, was the prime minister of Portugal from 1750 to 1778, and perhaps he never looked as puffed up and haughty in life as he does today in bronze. He is meant to be proudly surveying the lower city, which was restored during his regime, with its streets shooting off in a symmetrical pattern like the skeleton of a fish, after the disastrous Lisbon earthquake of 1755. Among Pombal's other accomplishments—he rescued Portugal from her abject dependence on Great Britain in foreign policy matters, he greatly encouraged trade, industry, and education; in short he was a colossus among Portuguese statesmen. His personal reputation was quite unsavory, though, and his admirers were far outnumbered by his critics. He was described as "baseborn, overbearing, and deceitful," or simply as "that madman," and his nickname was "the Butcher with the Ax"—harsh words, even for a politician.

But perhaps there had to have been a streak of madness in Pombal's makeup for him to have done what he did—he was the first European politician who dared to launch an all-out offensive against the Society of

Jesus, which, even in its decadence, was still a formidable opponent. It may seem strange that this happened in backward, reactionary Portugal rather than, say, in France, where, as we have seen, anticlerical feelings ran high and where philosophers, from Descartes and Pascal to Diderot and D'Alembert, had been in the forefront of the struggle against Catholic obscurantism. In fact there were two reasons for this. The first was that Portugal had turned her back on Europe and fixed her eyes on the horizon, on her empire overseas (her colonies would still determine Portugal's fate politically until 1974). Pombal needed to divert some of the riches of the colonies into his own empty treasury, but the Jesuits were disproportionately influential in the colonies as well, more so than an upstart prime minister in faraway Lisbon. The second reason has to do with Pombal's own (comparatively) lowly origins—he was the son of an impoverished family of gentry and he had always borne a grudge against the members of the higher nobility and their Jesuit hangers-on. (The feeling of antipathy was mutual, needless to say.)

In many ways Pombal was the first representative of a political species that has become all too common in our own century—the fascist dictator. He was not given to purely strongarm tactics, though; he was a political pragmatist who knew how to bide his time. The Lisbon earthquake of 1755, which totally destroyed the old city and killed thirty thousand of its citizens (and convinced Voltaire that God could not possibly exist), gave Pombal the opportunity he had been waiting for—first to construct a magnificent new capital city, work on which was begun almost immediately, and then to proceed against the Jesuits while he was still able to present himself in the unaccustomed light of a public benefactor. The Jesuits had not done their cause any good by sermonizing about the earthquake as a "judgment sent from God," specifically to chastise the current regime for its atheistic, pro-Enlightenment leanings—other preachers, of course, had also sounded this inevitable motif, but Pombal was not concerned with them.

Just a year after the earthquake he suddenly ordered the leading Jesuits in Portugal arrested, and a few months after that his ambassadors to the various courts of Europe and to the Holy See presented their hosts with a kind of government white paper entitled "A Brief Report on the Republic which the Jesuits had established in the Spanish and Portuguese Possessions in the New World, as well as on the War which they have waged against the Armed Forces of both Monarchies, all drawn from the Protocols of Ambassadors and Plenipotentiaries as well as other

Documents." (It had not been too long ago that the Jesuit army had fought with the Spanish against the Portuguese, and it was now bristling defiance at both of them.) This was not the covert diplomatic maneuver the Jesuits were accustomed to, a theological shouting match like the rites controversy, but rather the opening salvo in what was clearly meant to be an all-out offensive whose object was to drive the Jesuits out of Portugal. The time was certainly propitious for such a campaign, since the current General, Luigi Centurione, was a rather weak character who had relinquished most of his authority to his assistants.

For some time now, as we have seen, the leadership of the Order had been demoralized and uncertain of its direction; on Christmas in 1739 General Franz Retz had made the "request" that "in view of the critical nature of the times we should refrain from any public celebration of the two-hundredth anniversary [of the founding of the Order]."

Pombal, on the other hand, was spoiling for a fight. He released a torrent of anti-Jesuit propaganda in four languages, French, Italian, German, and Spanish—the first time any government had ever made such a concerted assault on European opinion. This included a provocative "deep background" for journalists that began with the sentence, "Is it not curious that Portugal was a rich and prosperous nation until 1540, when the Jesuits came?" Pombal's press handouts also profitably exploited the rather wide margin between what is unthinkable and what is merely unprintable, with titillating phrases like "scandalous conduct in their missions, so shameful that decency forbids that it be mentioned by name" and "crimes even more shocking than those of the Knights Templar." The apostolic nuncio in Lisbon was alarmed by these rumors, and Pope Benedict XIV—a broad-minded man but no friend of the Jesuits— ordered an investigation. Cardinal Saldanha was sent on an inspection tour of the *reducciones* in Paraguay in 1758, and he reported back that, if not necessarily steeped in unspeakable vice, the Jesuits were clearly too prosperous for their own good. "Their missionary station," he wrote, "smacks more of the warehouse than of a place fit for spiritual contemplation." (For insiders this was an especially pointed barb, since Benedict himself was one of the most mercenary popes on record since the days of the Medicis and the Borgias.) Nevertheless, Benedict was apparently about to pronounce some sort of sanctions against the order, but then both he and Cardinal Saldanha happened to die, within a month of one another—and, as a contemporary Jesuit, Father Hubert Becher, expresses it, "Our people interpreted this remarkable dispensation as a special sign from God." (A theory that met with wider popular approval, of course, was that the Jesuits had poisoned them both.)

At this point, however, Pombal was presented with a remarkable dispensation of his own, not so much by Providence as by a far less potent figure who had been lurking in the shadows all this time. This was Dom José I, the king of Portugal, a feeble and compliant monarch who was content to let Pombal look after the affairs of the nation while he carried on like a lusty student prince in a bad operetta. This is what happened: Dom José's clandestine intrigue with the young Marquesa da Tavora was discovered by her husband. The marquês waited in ambush not far from their accustomed trysting place in a secluded woodland glade. The marquês fired his pistol; the king was grazed lightly on one arm—perhaps the marquês imagined that his rival would simply take warning from this object lesson and that he would be too humiliated to make a fuss about it afterward. If so, this was reckoning without the king's colossal vanity— he could not imagine that the husband of one of his mistresses would not be honored by attentions to his wife—and of course without Pombal, who announced that the real authors of this treasonous attack on his majesty's person would be produced forthwith.

Actually what Pombal produced was a hodgepodge of insinuation about the Tavora family's suspiciously close relationship with their Jesuit confessors and reports of fresh instances of more Jesuit high-handedness overseas, but the frightened king swallowed this concoction greedily and in time it produced the desired effect. On January 19, 1759, he signed a decree denouncing the Jesuits as "traitors, rebels, and enemies to this kingdom" who were to be immediately expelled from Portugal and her dominions overseas. All property of the Order was forfeit to the crown, of course, and the Jesuit missionaries from overseas emerged blinking from the gloomy lower decks of the ships that had brought them back to Portugal only to be trundled off to equally gloomy cells in one of Pombal's prisons. The higher nobility hastily withdrew from court to their provincial estates, and Pombal was left unchallenged in his mastery over both king and country.

Some years later, when the Paris Parlement decided to proceed against the Jesuits in earnest, everything would be carried out with lawyerlike correctness, but perhaps it took a political bully-boy like Pombal to cast the first stone; otherwise his less ruthlessly anticlerical colleagues in other countries might never have dared to take on the Jesuits. Just how ruthless Pombal could be is dramatized by the case of his old archenemy, the Italian Father Gabriel Malagrida, who had begun to denounce Pombal's regime from his pulpit in 1755; in the wake of the "assassination plot" of 1759 Father Malagrida was arrested on a charge of high treason, but even with the worst will in the world, Pombal could not secure a conviction on a capital charge with no evidence at all. Instead Father Malagrida was handed over to the Inquisition and condemned as a heretic, which was a routine matter since the Grand Inquisitor was Pombal's brother. In the meantime the eighty-year-old Malagrida had succumbed to some kind of religious mania while in prison, but Pombal was determined to have his revenge. The old man was paraded through the streets of Lisbon with a halter around his neck; he was then publicly garroted and his corpse was burned. This was in 1761.

The new Pope, Clement XIII, was inclined to absolve the Jesuits of any wrongdoing, in Paraguay, Portugal, and elsewhere—he described the Order as "a special creation of Providence for the fulfillment of the Church's tasks on earth," but this flattering appraisal was only endorsed by twenty-three out of the more than three hundred Catholic bishops—an indication of how the power and prestige of the Holy See had dropped in this anticlerical age of Enlightenment. And even as a gesture, a vote of confidence for the Order, as it were, it was ineffective, since Pombal immediately broke off diplomatic relations.

Most of the Jesuits in Portugal fled by ship to Italy; those who had been arrested in connection with the alleged assassination plot were detained at Pombal's pleasure until 1777, when Dom José died, Pombal fell from power, and the surviving Jesuits were released by his successor, Queen Maria. Pombal himself died in poverty and isolation on his own estates in 1782; true to his anticlerical sentiments to the end, he refused the last rites on his deathbed. For reasons that are not entirely clear, Pombal's body was not given a proper Christian burial for another fifty years, and when his coffin was finally committed to the earth the priest who sang the funeral mass was a Jesuit, one of the first who had been permitted in Portugal after the resurrection of the Order. (As a footnote to this story, it is interesting that four of the marquês's great-grandsons were enrolled in the celebrated Jesuit college at Coimbra in the year 1829.)

SINT, UT SINT, AUT NON SINT—THE JESUITS ARE EXPELLED FROM FRANCE

The expulsion of the Jesuits from Portugal was the result of an historical accident, a political vendetta carried out by one man, but the crisis of the Order in France was over a century in the making and seems in retrospect to have been inevitable, the product of historical necessity—for those who care to subscribe to such a notion. The anti-Jesuit coalition in France came to include those who resented the Jesuits' privileged position at court on political grounds as well as those who opposed the Jesuits on doctrinal or philosophical grounds. (Both groups often received encouragement from other religious orders who felt that they had been slighted or unjustly neglected in favor of the Jesuits.) In old-fashioned history books this conflict was often described as a purely theological contest between Jansenism* and the Jesuit doctrine of accommodation, but in fact this controversy had long since been resolved (in favor of the Jesuits) by the middle of the eighteenth century, and "Jansenist" had simply become an all-purpose term of opprobrium that the Jesuits applied to their opponents.

But in fact this rather gloomy theological controversy did manage to strike a number of unexpected sparks before it died out. The political enemies of the Jesuits, whose traditional stronghold was the Paris Parlement, had been trying for many years to wean the kings of France away from their Jesuit confessors, whose comfortable laxity in matters of penance and absolution was too congenial to the Bourbon temperament to be dispensed with. Then in 1656 a series of pamphlets appeared, clearly written by a Jansenist sympathizer, which were intended to discredit the Jesuits' interpretation of the doctrine of free will and which incidentally provided the intellectual salons of Paris with the latest literary sensation.

*Named for Cornelius Jansen (1585–1638), a Catholic bishop whose posthumous work *Augustinus,* a commentary on St. Augustine, expressed the unorthodox view—somewhat similar to Luther's and Calvin's—that individual salvation or damnation is *predestined* from the beginning of time and thus that man cannot hope to save himself from hell by prayer and repentance alone (which was the more lenient position adopted by the Jesuits).

These *Lettres provinciales*—written by a pseudonymous author who called himself "Louis de Montalte" but was finally unmasked as the mathematician Blaise Pascal—appeared in eighteen installments, all of which sold out immediately, and treated both the learned doctors of the Church and ladies and gentlemen of fashion to a brilliant dissection of Jesuit morality. Many of the most arresting and most frequently quoted passages were (or were purported to be) quotations or paraphrases from Jesuit works of casuistry:

> The great difficulty is to avoid lying, in which our doctrine of ambiguous words is helpful. It holds, for example, that it is permissible to use vague and inexplicit language that will be taken in a different sense by one's neighbor than one intends oneself. . . .
>
> Père Lemayn judges dueling . . . to be permissible only when one engages in it with the intention of defending one's honor or property. But if one can kill one's man stealthily, so that it need not come to dueling, then so be it. Thus one avoids the twofold risk of losing one's life and in partaking of the sin our enemy commits by dueling.

None of the Jesuits' attempts to defend themselves against Pascal's attacks was successful (nor their efforts to have the publication of the *Lettres* suppressed). For the time the Jesuits were helpless against an attack; what was more, they had been routed on their own chosen terrain. "In the past," Voltaire was to write some years later, "they had always tried to make the Jesuits seem odious, but Pascal did even more, by making them look ridiculous." However, in the end it was the Jansenists, not the Jesuits, who were suppressed: The Jesuits were still far too strong, and well connected, to be laughed out of existence. But the real point of this episode was that Pascal had proved to the Jesuits' political enemies that they were vulnerable to attack and had even shown them how they might one day be destroyed. In the LaValette case, almost a century later, LaChalotais and the other government lawyers made use of the Jesuit *Constitutions* in much the same way that Pascal had used the writings of the casuists, and this time the political consequences for the Order were both immediate and devastating.

For the Jesuits, the LaValette case was something like the sort of nightmare in which one starts out with a traffic ticket and ends up in the electric chair. The final judgment incorporated a resolution, adopted by a vote of 112 to 98 on August 6, 1762, in which the Order was described as "endangering the Christian faith, disturbing the peace of the Church, and in general building up far less than it destroys." Moreover, it "outrages the laws of nature and as an enemy of the laws of France should be irrevocably expelled."

The Parlement, however, was purely an advisory body—apart from its capacity as the highest court of appeals—and this resolution was just another piece of parchment without the signature of Louis XV. But Louis was reluctant to sign, and the Jesuits seemed to have triumphed over their opponents, if only at the eleventh hour. Pope Clement XIII sprang once again to the Jesuits' defense, this time with more opportune effect, in the bull *Apostolicum,* of January 7, 1765, which explicitly places the Jesuits under the protection of the Holy See and ends with the ringing injunction, "Let no man dare to commit the folly of defying my instructions, which are hereby ratified and confirmed, without calling down upon him the wrath of God." No other order had ever received such an unqualified vote of confidence from the Holy Father, and no other order had ever stood in such desperate need of it. This made some impression on Louis, who was exploring the possibility of avoiding outright expulsion of the Jesuits by removing some of the offending passages from the *Constitutions.* When the French ambassador to the Holy See relayed this suggestion to Pope Clement, he is said to have replied with the trenchant phrase *"Sint, ut sint, aut non sint"* (" Let them be as they are, or not at all").

In the meantime the duc de Choiseul, Louis's current prime minister and the leader of the *non sint* faction, was actively trying to recruit his patroness, Madame de Pompadour, to their cause. That lady was still trying to patch together some sort of working compromise with the king's implacable Jesuit confessors, and she had just about reached the limits of her patience. So far, she had acceded to all their demands, however humiliating or inconvenient—she had absented herself from court on those days when the king was to take communion, she had effected a reconciliation with her estranged husband. One of the king's confessors, Père de Sacy, had even insisted that a hidden staircase be installed between the king's bedchamber and her own, which was directly overhead, "in the interest of decency"—though actually the notorious "secret staircase" would be remembered as the most provocative aspect of what seems otherwise to have been a highly conventional relationship. Pompadour had submitted to these and other trials proposed by the Jesuits very patiently and in a spirit of compromise and conciliation, but after some time it became clear that the Jesuits had no intention of agreeing to any kind of détente with the king's mistress and they were simply trying to wear down her resistance with a series of humiliating ordeals. At this point, when Choiseul approached her with a request to intercede with the king on behalf of the anti-Jesuit faction, it certainly must have occurred to her that her own personal life would be considerably simplified if the Jesuit confessors were removed from court. In addition, she generally had confidence in Choiseul's political judgment— even though she frequently had to take the blame when the king followed Choiseul's advice and things turned out badly. In this case, we have no idea what arguments, if that is the right word, she might have used to persuade the king to sign the order of expulsion,* but whatever they were, she succeeded in her mission, and he did. Thus, as a fairly direct result of their own intransigence in the prosecution of an inconsequential lawsuit and an inane court intrigue, the Jesuits were expelled from the kingdom of France.

La Pompadour was not as vindictive as Pombal, however, and the Order was dissolved with a minimum of unpleasantness. General Ricci released the French Jesuits from their vows, and they were free to remain in France as regular clergy, but the Society of Jesus itself no longer existed on French soil. Voltaire himself, a former pupil of the Jesuits who had been expelled as a *"grandis nebulo"*—a worthless ne'er-do-well— demonstrated that there were no hard feelings by taking on a Jesuit father who found himself at loose ends as a kind of paid companion to play chess with him in the evenings. "Now that we have broken up the

---

*According to the *Memoirs of the Marquise de Pompadour,* which was a spurious "autobiography" worked up in the nineteenth century to satisfy the French reading public's insatiable appetite for *ancien régime* reminiscences, what Pompadour actually said to the king was "I can well believe that the Jesuits are honest fellows, but can Your Majesty stand to sacrifice his Parlement to them when he has such need of it?" Louis XV was an absolute monarch, of course, but he generally found it easier to get along with both Parlement and Pompadour on his side, especially when he was short of money, as he had been for some time now. So perhaps this version of the story might actually have something to it—the authors of these heavily dramatized "memoirs" took great pride in their scholarship and the authenticity of background detail; their motto was "Not really the truth, but never far from it."

Jesuits," he announced contentedly, "it should be no great matter to be rid of the Pope as well."

The Sombrero Rebellion—the Jesuits Are Expelled from Spain

Charles III of Spain was a Bourbon, like Louis XV, the king of Naples, the duke of Parma, and a number of others. This fact was of more than passing significance in the year 1766, since all of them had signed what was called the "Family Compact," in which they pledged to consult with one another on all "important measures" and to present a united front to the rest of the world. Louis XV, the effective head of the family, had just expelled the Jesuits and was urging the other reigning Bourbons to do likewise. Charles III was not quite ready to do so, though the prevailing sentiment in his immediate circle was that the Jesuits would have to be dealt with eventually. For the moment, however, King Charles appeared to be more concerned with a recent edict that prohibited the wearing of sombreros whose brims exceeded a certain diameter—this was one of the so-called sumptuary laws that the fussier, more despotic monarchs, and Charles was such a one, were given to enacting from time to time in order to keep their subjects from wasting too much money on inessentials or from getting ideas above their station.

For some reason this seems to have touched a raw nerve; an angry crowd of protestors appeared outside the Palacio Real, the king hastily left his capital for the countryside, the Flemish palace guard fired shots over the heads of the crowd. A popular insurrection was only averted at the last moment by a group of stout-hearted Jesuit padres, who managed to pacify the demonstrators and send them back to their homes. This at any rate is the story you are likely to encounter in most of the history books, sometimes with a few extra embellishments, like Fülöp-Miller's ". . . and the Spaniards clung to this fashion [the broad-brimmed sombrero] with the righteous and heroic resolve of an aggrieved and down-trodden people." Unfortunately a glance at the primary source for these accounts, in the Spanish Historical Archives, reveals that there was a little more to it than that. The antisombrero edict had come right on the heels, so to speak, of a dramatic increase in taxes, and the combination of sartorial insult and fiscal injury was too much for the people to bear—in addition, the broad-brimmed sombrero was a convenient and highly conspicuous symbol of taxpayer disaffection. Peace was really only restored when the tax increase was rescinded, the finance minister dismissed, and the hated antisombrero ordinance repealed.

However, the Jesuits received no credit for quelling the initial outbreak in Madrid. King Charles was convinced that the padres would never have been able to disperse the crowds so quickly if the whole insurrection had not been carefully planned and rehearsed by the Jesuits—as a demonstration of how easily they could manipulate popular discontent and have an angry crowd surging through the streets on the slightest provocation. (There is no surviving evidence that indicates that this might be true.) The anti-Jesuit party at court was quick to exploit this opportunity for anti-Jesuit agitation; they began with the standard rumor of an assassination plot, a more inventive tale—to the effect that the Jesuits were in the process of assembling proof that the king was a bastard (in the strict, technical sense), or indeed that this proof might already be in their possession. This was a subject on which Charles III, as a hereditary monarch, was understandably quite touchy; he gave orders that a special royal commission be convened to prepare a master plan for the expulsion of the Jesuits. The commission's first meeting was in January 1761; the expulsion order was signed by King Charles on February 27.

The plan that the commission had come up with was modeled on the tactics that Philip the Fair had used against the Knights Templar in 1312. The element of surprise was essential, and during the month of March sealed envelopes were distributed to all the provincial viceroys and district military commanders, which bore the legend "Not to be opened before sunrise of April 2 on pain of death." The envelopes contained two documents; the first instructed these officials to surround the Jesuit colleges and residences with troops during the night of April 2, to take all the Jesuits into custody, and to arrange for them to be put aboard ships that would be waiting for them at various points. (King Charles was not a notably efficient despot, but the closing sentence of this order has a ring of twentieth-century thoroughness: "If a single Jesuit, even though sick or dying, is still to be found in the area under your command after the embarcation, prepare yourself to face summary execution.")

The second enclosure was a copy of the original expulsion order, according to which "all members of the Society of Jesus are to leave my kingdoms [i.e., Castile, Aragon, Navarre, and the other formerly independent kingdoms that made up the Spanish state] and all their goods are declared forfeit . . . by virtue of the highest power, which the Lord God Almighty has confided into my hands." The king went on to point out that "it is not for subjects to question the wisdom or to seek to interpret the decisions of their sovereign," but the keynote of high-handed absolutism was struck in the very first line, which begins, somewhat after the manner of a papal encyclical, "Being swayed by just and legitimate reasons . . ." but instead of leading into a forceful and detailed presentation of King Charles's side of the case, it merely trails off into the rather sulky admission ". . . which shall remain sealed within my royal breast forever."

Pope Clement was presented with a similar ultimatum only a few days before the decree was to go into effect by the Spanish ambassador to the Holy See. The language of this document was almost as brusque and patronizing as the decree itself; by the middle of the eighteenth century the temporal lords of Europe tended to treat the Holy Father not even as an equal but instead as a kind of shiftless poor relation. "Your Holiness knows as well as anyone else," the letter read, "that a sovereign's first duty is to ensure the peace of his dominions and the tranquillity of his subjects. In the fulfillment of this sovereign task, I have found it necessary to expel all the Jesuits residing in my kingdoms and to commit them directly to Your Holiness's wise stewardship in the States of the Church. . . . I beg Your Holiness to consider that my decision is unalterable and has been made as the result of mature reflection and all due consideration for the consequences. . . ."

The Pope's reply, on the other hand, began with almost a servile whine—"Of all the shocks I have had to endure in the nine unhappy years of my pontificate, this one, of which Your Majesty has informed me, is the worst of all. . . ."—and went on to remind King Charles, in a fairly perfunctory way, that he was facing the prospect of eternal damnation. Certainly Pope Clement had no earthly remedy at his disposal, and Charles was not bothered by this in the least. He had already taken the precaution of polling all sixty Spanish bishops on this very question, and forty-six of them had voted for expulsion. The padres were rounded up according to plan and stowed away in the lower decks of Spanish warships bound for the port of Civitavecchia, in the Papal States. The Society of Jesus no longer existed in the land that had given birth to its founder.

This would have been the end of the story right here, except for a sudden and unforeseen departure from the prearranged plan that occurred when the Spanish flotilla had entered Italian waters. Altogether there were twenty-two warships of various tonnages and some six thousand Jesuits (not six hundred, as at least one historian has stated) packed in below decks in very tight quarters indeed.* In May 1767 the Spanish fleet appeared off Civitavecchia, and, to the amazement of everyone (including most of the historians who have dealt with this incident), Pope Clement refused them permission to land their prisoners on papal territory. Shore batteries opened fire, and the Spanish warships were forced to look for an anchorage off Corsica. A rebellion had just broken out on Corsica, however, and the upshot of all this was that five months had passed before some of the Jesuits could finally feel solid ground beneath their feet (almost twice as long as it generally took to cross the Atlantic in those days).

But the question remains—why were the Spanish ships fired upon by the guns of Civitavecchia? How was it that Pope Clement, until recently a staunch champion of the Order, could have been unwilling to offer the privilege of political asylum to his most loyal servants? And, for that matter, how was it that the General of the Order had permitted this calculated act of treachery to take place? In fact, General Lorenco Ricci had been consulted and had acquiesced completely in Clement's decision not to allow the Jesuits to be put ashore. The reason for this was a simple one—the Vatican was unwilling to incur the displeasure of the great Catholic monarchs of Western Europe by so much as lifting a finger on behalf of the outcast Jesuits. Pope Clement was no longer even a sovereign prince in his own territory; malicious broadsides were circulating against him in the streets of Rome, and a troupe of actors who per-

---

*Fülöp-Miller says there were six thousand Jesuits deported altogether, but this figure includes the Spanish colonies as well; Heinrich Boehmer says that "about six thousand were arrested" in Spain alone. Father Hubert Becher mentions only that "about six hundred Jesuits are said to have died during the voyage," but David Mitchell's history of the Jesuits, published in 1950, maintains that "about six hundred Jesuits" were deported from Spain in the first place. The Spanish Admiralty records indicate that twenty-two vessels of various sizes were involved; unfortunately they are not identified by tonnage but only by the number of guns they carried. However, since it was a general rule of thumb that a slave ship could transport ten times as many Africans as there were crew members aboard, and assuming, with all due deference to King Charles, that the Jesuits were only packed in half as tightly, then a medium-sized warship like a frigate or corvette, which usually carried a crew of about seventy, could easily accommodate a human cargo of 350 Jesuit padres. This means that it would have been simple enough for King Charles's fleet to ferry six thousand Jesuits across to Italy (and the report that six hundred of them had perished during the voyage seems equally plausible under the circumstances).

formed a parody of the mass were playing to enthusiastic crowds while the churches were empty. The cannonade at Civitavecchia might just as well have been an artillery salute to the birth of the secular age, or a peal of ordnance fired off to mark the passing of the temporal power of the papacy.

Sympathetic historians have done their best to come up with a more creditable explanation for Clement's treatment of the Spanish Jesuits. According to some, the Holy Father was reluctantly compelled to turn them away because the Papal States could not cope with such an influx of refugees; the historian Christopher Hollis provides a more sophisticated variant. "The Pope had not been informed of their arrival, and Civitavecchia was already overflowing with refugees." However, we know that the Pope had had more than a month's notice (he received Charles's letter of warning at the beginning of April, and the refugees were certainly not obliged to remain in Civitavecchia for more than a few hours. Some of these writers seem to envision "the Papal States" as a tiny enclave on the order of the Vatican City; in fact, in those days the papal territories included most of central Italy from the valley of the Po to Terracina. From the vantage point of our own century, which has experienced all too many such migrations on a far vaster scale, it seems incredible that a country somewhat larger and more fertile than Switzerland could not possibly have accommodated an extra six thousand inhabitants—unless there were other compelling reasons for turning them away.

Father Becher has devised a far more ingenious argument (which almost has a hint of casuistry about it): "Clement's indignation knew no bounds. He protested bitterly to the king, who only persevered in his chosen course of action. To make his protest even more keenly felt the Pope forbade the Spanish ships to land in the Papal States." Leaving aside the problem of whether it was correct for the Pope to abandon six thousand Catholic priests to an unknown fate in order to underscore a futile diplomatic gesture—the question remains why Clement did not inform the Spanish ambassador at the beginning of April that he was not going to allow the Spanish ships to discharge their cargo, which might conceivably have convinced King Charles at least to modify his unalterable plan.

In the course of the next few years the Jesuits were expelled in turn from the remaining Bourbon states—Naples, Sicily, and Parma—as well as the island of Malta, which was ruled by the paramilitary Order of St. John. The Bourbons were still not satisfied, however, and they continued to badger the seventy-four-year-old Clement into accepting (in the words of a memorial that was presented by the French ambassador on behalf of the entire family) "the complete and utter suppression of the Society of Jesus." The following year, in 1769, Clement convened the College of Cardinals so they could address themselves to this question and then died unexpectedly of heart failure before they could come up with a solution. Since they were already assembled in conclave, the cardinals turned immediately to the business of electing Clement's successor; at the end of three months Cardinal Lorenzo Ganganelli, a Franciscan who took the name of Clement XIV, was chosen.

This Pope has not received very high marks, either from historians or from his contemporaries—the duc de Choiseul described him as "an unsociable weakling"—which seems highly unfair in my opinion. For one thing, he was an adroit and able diplomat when dealing with forces outside the Church, even though he was rarely left with very much room to maneuver. He also made an attempt to normalize the chaotic economy and fiscal structure of the Papal States, and, most notably, it was during his pontificate that the practice of castrating young boys to sing in the Sistine Choir was finally abolished (but only after some four hundred of these grotesque operations had been performed).

As a diplomat, the principal tactic that was available to him, of course, was simply to stall for time. He flattered Charles III, who was still the most energetic proponent of dissolution, with such assurances as "We have assembled all the documents that will be necessary to compose the *motu proprio** condemning [the Jesuits], which should proclaim to all the world the wisdom of Your Majesty's decision to expel the Jesuits as unruly and rebellious subjects." To the French king he made a similar promise to "present a plan for the complete suppression of this society," but when he was not addressing one of these monarchs he was inclined to take a broader view and insist that such a step could only be taken with the concurrence of all the Catholic powers—and the Jesuits still had a safe haven in Maria Theresa's Austria.

---

*Ironically, a *motu proprio* (from the Latin, "on one's own impulse") is a papal rescript—a clarification of a point of doctrine—which is issued spontaneously by the Pope and not at the request or on the advice or, as in this case, at the insistence of anyone else.

MARRIAGE À LA MODE—THE JESUITS ARE EXPELLED FROM THE EMPIRE

In October 1768 Empress Maria Theresa assured her Jesuit confessor, Father Koffler, "My dear father, there is no cause for concern; as long as I am alive you have nothing to fear." A year later her son, the Emperor Joseph II, was rumored to have gone to Rome incognito to inform the College of Cardinals that neither he nor his mother would have any objection to the dissolution of the Order, but this was only a rumor. Finally, like everyone else, she succumbed to political pressure applied by the Bourbon family. As empress she might have held out indefinitely, but as the mother of sixteen children, including several marriageable daughters, she was in a very vulnerable position.

Most of the eligible Catholic princes in Europe were Bourbons (even if they had little else to recommend them), and two of her daughters, Marie Antoinette and Caroline, were already betrothed, respectively, to the French dauphin (the future Louis XVI) and Ferdinand of Naples. Maria Theresa was given to understand that the Austrian princesses would have to look elsewhere for husbands unless she proved more cooperative in the matter of the Jesuits. The Jesuits were expelled forthwith, and Maria Theresa, now in her capacity as empress and a Hapsburg, turned her attention immediately to the problem of how the confiscated property of the Order could be disposed of most advantageously. On April 4, 1773, she wrote to one of her prospective in-laws, the king of Spain: "I hope that Your Majesty will be satisfied now that there is nothing left for you to wish for. And in this confident hope I beg that our friendship might be permitted to continue, particularly for the sake of our dear children in Naples and Tuscany and, when the time comes, in Parma as well." Ferdinand of Naples, the boisterous practical joker who married Princess Caroline, was one of Charles's sons; Leopold of Tuscany (the future Emperor Leopold II) was one of Maria's, and the duke of Parma was one of Charles's, another eligible Bourbon (though strictly in the dynastic sense) who had been suggested as a suitable match for another of Maria's daughters. Austrian diplomats had already arrived at the court of Parma to negotiate the marriage settlement, but

Maria Theresa had always felt that such things were best worked out at the highest level.

THE SUPREME SACRIFICE—THE FINAL SUPPRESSION OF THE ORDER

Pope Clement XIV had been putting off the inevitable with long delays and small concessions (shutting down the Jesuit seminary in Rome, for example), but the monarchs were getting restive again, Charles III in particular. Finally Clement was presented with another ultimatum—either the Order was to be dissolved, "utterly and completely," or His Catholic Majesty would be compelled to break away from Rome and establish an independent Spanish Church, something on the order of the Church of England. (The Spanish ambassador followed this up with a more immediate threat—to publish Clement's correspondence, in which he had repeatedly given his promise that the Order would be suppressed, unless a decree to that effect was forthcoming.)

Whether Clement was genuinely impressed by these threats or whether he had simply been worn down by the struggle (he was supposed to have been seriously worried that he was eventually going to be poisoned, either by the Jesuits or the Bourbons' political agents), a breve entitled *Dominus ac Redemptor noster* was signed on July 21, 1773. Instead of being posted on church doors for all to read, copies were sent directly to the bishops and then passed on to the Jesuits in their dioceses on August 16. The text of the breve that dissolved the Order presents an interesting contrast to the bull of Paul III by which the Order was originally established 233 years earlier; in its opening sentences the breve of Clement XIV invokes "Jesus Christ, the Prince of Peace," whereas the original bull had praised the Jesuits as an impressive new addition to the forces of *ecclesia militans.* The Church of Clement XIV was no longer militant; it simply wanted to be left alone, as the breve's closing sentences make clear:

> . . . for the rest it appears to be scarcely possible, or not
> possible at all, to establish a real and enduring peace within
> the Church so long as this Order remains in existence.
> Swayed by these weighty considerations and compelled by

other reasons which have been made known to us by the sagacity and the wise stewardship of the assembled body of the Church [the College of Cardinals, in other words] . . . and upon mature reflection and by the fullness of our apostolic power, we declare this aforesaid society to be dissolved, suppressed, disbanded, and abolished for all eternity. . . . We declare all their offices, authorities, and functions to be null and void, and all their houses . . . colleges, hospices, and any other places occupied by them to be hereby disestablished, no matter in what province, state, or kingdom they might be found. . . .

A panel of ecclesiastical dignitaries, including five cardinals, an archbishop, a bishop, and two theologians, were appointed to supervise the implementation of this decree. All existing records, correspondence, and accounts were confiscated, but this produced no fresh revelations—which came as a surprise to no one, since the Jesuits had had plenty of time to put their house in order. The remaining Jesuits were not treated at all harshly—most of them became regular clergy, and sixty of them were eventually made bishops—except for General Ricci and his two assistants, who were later imprisoned in the Castel Sant'Angelo and interrogated by the Inquisition for many months. Ricci was only released from these indignities by his death two years later; shortly before he died he swore out a deposition in which he calmly asserted his innocence of all wrongdoing:

I depose and say that the Society of Jesus that is dissolved offered no reason or pretext whatsoever for its dissolution. . . . And I further depose and say that I myself have not furnished even the slightest reason or pretext for my own incarceration, though I make this second declaration only insofar as it may be of some use in restoring the reputation of the Society of Jesus.

The General certainly must have realized that his imprisonment and interrogation were no more than an empty, if necessary, formality—just as an elite formation, such as the Jesuits, must realize that they may be sacrificed in the heat of battle to save their commander, especially if the enemy is pressing as furiously as the Bourbons were around Clement

XIV. It is difficult for us to imagine today that a country like Spain—which has frequently been described as being "more Catholic than the Pope"—could have broken away from Rome to establish its own national church. At the time, however, when the papacy had reached its lowest ebb of power and prestige in close to a thousand years, this may have seemed like a very real possibility—Charles III was more of a son of the Enlightenment than of the Holy Church—which Clement was finally prepared to make extraordinary sacrifices to prevent.

Clement himself survived the Jesuit Order by not much more than a year. He died on September 22, 1774, the same day as, as it happened, on which General Ricci was imprisoned in the Castel Sant'Angelo. The suppression of the Order had done nothing to diminish the popular image of the Jesuit slinking down murky passageways and skulking behind arrases, and, as with Benedict XIV, the Pope's death was commonly regarded as either a dispensation of a just Providence or from the Jesuits' poison cabinet. The report of the papal physician did nothing to discourage these speculations; he announced that Clement had died "of the natural process of a fatal disease" (this was merely a diplomatic way of saying that the Pope had died of a brain tumor, which was too closely connected with mental illness in the eighteenth-century mind to be regarded as a respectable cause of death). As a final note on Clement's passing—Father Becher suggests that it was not some hellish Jesuit potion that was gnawing at his vitals, but rather the simple pangs of remorse: "In spite of the blameless life that he had led, it was said that he had often been heard to cry out, 'Mercy, mercy. *Compulsus feci.* I was compelled to do it.'" This was no more than the truth—whether or not Pope Clement actually said it—but even though the Jesuits had been abandoned by the Pope, they were still not without sympathetic and influential friends.

EAST OF EDEN—THE JESUITS IN PRUSSIA AND THE RUSSIAN EMPIRE

Less than a month after the brief of dissolution was made public, the Prussian chargé d'affaires in Rome received these instructions from his sovereign, Frederick the Great:

... You shall tell everyone who will listen to you, but without ostentation or affectation, and you shall also take this opportunity to inform the Pope or his chief minister that, as far as the Jesuits are concerned, I have decided to allow them to remain in my territories. I undertook to guarantee the Catholic religion *in statu quo* in the Treaty of Breslau [with Austria, 1742], and I have never known any other Catholic priests to compare with them. You should also make it quite clear that inasmuch as I am to be numbered among the company of the heretics, the Holy Father cannot give me a dispensation to break my word or betray my duty as an honest man and a king. ...

This announcement created quite a sensation all over Europe, and Frederick the Great, "the Philosopher of Sanssouci," onetime crony of Voltaire's, and the very model of the enlightened despot, has astounded his critics and his admirers once again. D'Alembert, one of the stalwarts of the French Enlightenment, wrote to Frederick in response: "It may seem strange, Sire, that while Their Most Christian, Catholic, and Apostolic Majesties have wiped out the papal grenadiers to the last man, Your Most Heretical Majesty is the only one who has chosen to deal with them honorably."

There were actually two very good practical reasons behind this uncharacteristic gesture on Frederick's part. The first was political; though most of his Prussian subjects were Lutherans or Calvinists, the inhabitants of the newly conquered province of Silesia (which had been ceded to him, most reluctantly, by Maria Theresa by the terms of the Treaty of Breslau) were predominately Catholic. Frederick naturally hoped that the Silesians would eventually turn into loyal and contented Prussians, and he was reluctant to do anything that might be construed by them as interfering with the practice of their religion—such as suppressing the Jesuits, for example. Frederick was a great champion of religious tolerance in general; as he put it in one of his more famous remarks (apropos of a controversy about the establishment of Catholic schools in Berlin in 1740), "Here we must all be holy in whatever way we choose."

The second reason for Frederick's decision had to do with money, which was always in short supply. He was concerned that the abolition of the Jesuit schools might put too much of a burden on the state school system; the Jesuits, unlike lay teachers, did not have to be paid by the state, and Frederick had great respect for their educational abilities, though his evaluation of them in his dispatch as "the best priests" he had ever encountered would have to be taken as a backhanded compliment at best. Frederick referred to the Jesuits in his other writings in the same affectionately ironic tone: "I have so many different beasts in my kingdom, I would account it a great pleasure to secure a few specimens of this particular sort of fox. . . . If they could keep lions and tigers to fight in the arena, why not put up with the Jesuits as well?" Afterward he wrote proudly to Voltaire: "The good Friar Minor [Franciscan] in the Vatican has allowed me to keep my dear Jesuits, who are being persecuted everywhere else. I shall guard the precious seedlings very carefully, for the benefit of all who might one day choose to cultivate this exotic plant."

Pope Clement had not actually been quite so accommodating as Frederick's letter implies. He had only agreed to the proposal under protest and had insisted that a number of formal conditions be met. First, the Jesuits were officially no longer members of the Society of Jesus but "priests of the Royal Pedagogical Institute," the only one of a great many such scholarly and scientific bodies in Frederick's kingdom whose bylaws were modeled on the *Constitutions* of Ignatius Loyola.

Catherine the Great of Russia, another benevolent autocrat and disciple of the French Enlightenment, simply refused to acknowledge the fact that the Order had been abolished in the rest of Europe. She ignored the diplomatic entreaties of the Bourbons, who had offered her various commercial concessions (as a non-Catholic monarch, she was not obliged to let them marry her daughters); she even ignored a personal appeal by the Jesuit vice-provincial, who begged her to publish the brief of dissolution in her domains "in order to appease my conscience." The other Jesuits in Russia did not seem to be troubled by such scruples, and they were allowed to carry on as a fully autonomous order in Catherine's province of Byelorussia (which included a great many Polish Catholics). The Jesuits set up a separate Russian novitiate, and even went so far as to elect their own "Vicar General for life," also called "Superior General for Russia," in 1782. When Clement's brief of dissolution was rescinded by Pope Pius VII in 1814, this was to be the only province in which the Order had been able to maintain a continuous existence under its own name and under the original Ignatian rule (which had been somewhat modified for the good fathers of the Royal Prussian Pedagogical Institute). A few years earlier the emperor Napoleon, who was no friend of the

Jesuits and apparently had not been apprised of these developments,* was both shocked and chagrined to come across a number of Jesuit colleges along the road to Moscow.

In Italy, France, and Austria the Order had continued to have a kind of shadow existence in such organizations as the Society of the Faith of Jesus, the Society of the Sacred Heart of Jesus, and the Society of the Fathers of the Church, all of which were composed of former Jesuits who continued to observe the Ignatian Rule and, in fine equivocal style, managed successfully to defy the papal ban without actually disobeying it. Oddly enough it was one of the Bourbon princelings, Ferdinand of Parma, who became chief lobbyist for the Jesuits among the Catholic rulers of Europe. He had petitioned the Pope to restore the Order on the reasonable grounds that "Europe would not be in the situation it is in today if the Jesuits had been recalled earlier." When the Pope neglected to do so, Ferdinand took it upon himself to reestablish the Order in his own small state of Parma and Piacenza. Pope Pius VI responded with a rather plaintive letter in which he explained—a remarkable admission for a Pope—that such matters were really no longer in his hands. The existence or nonexistence of the Order had become purely a political question in which a political cipher like the Pope of Rome was understandably reluctant to interfere:

> When we have examined the methods of the dissolution and the ideas upon which it was principally based, we have never been able to find ourselves in agreement with them. Nevertheless, this is the law, and we must obey it. But even so we shall still behave as if we know nothing of all this, just as we have done in the case of those [Jesuits] who have sought refuge in the north. If certain rulers do not approve of what Your Highness has done, we would certainly be loath to condemn Your Highness's decision, of which we choose to take no notice, even though we know full well what it is.

---

*In October 1804 Napoleon wrote to his minister of the interior, the infamous Joseph Fouché: "Kindly convey to the editors of the *Mercure de France* and the *Journal des Débats* that I never wish to see the word *Jesuit* in print again. Any allusion in the newspapers to the existence of this society should be avoided. I shall never allow the Jesuit Order to be reestablished in France."

PART ❧ XII

THE ALLIANCE BETWEEN THE CHALICE AND THE SWORD

*Like you, I disapprove of the restoration of the Jesuits, which
seems to portend a backward step from light into darkness.*

> —Thomas Jefferson to John
> Adams, 1816

*Above all, the Society of Jesus has been restored for the purpose
of instructing our youth in wisdom and virtue.*

> —Pope Leo XII (1823–29)

The End of an Eternity—
the Jesuits' Second Chance

The papal breve of 1773 had abolished the Order "for all eternity," an eternity that lasted for all of forty-one years and even then was only prolonged by the French Revolution and the advent of Napoleon. The eighty-year-old Pius VI was held captive in France; he died in Valence in 1799, and the town notary, a true son of the Revolution, made the following entry in the register of births and deaths: "This is to record the passing of the aforesaid Giovanni Angelo Braschi, a pontiff by profession." Five years later Napoleon had proclaimed himself emperor of the French and had Pius VII brought to Paris to officiate at his coronation (though he insisted on placing the imperial crown on his head himself). Still, relations between Pope and emperor were badly strained, and in 1809, when Napoleon decided to annex what remained of the Papal States, he was promptly excommunicated, and Pius VII was obliged to follow his predecessor into French captivity. Finally, on April 11, 1814, Napoleon was packed off to the isle of Elba, and within a few weeks Pius was en route back to Rome. One of his first official acts as pontiff was to hand down the bull by which the Society of Jesus was officially restored to life. The inaugural ceremonies were nicely calculated to have the maximum visual, emotional, political, and theatrical effect; to begin with they were held on August 7, 1814, the Sunday following the Feast of St.

Ignatius (which is July 31), and in Il Gesù rather than in St. Peter's—so that Pope Pius was, in effect, welcoming his Pretorian Guard back to their old regimental barracks. The phrase is hardly in keeping with the actual splendor of the proceedings, however: the Pope, enthroned, surrounded by seventeen cardinals in full regalia (all there were to be found in Rome, save one who was too ill to attend) plus high-ranking representatives of all the ruling houses. The exiled king of Spain, Charles IV, who was living in Rome at the time, did not put in an appearance—"He dared not show his face," the Jesuits said. A hundred and fifty Jesuit fathers (all of pre-1773 vintage, of course) filed in and knelt on creaking knees before the papal throne; the oldest of them was in his nineties, the youngest over sixty. The Pope gave each of them his blessing, one by one.

The bull, entitled *Sollicitudo omnium ecclesiarum,* was concise but lavish, almost rhapsodic in its praise of the Jesuits, and was read out loud by a cardinal to the assembled notables. (Curiously enough some of the same phrases occurred in the original brief of dissolution; in both, for example, the Pope invokes "the aid and inspiration of the Holy Ghost," though it is not clear whether this occurred by accident, by design, or merely out of force of habit.) In the final dazzling sequence of metaphors, the Jesuits were soothed, flattered, appeased, deferred to, and, finally, reassured, as the document swoops down in its closing phrases from the rhetorical stratosphere to the realm of practical politics:

> We should think that we should have been guilty of the most grievous sin before God if we had neglected to apply the healing unction to those in such great need, as Divine Providence bids us do . . . or if we had failed to recall the skilled and practiced steersmen to guide once more the storm-tossed barque of Peter. . . . And we commend this society . . . to all anointed kings and princes, likewise the rulers of every nation. We urge, no, we implore [this society] to have no fear that any of its members will be in any way molested or detained, but rather to take care that they are offered all favor and deference to which they are entitled.

Certainly the Jesuits and the unenlightened monarchs of the Bourbon Restoration had very little to fear from each other this time because they had so much in common—they both devoted a great deal of their energies to blotting out the memory of the last twenty-five years of European history, and the Jesuits were especially active in promoting an alliance between religion and reaction, a cause that was taken up by a number of these monarchs and their secular apologists. The main problem with this was that neither the anointed kings and princes of Europe nor the hierarchy of the Church was prepared to face the problems of what really was, as much as they have liked to deny it, a new era.

The editors of the newly founded Jesuit newspaper, *Civiltà Cattolica,* which was sponsored and encouraged by Pius VII himself, set standards for backward thinking and sheer reactionary wrongheadedness that prevailed until the third decade of the present century. Anyone who might have expected the Order to have awakened from its sleep of forty years with a refreshing new outlook on social or pedagogical problems was bound to be cruelly disappointed. The Jesuits had allowed themselves to be degraded to the role of ink-stained toilers in the papal propaganda mills, and this is what they would remain for some time to come. General Jan Roothaan summed up his reaction to recent political developments in a single sentence: "It is in the nature of liberalism that its consequences are beyond human control . . . as the bitter harvest of many lands with liberal regimes has amply borne out." Faced with the challenge of a new age, the Jesuits responded by carrying their old principle of cadaveric obedience to a new extreme and becoming at the same time increasingly rigid and increasingly moribund. But the tenor of the times was such that there were still places in Europe where the Jesuits were looked at askance as dangerous firebrands and potential subversives.

THE HOLY ALLIANCE AND THE SEPARATIST LEAGUE— FRESH REVERSES FOR THE SOCIETY OF JESUS

Between 1824 and 1860 the reconstituted Jesuit Order was expelled, reinstated, outlawed, redissolved, and rerestored no less than seventy times in various countries of Europe. Ironically enough, the first to expel them after 1814 was Russia, their last safe refuge on the frontiers of Europe from the papal decree of dissolution. Pro-Jesuit historians are inclined to attribute this surprising reversal of policy to the fact that Tsar Alexander I had fallen in love with a woman whose Jesuit confessor instructed her to spurn his advances, and accordingly the autonomous Russian branch of the Order was dissolved only a year after it had been reunited with the restored Society of Jesus, in 1815. (You may recall that a similar story has been offered as an explanation of the Tokugawa persecutions in Japan.) Fülöp-Miller tells a different tale, however; according to him, and a number of other historians less well disposed toward the Order, it was the Jesuits' persistent attempts to convert young men of prominent Russian families that had made them *persona non grata:* "When at last a member of the higher nobility, the young Prince Golitsyn, who had become a Catholic under their influence, began to go about in a hair shirt festooned with devotional images and to devote himself to various eccentric and fanatical practices of this kind, the Emperor Alexander was so enraged by this that he ordered the expulsion of the Jesuits." As usual, then, we have two different accounts to choose from—on the one hand, we have Tsar Alexander repelled by a virtuous Polish maiden (or matron); on the other, Tsar Alexander appalled by a kind of walking Grotto of Lourdes. Unfortunately, neither of these stories seems to fit all the facts as we know them.

First of all, 1815 is better known in Russian history as the year in which Alexander brought his so-called Holy Alliance* into existence; the actual treaty by which the alliance was created bears ample evidence of Tsar Alexander's pronounced if not always well-defined mystico-religious bent. For example, the treaty, according to its preamble, is to be ratified "in the name of the indivisible Holy Trinity" and the monarchs were bound "to apply no other criteria but the precepts of Holy Gospel" . . . "The three monarchs who are joined in this alliance feel themselves to be no more than the earthly deputies of Divine Providence, who intend to rule as three kinsmen of the same family." This document was not endorsed, however, by the Turks, who were put off by all these explicitly Christian sentiments, however broadly ecumenical in tone, or by the British, who simply thought the whole project was too vague and impractical—the British prime minister referred to Alexander as "half Bonaparte, half idiot." A third prominent holdout was Pope Pius himself, who was naturally mistrustful of any prince who was even a fraction of a

---

*Originally a mutual-defense pact signed by the Russian and Austrian emperors and the king of Prussia, to which the other more conservative European rulers eventually subscribed. It was not really a nonaggression pact, but it gave the signatory powers the right to intervene in each other's affairs under certain conditions, namely, to help stamp out the sparks of "liberalism" and nationalism wherever they might appear—a right that was exercised several times by Russian rulers in the course of the next few decades.

Bonaparte, especially one who spoke of himself as an "earthly deputy" of Divine Providence and who took such a proprietary attitude toward religion and the Holy Trinity. Alexander had probably not had such great hopes for the English or the Turks, but the Pope's defection was a bitter blow, and thus—in much the same spirit that Western diplomats are often expelled from Russia today when their governments have done something to offend the Kremlin—the Jesuits, as the Pope's earthly deputies in Russia, were accordingly expelled.

The expulsion of the Jesuits from Russia was the caprice of one absolute monarch, and their expulsion from France came as the result of the rocklike immobility of another. This was Charles X, the last of the Bourbons, in whom the Jesuits thought they had found a true champion of religion and reaction; he himself was a monarch who thought that humanity began with the upper-middle classes and that the greatest danger to a strong monarchical government was posed by freedom of the press. Charles was a relic of the seventeenth century (reminiscent in many ways of James II, the last of the Stuarts) who managed to withstand the tides of change for no more than five years before he was deposed by a popular revolution. While he still ruled, the Jesuits had allowed themselves to take the blame for many of his more conspicuously high-handed blunders, so that the *Journal des Débats* (which had once been forbidden even to mention the Order by name) could write: "The name Jesuit is on everyone's lips, but only with a curse to follow; it echoes through the columns of every newspaper in the land, always with fear and sorrow, and it has been carried all throughout France on the wings of terror."

The Jesuits simply read this sort of thing and shrugged, at least until the first shots were fired in the July Revolution of 1830. The rebels (almost everyone, that is, but the deepest-dyed reactionaries) stormed the Jesuit houses. The king fled to England; the fathers fled to Italy and Spain.

They returned during the reign of Charles's successor, "the Citizen King" Louis Philippe, but only to become the target of literary brickbats rather than revolutionary bullets and cobblestones (though the Jesuit seminary in Avignon was forced to relocate to Nice, which was then in Italian territory). For the rest of the century every French writer with genuine liberal or radical credentials was expected to take a few potshots at the Jesuits, and the prevailing standards of marksmanship were not always of the highest. Eugène Sue's *The Wandering Jew,* an enormously successful potboiler of the 1840's, is full of seductive "Jesuitesses" whose beauty deprives men of their reason, and sinister Jesuits, steeped in all sorts of political iniquity and seeking whom they might destroy. In 1889 a character in one of Zola's novels expressed a view of the Jesuits that was only slightly less fantastic but was probably shared by millions of Frenchmen:

> It's them—and it's always them—hiding behind everything. You think you know all about it, but really you know nothing of their abominable deeds and their unseen power—the Jesuits! You should suspect the worst of every one of them you see slinking along in his shabby old cassock, with a flabby, deceitful face like a sanctimonious old nun . . . all of Rome belongs to the Jesuits, from the most insignificant priest to His Holiness Leo XIII himself!

In 1894 Captain Alfred Dreyfus, a Jewish Alsatian officer on the French general staff, was convicted of spying for the Germans; the evidence was forged, as it turned out, and the public outcry against him was led by the Jesuits' perennial allies—the right-wing nationalists, anti-Semites, Catholic diehards, and miscellaneous partisans of "the honor of the Army and the Nation." As *Civiltà Cattolica,* the official organ of the Jesuit hierarchy, helpfully observed, "The Jews were created by God, everywhere and always for the purpose of playing the role of traitor." The pro-Dreyfus party—galvanized by Zola's famous editorial, *"J'Accuse!"*—eventually prevailed; Dreyfus was recalled from exile on Devil's Island, retried (twice), and finally acquitted in 1906. One of the indirect results of "the Affair," as it was called, was the official separation of church and state, which meant that, without government subsidies to support them, many Catholic schools, and even many Catholic churches, were closed.

The history of Switzerland is notoriously placid and uneventful, but the Swiss have engaged in a number of poorly publicized civil wars, the last of which was fought in 1848 between a coalition of Protestant cantons and the Catholic cantons of Uri, Schwyz, Unterwalden, and Lucerne, which intended to form a "separatist league" (*Sonderbund*) of their own and secede from the Swiss Confederation. The Protestant cantons were victorious in the ensuing "War of the Sonderbund," and, as a precautionary measure, the 250 Jesuits in the 4 cantons were expelled.

A more permanent legacy of the Sonderbund War was Article 51 of the Swiss Constitution, as incorporated in 1848 and restated in 1874: "The order of the Jesuits and its affiliated societies may not be received into any part of Switzerland, and its members are forbidden to keep schools or engage in any other activity. This prohibition may be extended by the decision of the confederation to include other religious orders whose activities endanger the security of the state or the harmony of the various confessions."

And so the reunited cantons agreed to differ—the Catholic cantons continued to furnish the Pope's palace guards, the Protestant cantons to defy "the Pope's black battalions." An honorable exception to Article 51 was made for the Superior General of the Jesuit Order, Wlodomir Ledóchowski, and his two assistants, who sought asylum in Switzerland when Italy declared war on Germany in 1915. After that, when the odd Jesuit or two turned up in Switzerland, the compatriots of Calvin and Zwingli were content to look the other way—all but a vigilant deputy to the federal assembly, Dr. A. Frey, who informed his bemused colleagues that three Jesuits were currently serving as parish priests in Switzerland. Article 51 was invoked, the Jesuits were dismissed from their parishes, and the assembly was treated to a little homily from Dr. Frey on the geopolitical folly of harboring the agents of an alien creed:

> It is no accident that none of the great dictators was a Protestant, and that all of them were the products of Catholic education. By the same token, Czechoslovakia, Poland, etc., have fallen prey to the Communists, while Protestant Finland successfully resisted them. Protestant Scandinavia and England remain free of Communist influence, which is on the rise once again in Catholic Italy.

One positive result of Dr. Frey's vigilance was to focus a certain amount of attention on Article 51, which was resented by Catholics as discriminatory, derided by those who were not impressed with Dr. Frey's inductive powers as a pointless anachronism, and finally repealed by a national plebiscite in 1974.

The Synod of the Sycophants—The Jesuits and Papal Infallibility

Of all the revolutions that swept over Europe between 1789 and 1848, it was the Industrial Revolution—perhaps the only one that was not deplored by the Jesuits—that brought about the most permanent, and often the most catastrophic, changes in the lives of ordinary people. The spiritual and psychological effects of the factory system were only beginning to be observed, most notably by Karl Marx and Friedrich Engels. In our own century a Jesuit scholar and social reformer like Professor von Nell-Brenning could readily make an observation like "We are all standing on the shoulders of Karl Marx, but some of us are simply not aware of it," but at the time it was certainly not apparent that the Catholic Church and the authors of the *Communist Manifesto* could possibly have any common ground between them.

It was an age of superficial, old-fashioned piety, in which respectable men and women went to church on Sunday, organized evening Bible classes, and handed out Christmas packages to the children of the poor (as long as they came around to the back door, by the kitchen). The official Protestant churches of Northern Europe were completely secularized, a vicarage or a pastorate was a career, a "living," rather than a calling, and the clergy were occupied for the most part with the singing of loud hosannas to His Majesty of Prussia or Denmark or Her Majesty of England. The Danish philosopher Søren Kierkegaard (1813–55) summed it all up by saying, "Luther had ninety-five theses; I would have only one, that Christianity has ceased to exist."

At least the Catholic Church seemed to be more fortunate in Pope Pius IX ("Pio Nono"), elected in 1846, who had already declared an amnesty for all political prisoners in the Papal States and had endorsed the nationalist cause of the political reunification of Italy—a Supreme Pontiff, in other words, who had finally emerged from the eighteenth century. But Pius neglected to fulfill the liberal promise of the first few years of his reign. When the Revolution of 1848 broke out all over Europe (including Rome), he fled to Gaeta, in the kingdom of Naples, on the advice of the Jesuit Superior General and only returned in 1850, in the company of a French expeditionary force. Henceforth Pio Nono was to be a confirmed reactionary, a helpless champion of the *status quo* who only looked on sulkily while the new kingdom of Italy gradually absorbed the Romagna, Umbria, and the Marches, and then Rome itself. He was finally left as the temporal ruler of an acre or two of gardens and palaces or, as he preferred to put it, as "the Prisoner of the Vatican."

But Pius continued to reign as an absolute monarch in his principal capacity of Supreme Pontiff of the Catholic Church, and perhaps it is not surprising that he was now determined to safeguard the spiritual frontiers of the Church at least—or if possible even to expand them at the expense of the secular forces of liberalism and modernity—by means of three dramatic measures. The first of these was to elevate the doctrine of the Immaculate Conception, previously the subject of considerable philosophical speculation, to the level of unquestionable dogma. The second was to draw the boundaries between the higher ground of Catholic orthodoxy and the insalubrious lowlands of modern thought much more sharply in the so-called Syllabus of Errors and the encyclical *Quanta cura*. The third was to affirm his own position as the supreme arbiter of all such matters of belief by enunciating the doctrine of papal infallibility.

The Jesuits played a prominent role in the adoption of all three of these measures, especially the first, a goal that was also pursued, of course, energetically and even autocratically, according to some historians, by Pius himself. The bull *Ineffabilis Deus* was handed down on December 18, 1854, in the presence of two hundred bishops, which concerned the dogma of the Immaculate Conception, that is, that the Virgin Mary herself was "from the moment of conception by the particular grace and goodness of Almighty God . . . immaculate and free from all taint of Original Sin." (This is not to be confused with the doctrine of the Virgin Birth, by the way, which refers to Christ's conception rather than Mary's.) The Syllabus of Errors was published ten years later, in 1864, in which eighty "erroneous propositions" were specifically rejected—and of course all good Catholics were intended to do the same. Among them:

11. The Church should never interfere with philosophy, but should leave it free to correct itself. . . .
16. Mankind can find the path to Eternal Salvation in every religion. . . .
55. The Church is to be separated from the state, and the state from the Church.

Basically the syllabus was intended as a warning to liberal Catholics that any attempt to contaminate the teachings of the Church with the bacilli of "progress, liberalism, and modern civilization" would not be tolerated, though it was hard to avoid the impression that the Church was really abdicating its primary responsibility of providing spiritual guidance to concerned Catholics by condemning all these propositions, from Darwinism to socialism, out of hand and, rather in the manner of Cardinal Bellarmine some 250 years earlier, simply drawing a shroud of medieval obscurity over the whole perplexing question. The reaction within the Order was mixed. A group of German Jesuits founded a periodical called *Voices from Maria Laach* in 1865 (renamed *Voices of the Times* in 1915) with the express purpose of defending the syllabus, though on the other hand the Jesuit editors of the French-language journal *Etudes* maintained such an eloquent and expressive silence on the subject that they were quickly compelled to cease publication altogether. In general, however, the majority of Jesuits were quite content to retain their place of honor in the vanguard of this papal crusade against a comparatively small minority of liberal Catholics—rather than doing battle with the real ogres of the day, such as the idealist philosophers Hegel and Fichte and their numerous disciples, who had made a god of human reason and dispensed with the Christian God altogether. The Jesuits of the nineteenth century preferred to ignore these disturbing phenomena, or to condemn them from a distance, rather than to contend with them *mano a mano,* as Ignatius would certainly have recommended: "Spiritual tendencies," he observed, "can only be arrested by spiritual means." (This was one of the lower ebbs in the history of Jesuit education as well, and the classic cut-and-thrust approach to philosophical disputation for which the Jesuit colleges had once been famous had long since been supplanted by a system that merely emphasized the passive absorption of an extremely limited body of doctrine.)

On July 18, 1870, the doctrine of papal infallibility was affirmed by the First Vatican Council—"the Synod of the Sycophants," as its severer critics called it. Actually, though, this decision was only arrived at in the face of serious opposition, spearheaded by the German bishops, and up until the present day this particular point of doctrine (which states specifically that the Pope is infallible when pronouncing *ex cathedra* on a question of faith or morality) has created more breaches in the Catholic ranks than it has healed, even though it was intended as the keystone of Pius's twenty-year program of consolidation of the spiritual prerogatives of the papacy. It has also caused a certain amount of enmity and hostility to be deflected onto the Jesuits, who for the most part applauded it and were soon to become its most vociferous defenders. Here is the exact wording of the passage from the conciliar resolution in which the dogma of papal infallibility was both established and defined:

> ... for the glory of Almighty God and Jesus Christ our Savior, for the advancement of the Catholic faith and the salvation of all Christian people, and by the authority of the sacred Council, we hereby do profess and proclaim this to be an article of dogma and divine revelation: If the Roman pontiff is speaking *ex cathedra,* that is, when he is acting in his capacity as pastor and teacher of all Christians by virtue of his supreme apostolic powers as the deputy of Christ and when he proclaims a certain doctrine to be binding upon the entire Christian Church, then he is exercising that office, with the help of God, that was vouchsafed to him through Peter and which partakes of the infallibility with which our Redeemer intended His Church to be endowed for the purpose of determining the correct doctrine in matters of faith or morality. . . .

The liberal Catholic movement had already been thrown into headlong rout by the publication of the Syllabus of Errors. The idea that it was not absolutely necessary to choose between the catechism and liberalism, or Darwinism, or even socialism, would have to be deferred until the twentieth century (when, of course, it would include a great many Jesuits among its proponents). Unfortunately for the Jesuits the great religious conflict of the nineteenth century was to pit them against secular statesmen—anticlerical French Radicals and crusty Lutherans like Otto von Bismarck—who were not to be kept from doing their worst even by such potent theological weapons as the Syllabus of Errors and the declaration of infallibility. This time the papal grenadiers found themselves more or less in the situation of conscripts sent into battle with wooden rifles, who are only likely to prevail if their enemies are no better equipped or not much disposed to fight.

"First the French and Then the Jesuits"—The Jesuit and Bismarck's *Kulturkampf*

The Prussian chancellor, Otto von Bismarck, had created the German Empire out of a dozen or so princely states essentially by defeating the Danes, the Austrians, and the French in rapid succession—"unification," as he put it in his gruff Pomeranian way, "had to be fought for on the field of battle." And once unification was achieved, he decided to continue the struggle by only slightly less belligerent means by taking on the Ultramontanes,* those Catholics who felt that their primary allegiance lay with Pio Nono rather than Kaiser Wilhelm. This was what Rudolf Virchow, the eminent pathologist who led the liberal opposition in the Reichstag, liked to call Bismarck's *Kulturkampf* ("culture battle"), a term that has since caught on with historians as well.

The declaration of papal infallibility had come at just the right moment, since it gave Bismarck the opportunity to offer the numerous priests and scholars who had spoken out against it the "protection" of the Prussian state against reprisals by the Catholic hierarchy. Even more opportune was the founding of the Catholic Center Party in Germany— "one of the most monstrous developments I have ever witnessed in the realm of politics"—which may have lent a modest amount of credence to some of Bismarck's rather wild-eyed utterances in the Reichstag about the international Catholic conspiracy. On various occasions he rose to warn "the nobility of Upper Silesia and Westphalia, who are all under the influence of tne Jesuits and have been seriously and deliberately misled while under their tutelage," or to convince the deputies themselves "of the danger that is represented by the Jesuits," both "on account of their international organization" and "their renunciation and deliberate subversion of all national ties," to say nothing of "the patriotic impulses they seek to destroy and set at naught."

In fact, Bismarck was simply exploiting the rich vein of anti-Catholic hysteria that was never too far beneath the surface of the North German

---

*From Latin *ultra montes*, "on the other side of the mountains," i.e., the Alps. The term was originally used in France in the seventeenth century and has frequently been invoked as a kind of code word for the Jesuits and their sympathizers.

psyche. On August 5, 1870, three days after the outbreak of the Franco-Prussian War, a provincial paper, the *Gottinger Zeitung,* had run as a banner headline "FIRST THE FRENCH, AND THEN THE JESUITS!" The Prussian court chaplain Bernard Rogge, otherwise a thoroughly respectable clergyman, recorded in his memoirs a vision, inspired by a fever, that is worthy of Eugène Sue: "During those sleepless nights I was plagued by the most frightful fancies. . . . For one entire evening I saw a number of Jesuits sitting around my bedside, and I knew that they had come to torment me."

Once again the Jesuits had become the scapegoat for all the excesses, transgressions, and omissions of the Church. They were expelled from Germany—or perhaps *exorcised* would be the better word—on July 4, 1872, when Kaiser Wilhelm I signed the so-called Jesuit Law—and took the opportunity to castigate the Jesuits personally as "enemies of the Reich" who had corrupted "our German youth with an unpatriotic spirit of internationalism." The Order was given six months to liquidate its establishments in Germany; foreign-born Jesuits were faced with immediate expulsion, while German Jesuits were allowed to wait out the six-month grace period, as long as they remained in certain designated areas. All in all, 550 Jesuits were expelled from the German Empire, which hardly seems to amount to the Jesuit "diaspora"—he also likened it to "a plague of aphids"—that Bismarck had been thundering about in the Reichstag. "If it came to that," he informed the deputies after the danger, if any, had been averted, "I would still prefer to be ruled by the Social Democrats than lorded over by the Jesuits." He also predicted that "one day the Jesuits will be the leaders of the Social Democratic movement," which was not so much a prophetic vision of things to come (i.e., the Order's dramatic shift to the left since the Second World War) as simply his cryptic Prussian way of saying that politics makes strange bedfellows; the violence of his "*Culturkampf*"(he stubbornly insisted in spelling the word with a *c,* perhaps merely to do it differently from Virchow) had endeared him to the anticlerical left, for a short time, and had alienated many of his reactionary old friends on the right. Certainly some strange political repercussions were to be expected after the collision of two immovable objects like the Prussian-German state and the Catholic Church. When Bismarck realized that the *Kulturkampf* had already outlived its original purpose, he was prepared to reach a compromise with Rome. Most of the religious orders that had been expelled were permitted to return to Germany, all except the Jesuits, who remained officially under the ban until 1917.

These were difficult years for the Order in all the Catholic countries of Europe. The Italian Parliament dissolved every one of the religious orders as part of its perpetual feud with the Vatican, and all the Jesuit colleges, and related facilities (including museums, libraries, and observatories) were taken over by the state. The headquarters of the Superior General had to be transferred from Rome to Fiesole, and anti-Jesuit feelings were running so high in Rome in the year 1892 that the Twenty-fourth General Congregation of the Order decided to convene instead in Ignatius's native town of Loyola, though more for reasons of security than sentiment. The French Third Republic had turned bitterly anticlerical by century's end, and when the monarchy was overthrown in Portugal and a republic was proclaimed in 1910, the Jesuits were promptly expelled from Portugal. The mythical Jesuit that had sprung full-blown from the imagination of such divine personalities as Emile Zola and Otto von Bismarck continued to work his will behind the scenes—sometimes in concert with the Freemasons and Rosicrucians—and to glide invisibly down the corridors of the chancelleries of Europe, a myth that was finally to be exploded, like so many other *fin-de-siècle* delusions, by the outbreak of the First World War. In contrast to its fictional or rhetorical counterpart, the Order itself seems to have declined into a sort of medieval apathy in the face of so much hostility and persecution. Even in the realm of the spirit, where the Jesuits had once stood alone, they had finally relapsed from ultraconservatism into mere barbarism, where they now stood shoulder-to-shoulder with those Late Victorian relics who swathed their children in ankle-length bathing dresses before they stepped into the bathtub, never let brothers and sisters play together, and kept ample supplies of "St. Ignatius water" on hand as a specific against all the ills that afflict the flesh and spirit. And as far as the realm of the intellect was concerned, it is ironic that while Edison and Lumière were finally perfecting the method of projecting images on a screen that was devised by Athanasius Kircher,* the Jesuits were more profitably occupied in manufacturing devotional images of the Blessed Virgin that could be dissolved in water to produce an elixir that was said to have miraculous curative powers.

---

*The Jesuit Father who read over this portion of the manuscript correctly pointed out that Father Joye, of Basel, was in fact one of the first scholars and teachers of the art of film. Father Friedrich Muckermann deserves to be mentioned in this context as well.

"I WOULD RATHER HAVE HANDLED A MACHINE GUN"—
THE JESUITS AT THE FRONT

August 1914 was the centennial year of the restored Jesuit Order, and the twenty-fifth General, Franz Xaver Wernz, was determined that no unpleasantness of any kind should mar the celebration of this particular anniversary. The fortunes of the Order had improved demonstrably in recent years; five new provinces had been established around the world (Mexico, Canada, California, New Orleans, and Hungary), and, as was pointed out in the Order's annual report with a touch of corporate smugness, "In the Calcutta mission 130,000 heathen have been won for the faith and 12,000 in one Chinese mission alone. These figures could have been doubled if more missionaries were only available." Throughout that summer General Wernz had been largely preoccupied with the upcoming celebration—he, like virtually all other Europeans, had no idea war was only a few months away—though he did take the time during June to send off a crisp note to the superiors of the province of Maryland in which he explored, with commendable German thoroughness, the subject of unnecessary roughness in high-school athletic competition:

> Considering the savagery with which the game [of football] is generally played, certain modifications seem to be in order
> . . . at the very least our colleges should not compete with other colleges [i.e., non-Jesuit high schools] who are known to play the game with particular brutality. . . . In addition, only a certain number of games should be scheduled with other colleges. . . . I ask that these points should be drawn up in the form of a memorandum that can be read aloud during meals and thus immediately be put into effect in all our colleges.

A more serious problem had been created by Pope Pius X himself, who had accused a number of Jesuits of disseminating "Modernist" opinions, an offense that in extreme cases had been made punishable by excommunication in recent years. What was meant by Modernism had already been clarified in several encyclicals, and the term was quite literally intended to cover a multitude of sins. In this particular case the offenders had suggested that the Catholic interpretation of Scripture could stand to benefit from an infusion of new ideas generated by the so-called higher criticism, which was primarily dependent upon sources outside the text itself (philological inference and archaeological discovery) rather than the more traditional props of meticulous scholarship and divine revelation. Unfortunately this matter had already been looked into by a papal commission on biblical studies in 1909, which had ruled that anything other than a strictly literal interpretation of the Bible—particularly the first three chapters of Genesis—was a Modernist error that should be scrupulously avoided by all good Catholics. (For example, biblical scholars had established about twenty or thirty years earlier on philological grounds that "the first five books of Moses" were actually written by a great many different authors—probably not including Moses himself—over a span of several centuries, but as far as the papal commissions and Pope Pius X were concerned, they were still the first five books of Moses.)

Some of the anti-Modernist excesses that Pius IX had included in the Syllabus of Errors had been quietly dispensed with during the pontificate of Leo XIII, his successor, but the Church was essentially still very mistrustful of science in any form, and a few of the leading Jesuit intellectuals—which was greatly to their credit in those dark years—were trying to make amends by proposing a kind of détente, or relaxation of hostilities (if only in the rather limited terrain of biblical scholarship). However, this was not regarded as a praiseworthy endeavor by Pope Pius X, and in order to dispel the lingering taint of unorthodoxy in this centennial year, General Wernz had circulated a kind of position paper in which the Order was specifically acquainted with the dangers of Modernism, as well as its three chief symptoms—frivolity, novelty, and worldliness.

This did not seem to help. General Wernz was personally chastised by the Vatican because he had not dealt more severely with the Modernists who had already been identified within the Order. It had even been asserted that Pius X intended to have the General removed from office, which is confirmed by the overall tenor of his relations with the Jesuits but not by any specific evidence. In any case, this impasse was resolved, fortuitously as usual, by the death of General Wernz on August 19, 1914. Pope Pius X himself died on the following day, but the usual spate of rumors and lurid speculations was largely preempted by the fact that Germany, France, Britain, Austria, and Russia had been at war for almost two weeks. (Pope Pius was canonized in 1954, and the Jesuits can apparently afford to be generous in their recollections of the formative years of the modern Order. As the Jesuit scholar Karl Rahner observed not long ago, "Many of the decisions of the papal commission on biblical studies in the early years of this century were, as we know today, objectively false, and yet they had a providential role to play, since they opposed a kind of rationalism gone mad that sought to destroy the Holy Scriptures altogether.")

As soon as the powers began to mobilize, the Jesuits immediately began to disprove their ancient reputation as "stateless persons" "who would serve no prince but the Pope." In fact, in the martial phrase of the day, the Jesuits flocked to the colors; almost two thousand (about one tenth of the current membership of the Order) were to serve as chaplains, medical orderlies and stretcher-bearers, and even frontline troops with various armies on both sides. Six hundred Jesuits who had been deported by the Third Republic returned to France to offer their services; 375 German-born Jesuits, many of whom had come from overseas, volunteered to serve as chaplains with the Kaiser's forces, even though technically they were still barred from entering the country by Bismarck's Jesuit Law. Strangely enough, another internationalist bogey of prewar politicians—the Socialist International—proved to be no less patriotic than the Jesuits, and both the Jesuit and the Socialist press were soon full of dispatches and decorations and the great feats of gallantry their subscribers had performed.

Father Teilhard de Chardin was awarded the Croix de Guerre for bravery in the face of the enemy while serving as a stretcher-bearer in the French Army. "I would rather have handled a machine gun," he wrote to a friend, "since it seems to me that this is quite appropriate for a priest. Isn't a priest supposed to bear the sorrows of the world in whatever form they might present themselves?"

Father Rupert Mayer, the Jesuit chaplain who was personally decorated by a reluctant Kaiser Wilhelm II, won his Iron Cross on the Somme in 1915. A team of stretcher-bearers had come under fire and had taken shelter in an empty shell hole, leaving the wounded man they had been carrying lying exposed on the open ground overhead. The wounded man, quite naturally, panicked and began to scream for help. Father Mayer was suddenly stretched out at his side, telling him, "Be still now, comrade, because if anyone gets it, it's going to be me." The citation written by his company commander was quick to acknowledge that such a remarkable display of brotherly love could also provide a great boost to morale: "That my brave, fearless company could get through this at all is entirely due to our divisional chaplain, Father Rupert Mayer."

On December 30, 1916, Father Mayer's left leg was shattered by an exploding shell, but he was lucky enough to fall into the hands of a gifted and compassionate surgeon (rather than the sort of bloodstained regimental sawbones who looked after Ensign Iñigo de Loyola in similar circumstances). This was Dr. Hans Carossa, much better known as a writer than a doctor, who later described his first encounter with Father Mayer in his book *Führung und Geleit* ("Leaders and Followers"):

> The smile with which he greeted us was clear and very much of the present moment—it had not come to us out of the darkness—and for the first time we were encouraged to think that we might be of some use hereabouts. . . . The father began to speak. . . . His voice, which was almost inaudible, betrayed no trace of fear or pain . . . and you would have been ashamed to pity him. The man was lying there in his own blood, in the most wretched circumstances imaginable, and yet you still got the impression of an uncommon kind of self-awareness. While you were in his presence you couldn't help get the feeling that everything was going according to plan somehow, and that even his current predicament had long since entered into his calculations and was by no means to be reckoned as a casualty.

And as the casualties came to be reckoned in the millions, and the rations grew sparser and leaner, and the victories harder to come by, the German Nationalist pamphleteers began to look around for excuses. Actually all they needed to know was that Mathias Erzberger, a deputy from the Catholic Center party, had visited General Ledóchowski in Switzerland in 1917. By war's end it had become the unshakable conviction of the German Nationalists that

> in the course of these conversations the Jesuit General succeeded in convincing Erzberger to lend his support for the Jesuit political strategy vis-à-vis Germany and the revival of the original program of the Center Party, which was first brought to light by Bismarck [more or less the same program that he attributed to the Jesuits—the destruction of a unified German Reich as presently constituted, ruled by a Prussian Lutheran Kaiser]. And every political maneuver that Erzberger has engaged in since his discussion with the Jesuit

General has only served to advance this Jesuit political strategy, insofar as they undermined the spirit of resistance of the German people and helped bring about the surrender and the scourging of Germany of the Diktat* of Versailles.

This, then, was the source of the legend that "Germany was stabbed in the back."

As we have seen, General Ledóchowski was obliged to sit out the duration of the war in a castle in Switzerland—Schloss Zizers, near Chur, to be precise—though this was not in furtherance of any sinister design but simply because he had been expelled from Italy as an enemy alien; his family was Polish, his father had been a baron of the Austro-Hungarian Empire, and this Alpine interlude gave him the additional distinction of being the only Jesuit General to move his headquarters away from Rome. His long tenure in office overlapped with three pontificates (Benedict XV, Pius XI, and Pius XII) and two world wars, as well as the rise of Hitler, the Spanish Civil War, and the Russian Revolution. It is always difficult to trace the political activities of a Jesuit General in any detail—Jesuit sources always blandly insist that he concerned himself entirely with spiritual and administrative matters and never gave politics a thought, in much the same way that the Russian Collegium (the "Russicum") founded by Pius XI at Ledóchowski's behest was said to be exclusively intended for the training of priests to minister to the spiritual needs of White Russian emigrés in Western Europe, America, and Australia (and was not the least bit concerned with those Catholics who had remained behind in the Soviet Union). At any rate it appears that General Ledóchowski pursued a fairly aggressive, eastward-looking policy, as befits a scion of the Polish nobility, though not so aggressive as that contemplated by Père Michel, the Vatican emissary to the Soviet Union in the late 1920's and the central figure in one of the strangest episodes in the history of Jesuit diplomacy.

MISSION TO MOSCOW—A JESUIT IN THE SOVIET UNION

When the Russicum opened its door in 1929, the official explanation of its purpose was widely disregarded as a pious fiction, since, after all, the

---

*"Dictated peace," postwar Nationalist (and later Nazi) jargon.

Germanicum, the prototype of all the foreign seminaries in Rome, had been established as a kind of training camp for the shock troops of the Counter-Reformation with the avowed purpose of carrying the battle into the enemy's own territory—and the million and a half Russian Catholics were still largely to be found at home in the Soviet motherland, not in the emigré colonies of Paris and New York. The seminarians of the 1920's and 1930's dreamed, instead of being sent out to the Indies, of joining the "Vatican Airborne" and of floating down by parachute onto Russian soil to defy the Bolsheviks and to help bring the patient Orthodox masses back into communion with Rome. Whether such things actually happened is a different question, and there is no evidence to suggest that the students at the Russicum were taught how to wear fake beards or mix invisible ink (like the English seminarians of the 1570's) or to operate clandestine radio sets, for that matter. Although the Russicum has been denounced in *Pravda* as a "training installation for Vatican agents," no such agents, as far as we know, have ever been apprehended on Soviet territory. (Here we are confronted with the usual difficulty that arises in discussing such matters, namely, that it is not always that easy to distinguish between things that are top secret and things that are merely nonexistent.)

As early as 1918 a curious document was making the rounds of the foreign ministries of Europe that contained a series of proposals that were too audacious to be ignored, if a bit too unrealistic to be taken completely seriously. This was a memorandum, purportedly written by General Ledóchowski himself, which called for the establishment of a Catholic confederation of states in Central Europe—Bavaria, Austria, Slovakia, Bohemia, Poland, Hungary, and Croatia—that would keep the Bolsheviks from contemplating any further encroachments in the East and would also set a limit to the future pretensions of Protestant North Germany (Ledóchowski was thinking of Bismarck and the Kaiser rather than of Hitler, who had not yet come to prominence politically). The theory was apparently that this godfearing Catholic superstate would be particularly resistant to the Bolshevist contagion, which provided a unique new angle to the then-prevalent idea of creating some kind of political buffer zone—*cordon sanitaire* was the diplomats' catchphrase—to make certain that communism spread no further than Russia's western borders.

This kind of high-flying political fantasy makes a good introduction to the story of Père Michel d'Herbigny, the French Jesuit who became the Vatican's secret emissary to the Catholics of Russia during the 1920's. Père Michel rated an entry of seventy-six lines in Hock's *Jesuit Lexicon* of 1934 (twenty is about average for prominent Jesuits of the day), most of which are given over to a complete list of publications, scholarly attainments, and offices held. The biographical section ends abruptly with the notation *"Pâques 1926 en Russie"* ("Easter 1926 in Russia"), the bibliography breaks off as well, since, as the editor of the *Lexicon* explains, "He was sent to Russia by the Pope in 1925 and in order to expedite his dealings with the Russian bishops he was made titular bishop of Ilion. In 1925 the Vatican was able to obtain permission for him to enter the Soviet Union, which had been revoked when he attempted to intercede on behalf of Patriarch Tikhon at the latter's trial in 1922."

The rest of the story was provided by the English historian David Mitchell in 1980. It seems that early in 1926 Père Michel was summoned to the offices of the apostolic nuncio on the Rauchstrasse in Berlin, where he was consecrated Bishop of Ilion (Troia) by the Nuncio, Msgr. Eugenio Pacelli (later Pope Pius XII). This was done in strict secrecy, with only one witness present, and not just to enhance his prestige among the Catholic hierarchy in Russia but primarily to enable him to consecrate Russian bishops himself as he saw fit. The more critical part of his mission was simply to encourage the million and a half Russian Catholics to be steadfast in their faith and to stiffen the spirit of resistance against bolshevism.

Père Michel had proposed himself for this mission, and his qualifications for an undertaking of this sort were most impressive: He spoke fluent German and Russian as well as French, he had an expert knowledge of the Russian Orthodox Church and even some background in the field of espionage. In 1918 he had received the rosette of the Legion of Honor for providing the French Army with certain "useful information" about a forthcoming German offensive. General Ledóchowski had no great hopes for the success of this scheme, but he was obliged to do no more than watch and wait, since Pius XI had taken a personal interest in Père Michel's mission to Moscow.

Apparently he picked an escort of GPU agents (as the KGB was called in those days) at the border; his comings and goings in Moscow were closely watched, which, since he was frequently in contact with French ambassador Herbette, became the source of a certain amount of friction between Paris and Moscow. Père Michel himself was allowed to go about his business (including the consecration of three Catholic bishops in Moscow) and then to return to Rome quite unmolested. In 1929 he became director of the Russicum (a fact not mentioned in the *Jesuit*

Lexicon), where he soon began to pick up all sorts of disquieting rumors from the Soviet Union. Two of the three bishops he had consecrated had been sent to labor camps and a number of Catholic priests he had been in contact with had been arrested; by now it was clear that Père Michel had not been careful enough in covering his tracks, but apparently he was no less haphazard in his management of the Russicum, which was infiltrated by Soviet *agents provocateurs* who, posing as "religious fanatics," subsequently set up underground printing presses in Russia and generally did whatever they could to discredit the Collegium.

At this point it seems to have been decided at the highest levels that Père Michel had outlasted his usefulness and was likely to become a major source of embarrassment. The Vatican proceeded to launch a kind of preemptive scandal instead, and, at the express request of Pope Pius XI, a report was inserted in the official Vatican newspaper, *L'Osservatore Romano*, that "the Bishop of Ilion" had celebrated a pontifical mass in Moscow. Père Michel's cover was blown, and the European press immediately picked up the story, along with the usual sidebar speculations about Jesuit "backstairs diplomacy" and the like. General Ledóchowski finally felt compelled to intervene as well, and Père Michel was brought before an ecclesiastical court of inquiry (presided over by two Jesuits). The court's proceedings brought very few material facts to light that all the interested parties were not familiar with already—except that the suspicion was raised, apparently on the strength of a dossier supplied by the GPU, that Père Michel, while *in partibus infidelium* ("in the lands of the unbeliever"), had had two Russian women competing for his favors, one of whom had borne him a child. The verdict was a foregone conclusion—culpable negligence, which in this case really meant unpardonable naiveté—but there was some dispute about the defendant's state of mind when he committed these indiscretions. Some maintained he was a Soviet agent, or an unworldly scholar destroyed by his own vanity, or a renegade who had turned against Catholicism, or an out-and-out psychopath, but there was a strong consensus that Père Michel should be whisked out of the spotlight of publicity with all possible speed. The judges issued a statement to the effect that Père Michel, though not entirely a traitor, nor a certifiable madman, was probably a bit of each.

In Père Michel's first proposal for his mission to Moscow he had suggested a cover identity for himself to divert suspicion from his proselytizing activities in Soviet Russia—namely, a missionary en route to China. This time he was sent there in earnest, though there is no record of his ever having encountered his fellow exile, Teilhard de Chardin, in Peking. Père Michel was kept under house arrest in various Jesuit residences in France and Belgium for the last twenty years of his life. He had been, as he put it, "buried alive," and though he continued to write prodigiously, none of these later manuscripts was ever published, and they remain, presumably, in the possession of the Order. My own attempts to enlarge upon, or at least to corroborate, the account provided by David Mitchell were not notably successful. For example, I received the following reply to my request for more information about Père Michel from the archivist of the Jesuit province of Upper Germany:

> Michel d'Herbigny was an Orientalist. From the end of 1926 until 1937 he appears on the rolls of the Order as a bishop. This means he was so identified on the rolls (which are by no means secret) for over ten years before the General interceded in his case. From December 1926 until 1932 he was the director of the Oriental Institute, not the Russicum, which is a residential college (with eleven students in residence in 1979!). In 1932 he was named praeses [president] emeritus of the Institute. There is no room in his curriculum vitae for a trip to China. Since he had always been the editor of a newspaper (of which there are not any copies in my possession), it strikes me as very odd that he would not have written anything further.

I was certainly left none the wiser than I was before, and I can only hope that the appearance of this book might somehow impel the Vatican or the Order to be a bit more forthcoming about the details of Père Michel's career, perhaps to release some of the original documents, for example. There is one final detail, however, that all can agree on. Michel d'Herbigny died at a Jesuit residence in Aix-en-Provence on Christmas Eve, 1957. He was seventy-seven years old. His gravestone is simply inscribed "Père Michel," with no mention of his having been titular bishop of Ilion, director of the Oriental Institute (or possibly the Collegium Russicum), or even a member of the Society of Jesus.

If many of the actions and omissions of both the Vatican and the Order during the 1920's seem unaccountable to us today, perhaps this is because the Church had remained faithful to the principles of its nineteenth-century alliance with the forces of security and stability (even though most of these had long since defected to the other side). This resulted in a certain shortsightedness and parochialism, as well as a lingering tendency toward authoritarianism—a gross instance of the former being revealed by Pius XI, who found himself too busy to receive Mahatma Gandhi when he came to Europe in 1924 to enlist support for the cause of Indian independence, a more trivial instance of the latter by a German Jesuit called Father Robert von Nostitz, who addressed a conference at Innsbrück in the same year. Father von Nostitz proposed that one way of making the New Testament more acceptable to modern Catholics might be to stop comparing the Kingdom of Christ to the realm of an earthly prince or king and instead "to substitute an image of authority [*Führergestalt*] that would still have an impact on people living today." Father von Nostitz was to have his wish granted in the decade that followed, when a copy of *Mein Kampf* was placed beside the Bible on the altars of German churches.

The papacy's first real attempt to address itself to the other burning question of the day—the conflict between socialism and capitalism—was the encyclical *Quadragesimo anno,* which appeared in 1931. The encyclical affirmed not only the rights of property but also the property owner's inherent duties and obligations to the community at large, a truly radical innovation for the papacy for which one of Pius XI's circle of advisers, Professor Oswald von Nell-Brenning, was largely responsible.

Even this tentative endorsement of socialist principles was bitterly resented by the Communists, who preferred to keep the field entirely to themselves; the Social Democrats were stigmatized as "Social Fascists," and, when no more compelling argument was at hand, they sullenly intoned, "Christian Socialism is the most insidious form of Fascism." The use of the word *Fascist* as a casual verbal missile in political arguments soon began to seem very childish, when both Communists and Jesuits were to have a much closer acquaintance with the real thing.

FROM CONCORDAT TO CONCENTRATION CAMP—THE JESUITS IN ITALY AND GERMANY, 1922–1945

When Mussolini and his Blackshirts came to power in Italy after the March on Rome of 1922, the principal intermediary between the Duce and the Pope was a Jesuit, Father Tacchi-Venturi, who continued to exercise this demanding office until the end of the Fascist regime in 1945. Father Tacchi-Venturi also played a leading role in the negotiation of the Lateran Treaty, by the terms of which the Duce recognized the sovereignty of the Pope over the Vatican City State and relations between the Italian government and the "Prisoner of the Vatican" were normalized for the first time since 1848. He also had a hand in the drafting of the concordat that officially established the Catholic Church as the national church of Italy, and, according to the diary of Count Ciano, Italian foreign minister and the Duce's son-in-law, he persuaded the Duce to edit out a number of scurrilous attacks on the Church from the manuscript of a great many of the public speeches.

When Hitler seized power in 1933, a similar concordat was concluded with him almost immediately, though only after what was perceived as a healthy exchange of ideas in the party and the Catholic press. Catholic intellectuals thought it no great harm that the Church had had its feathers ruffled a bit, so long as it had been compelled to clarify exactly where it stood in relation to this new one-party state. Peaceful coexistence appeared to be the order of the day, and unfortunately the Catholics of Germany seem to have had the shining example of the Italian solution constantly luring them on, like a mirage of the desert horizon. Here, for instance, is an account of the concluding ceremonies of the Eucharistic Congress in Taranto in 1937, reverently reprinted from the *Corriere della Sera* by the German Jesuit paper *Voices of the Times* to illustrate the way in which "the Italian government pays tribute to the Catholic state religion in observing this festive occasion":

> The cardinal accompanied His Holiness aboard a battleship that was flying the papal ensign, where the highest-ranking officers had assembled to pay their respects; meanwhile the other dignitaries who had attended the Eucharistic Congress were afforded a similar reception on board the other vessels of the fleet. . . . A squadron of seaplanes swept by slowly in the clear sky overhead, and the crews of every vessel in the harbor were drawn up on parade to receive His Holiness's blessing. At the torpedo-boat station the cardinal, bearing the monstrance, stepped into a splendid automobile that was fitted out as a mobile altar and was driven through the city, accompanied by a glittering assemblage of the civil and ecclesiastical authorities as well as the various armed services and all the organizations of the Fascist party.

The tone of breathless admiration for the artifacts of the Italian war machine, soon to prove doubly misplaced, seems all the more incongruous when it is uncritically repeated in a German Jesuit publication in 1937—a year after the Nuremberg Laws were adopted for the purpose of "protecting German blood and German honor" and of preventing "any further infusion of non-Aryan, particularly Jewish blood into the body of the German *Volk.*" In fact it was already three years after the Nazi "chief ideologue" Alfred Rosenberg had launched the first wave of the party's propaganda attack on the Catholic Church. By 1937, in other words, it should already have been apparent, to a Jesuit journalist especially, that the Italian example was not necessarily relevant to what was happening in Germany.

The Nazi campaign against the Church was aimed at the Jesuits in particular, and Nazi officials discovered a number of ways of hampering their activities, ranging from mere bureaucratic harassment to systematic repression. First, the five Jesuit colleges in Germany were closed; the rector of the Canisius College in Berlin was tersely informed: "The Ministry has decided that it can see no further need for the school conducted by you." Jesuit publications were crippled by party censorship and by state-approved sabotage—the allocation of paper and newsprint was sharply reduced for "strategic" reasons, and many bookstores were persuaded to cut back on the quantity of Catholic literature that was offered for sale.

In wartime hundreds of Jesuits were arrested on meaningless charges of disloyalty and "defeatism"—an especially strange accusation to be leveled against a priest—and sent to prison or a concentration camp without benefit of a trial. One example will have to serve for all—Father Clemente Pereira was picked up in Trier in 1944 simply because he had been trying to serve as unofficial chaplain to a group of teenage airplane spotters—"Luftwaffe auxiliaries," in the current parlance—and was denounced to the Gestapo by the local Hitler Youth leader. The Gestapo kept a card-file "registry" for the Jesuits, as they did for the Jews, but when the Jesuits were discharged summarily from the Wehrmacht in 1941, by a special decree of the Führer, as reclassified "unfit" for future service, this ruling was largely ignored by the military, and only 63 of the 156 Jesuits in the province of Upper Germany who were serving with the armed forces were actually discharged. And finally, whenever a Jesuit was brought before a court, no matter what the charge, this furnished a pretext for an elaborate show trial, heavily publicized in the press, which turned every one of these proceedings into an exercise in public defamation of the Order.

In late 1943 Father Oswald von Nell-Brenning, mentioned earlier in connection with his activities as a papal adviser on social issues, was charged with violating the currency regulations and brought before a Nazi tribunal by Munich. In his capacity as acting administrator of the province of Lower Germany, he was accused of having supplied a confederate in Holland with forged tax vouchers as part of a scheme to smuggle a large amount of German currency out of the country. That was a familiar tactic of black marketeers in those days, since anyone who could produce a plausible-looking bill of some kind from a foreign creditor was automatically entitled to transfer an equivalent amount of Reichsmarks to the person in question. Consequently the press coverage of the trial made it appear that this was simply a case of another stateless Jesuit scoundrel trying to fatten his foreign bank account with irreplaceable German Reichsmarks at the expense of the Fatherland.

As it turned out, however, the tax vouchers were genuine, which meant that the prosecuting attorney was obliged to modify—but not to drop—the original charges. There was no question that a defendant could be acquitted of such a serious charge in a Nazi court, and accordingly Father von Nell-Brenning was sentenced to three years' imprisonment and fined five hundred thousand Reichsmarks (plus restitution of the full amount of the vouchers) for the crime of transferring money abroad "out of mistrust for the National Socialist state" and "through illicit channels." As he was to recall after the war, "They managed to make out a case for premeditated black marketeering, even though there was not a scrap of evidence to suggest that I intended anything of the kind—rather than merely to pay my taxes because it's the conventional thing to do, to discharge an obligation of that kind." However, Father von Nell-Brenning's sentence was deferred on the grounds of ill health, although he discovered in 1946, when he applied for a passport to attend the General Congregation of the Order in Rome, that the stigma of black marketeering had survived the collapse of the Third Reich, the special tribunals, and all the rest. The functionary at the passport office who turned down his application reasonably pointed out that if he felt well enough to travel, then he was certainly well enough to sit quietly in a cell, and there the matter rested until 1950, when his original conviction was finally vacated as a politically motivated "Nazi judgment."

Collectively the Jesuits in Germany did not engage in any organized resistance against the Nazi regime, or at least not in the usual sense of the term. "Their weapons," wrote the Jesuit historian Father Wilhelm

In 1939 there were 836 Jesuits on the rolls of the two German provinces. Of these 456 were abroad, most of them on missionary service, which left 380 Jesuits in the Third Reich.
20 houses were expropriated or commandeered.
226 Jesuits were dispossessed.
12 were sent to concentration camps (3 died at Dachau).
2 were condemned to death,
6 to lengthy prison terms,
about 20 to lesser terms of imprisonment.

Flosdorf in 1946, "were confined to those that are suitable to the cloth, unmasking the secret baseness of the enemy's thoughts and actions, refuting his arguments and meaningless slogans, resisting his efforts to corrupt all morality, upholding the constancy and convictions of the Catholic people through the written and spoken word." According to some accounts, about a hundred Jesuits were active in the French Resistance, twelve of whom gave their lives, but the two German Jesuits who were condemned for "resistance" activities were merely victims, or martyrs, rather than heroes of this sort. Father Alois Grimm, who was executed for uttering "defeatist sentiments" to an informer in 1944, was a victim of entrapment, pure and simple. A soldier came to him, ostensibly to seek advice on a spiritual matter, their conversation drifted into the forbidden domain of politics, and the next day Father Grimm found himself under arrest.

Father Alfred Delp was arrested during the mass roundup that followed the attempt on Hitler's life and the abortive coup d'état of July 20, 1944; he was an associate of several young officers who were involved in the conspiracy, though he himself was not a conspirator, nor was he aware of their plans to assassinate Hitler. Nevertheless, the prosecutor of the "People's Court," Dr. Freisler, was generally able to obtain a conviction on a great deal less evidence than that. He argued that a Jesuit could "only have had some motive that was inimical to the security of the state that caused him to cultivate the acquaintance of so many high-ranking army officers," and the court agreed that this was sufficient to justify a guilty verdict.

LAST LETTER FROM PRISON

Dear Brothers,

The death sentence has been confirmed, and the atmosphere here is so full of hate and anger that I must seriously consider the possibility that it will be carried out today.

I wish to thank the Society of Jesus and my brothers for all the goodness and loyalty and help they have given me in these last difficult weeks. I beg your forgiveness for much that I have said and done that was wrong or false, and I beg you also not to forget my parents, who are old and sick.

The only reason that I have been condemned is that I am and I remain a Jesuit. There was never any question of connecting me with July 20 or of finding some incriminating link with Stauffenberg [the ringleader of the conspiracy].

Hypothesis: A Jesuit is a priori the enemy and the adversary of the state. The whole thing has not entirely been a farce, since it contains the germ of this important truth. I was not condemned by a court but by a manifestation of the instinct for self-destruction.

May the Lord God protect you all. I earnestly solicit all your prayers, and I shall take some pains to make up for everything up there that I have not yet atoned for here below. When it gets on toward noon, I shall still be celebrating, and then in God's name I shall entrust myself to his divine guidance and direction. May God bless you all.

Gratefully,

Alfred Delp, S.J.

While awaiting execution in Plötzensee prison, near Berlin, Father Delp was permitted to subscribe to a written profession signifying his acceptance of the fourth vow and his submission to the Order. His wrists were handcuffed together as he signed this document, and his signature was witnessed by his jailers. Now at least he was free to speak his mind and, in spite of his formal profession of obedience, he was not entirely uncritical of the Church, which in a certain sense was responsible for his predicament. This was the subject of one of his final meditations in his cell: "A cultural and intellectual history . . . that is truly honest would have to include the contributions of the churches to the rise of the "mass man," of collectivism, and the various dictatorial forms of government."* This chapter would also have to have some mention of the delegates to the Eucharistic Congress reviewing the fleet at Taranto, of the swastika banners in the German churches, and the pastoral addresses conveying the bishop's birthday greetings to "the Führer."

Even ten years earlier, by the mid-thirties, it was clear to the average German Jesuit that the Church's loss of perspective where the dictatorships were concerned was a catastrophic failure of judgment. It was clear, in other words, that Nazi Germany had not turned out to be one of those reliably autocratic states to which the Church and the Order had so often linked their fortunes in the past. In 1945 the remaining Jesuits in the German provinces were only one among many small communities in that bombed-out generation who had learned the art of living under ground, like the early Christians in the catacombs. They had dutifully subscribed to the terms of the papal concordat with the Nazis, though not without some misgivings, and the dictatorships had repaid them very badly for their trust. Still, it was also during this period that the Order really began to take on its modern character, and the Jesuits of Germany, Italy, and Spain had learned more political wisdom at first hand than the Vatican itself.

---

* Hermann Rauschning (died 1982), a onetime crony of Hitler's who fled from Germany in 1936, reported a conversation in which Hitler himself acknowledged a much more direct connection: "Above all I have learned from the Jesuits. And so did Lenin too, as far as I recall. The world has never known anything quite so splendid as the hierarchical structure of the Catholic Church. There were quite a few things I simply appropriated from the Jesuits for the use of the Party."

PART ✤ XIII

ORA IN LABORAE—THE JESUITS TODAY

The gospel of Loyola was the most portentous of all times.

— *Thomas Carlyle (1795–1881)*

The entire purpose of the Jesuits is to promulgate the doctrine that the blackest deeds can be forgiven and to point the way for the most unregenerate sinners back into the good graces of the Church.

— *Adolf von Harnack (1851–1930)*

SPIRITUAL SUICIDE—THE JESUITS ON THE DEFENSIVE

If the Jesuits prewar reputation as curators and conservators of the old European order had survived the 1960's intact, then it was certainly shattered in September 1972, when a speaker arose in the Swiss cantonal assembly to address the proposition that Article 51 should be repealed. "The Jesuits," he observed, "are among the most progressive forces in the Catholic Church today." The speaker was none other than the leader of the *Partei der Arbeit,* the Swiss Communist party, and over a hundred years after the Syllabus of Errors, the Order at last had come to terms with modernity, or at least vice versa. But during the sixties the closer they came to Karl Marx, or so it seemed, the further away they got from the Pope, and in spite of all the brave talk of reform, by the early 1970's the Order was facing the most serious crisis of its four-hundred-year history. This, at least, was the view of Father Ludwig Volk, a German Jesuit who apparently felt that these desperate times cried out for desperate remedies, since he broke one of the Order's strictest unwritten laws by allowing his analysis of the current crisis to appear in print, in the German weekly *Die Welt,* under the title "Christian Soldiers Out of Step" (July 7, 1973). The following week a second unwritten law—that one does not publicly criticize a fellow Jesuit—was broken when *Die*

Welt also printed a reply to Father Volk's article by Professor Karl Rahner, S.J., in which he raked his Jesuit compère over the coals for 120 lines of closely printed text: "written in a flashy tabloid style that strays very far from the truth indeed," "simply ludicrous," "subjective bias," "distorted," "misunderstandings of history on the part of would-be historians," and so forth. Finally Father Rahner gets to the heart of the matter: "It is not so much that we have gotten out of step, it is simply that we have gotten out of the habit of goosestepping in unison, which by the way was not a maneuver that was introduced by Ignatius but rather developed during the restoration of the Church during the nineteenth century." (This sounds plausible enough, but it is also true that, as Jesuits are admonished in the *Constitutions*, "Insofar as possible we should, according to the words of the Apostle, feel as one and speak as one.")

In fact, the more immediate origins of this dispute are to be found in the events of the 1950's, when, as far as Pius XII and his circle of Jesuit advisers were concerned, God was in his heaven and all was right with the world, or almost all at any rate. As you may recall Pius had served as apostolic nuncio in Germany before the war and most of these advisers were Germans, including Fathers Robert Leiber and Wilhelm Hendrich; many of Pius's public statements on social issues were drafted by Father Gustav Grundlach, and Father August (later Cardinal) Bea was the Pope's confessor. In those days it seemed that all things really needed was a few timely adjustments to set them right again—the Jesuits thought that, as far as the Church's inglorious record on social and political issues was concerned, they could repaint the whole murky canvas with a series of delicate brushstrokes, like the tiny dabs of color in a pointillist painting. The ecclesiastical year was remodeled one day at a time, for example, so that May Day, the international socialist holiday, became, with Pius's blessing, "the liturgical feast of St. Joseph the carpenter," chosen as the heavenly representative of the industrious laboring classes on May 1, 1955. Pius's one recorded attempt to reform the Jesuits did not meet with much success, perhaps because it was couched in the form of a fatherly suggestion rather than a pontifical edict: "Among the superfluous things that a Jesuit could very well do without is the habit of smoking tobacco."

This pronouncement did not result in an immediate auto-da-fé of all the cigarettes and tobacco pouches in the Jesuit residence houses; the Jesuits responded instead with a casuist interpretation (provided by Professor Burkhart Schneider, S.J., of the Gregoriana) that considerably blunted its force. The Pope had suggested that "superfluous things" should be dispensed with, and yet, Professor Schneider reasoned, "for many of us smoking is an absolute necessity that permits us to get on with our work. This is a matter that each of us must work out with his individual conscience."

But in those days there was still very little that was left up to the dictates of one's individual conscience, and fathers who were at all premature or incautious in their inquiries into these questions of social reform were still likely to be reprimanded. Manuscripts intended for publication still had to be submitted for the approval of the office of the Superior General, and on one occasion (according to *Der Spiegel,* which is usually well informed on matters concerning the Jesuits) Professor Karl Rahner himself had to be rescued by a last-minute petition campaign from the doctrinal watchdogs of the Holy Office. This was not too long before the Second Vatican Council—Vatican II—convened in 1962, and although the new Pope, John XXIII, was not really inclined to be any less conservative than his predecessor, he was not able to hold out very long against the reformist enthusiasm of the majority of the bishops in the council. The impulse for spiritual renewal and reform appeared to be irresistible, and, at the time at least, it was no less astonishing that so many of the more radical items on the council's agenda were first proposed and sponsored by Jesuits: the principle of collective (collegial) responsibility of the bishops assembled in council (sponsored by Professor Rahner), the separation of church and state (Father John C. Murray), freedom of conscience and the principle that all religions should enjoy the same rights and be afforded the same treatment (Cardinal Bea). These three examples are all drawn from the council's initial agenda for 1962—which also brought up a number of old heresies to be reexamined (skepticism, the possibility that Catholics might reasonably question the historical existence of Jesus Christ) and new ethical alternatives (most notably the practice of chemical birth control, the Pill) to be debated for the first time.

The final resolutions adopted by the council in 1965 really signaled the end of the Counter-Reformation and the inauguration of this new "ecumenical" era in the history of the Church. The Jesuits had swept the opposition before them on virtually all fronts, but this tactical triumph threatened to turn into a strategic defeat—since, as their opponents were quick to point out, it was questionable that there was any need for a militant Society of Jesus in a pacifist, ecumenical, egalitarian Catholic

Church. The Thirty-first General Congregation of the Order was convened on May 7, 1965, and essentially its purpose was to provide an answer to this very question. The sessions, which lasted until November 17, 1966, were attended by the eighty-four Jesuit provincials, as well as the elected delegates of the individual provinces, in the Curia of the Superior General in Rome. In the interim John XXIII had been succeeded by Paul VI in 1963, and in 1965 General Johan Baptist Janssens died after a reign of eighteen years (though in his last few years he was really too infirm to carry out the responsibilities of his office in much more than a nominal wày). His successor was Pedro Arrupe, the first General of Basque descent since Ignatius himself, a small man with a lively and penetrating gaze who had studied medicine before entering the Order and then had gone on to complete his education by studying philosophy in Belgium and theology in Holland. His career as a Jesuit had been spent primarily in Japan, where, as provincial, he had had no more than 325 in his charge. Now, as Superior General, he had become chief executive of his organization with thirty-three thousand members, and his first departure from tradition was the atmosphere of openness and intimacy—of "dialogue," to use the signature phrase of the ecumenical era—that characterized his regime from the outset; it certainly would never have occurred to anyone to give him a nickname like "the Black Pope" or "the Old Man of the Mountains."* Arrupe embraced the concept of publicity in all its forms, gave press conferences, TV interviews, and allowed a collection of his speeches to be published. In two years' time he had traveled more miles than all ten of his predecessors put together.

It was General Arrupe who had decided to convene the Thirty-second General Congregation, the principal business of which was expected to give substance to the General's wish that "the Order should be completely pervaded by the spirit of Vatican II." The council had formally acknowledged that the Church was at least partially to blame for the destruction of the unity of Christianity, and although it had been some time ago that this had all taken place, a serious effort to make amends was clearly in order. Cardinal Bea was named as the first director of the Papal Secretariat for the Unity of Christianity—an unmistakable signal that the Order, originally devised and frequently employed as the cutting

---

*A name that was originally given to the head of the medieval Muslim sect of the Assassins, who were renowned both for their ruthlessness and ferocity and their fanatical attachment to their chief.

edge of the Counter-Reformation, was now intended to advance the cause of ecumenical dialogue in a sincere and practical way. This also provided an answer to the troubling question, What place remains for the Jesuits in an ecumenical Church?—which was, apparently, The same place where they have always been, at the very center of things, where policy is determined and the real decisions are made. (Another, more tangible relic of the Counter-Reformation, the *Ratio Studiorum,* the governing statute of the Jesuit education system, was significantly revamped at the same time; the number of compulsory lectures was reduced, the provision that lectures be delivered only in Latin was dropped, and the examination system was made somewhat less rigorous.)

General Arrupe's opening address to the Congregation was disarmingly candid; he announced that the Order was undergoing a "crisis of confidence," which he explained by saying, "Today it is no longer a question of bringing people the light, as it once was, but of teaching them how to lead independent lives and to develop their individual personalities." This was interpreted by the radical wing of the Order as a signal that this new dispensation should apply to Jesuits as well; they wanted to eliminate the stricter provisions of the *Constitutions* that established a kind of statutory minimum for prayer, penance, and other individual observances, as well as to replace the hierarchical principle of obedience with something more along the lines of parliamentary democracy. This, the delegates decided, was going too far, especially since Pope Paul had already made it clear that he felt that a number of the reformers had imbibed the spirit of Vatican II perhaps a bit too freely and that it was time to call a halt.

On the final day that the General Congregation was in session, November 17, Pope Paul celebrated mass before the delegates in the Sistine Chapel, which was intended as a particular mark of favor, though it also furnished the occasion for a confrontation of sorts. Afterward he delivered a brief address to the delegates that began with an allusion to the extraordinary works of art by which they were surrounded—Michelangelo's *Last Judgment,* for one, is directly above the altar—and went on to ask a question of the delegates that may not have been entirely rhetorical: "Do you, Sons of Ignatius, wish to remain for today, for tomorrow, and for eternity, what you have always been for the Catholic Church and for this Apostolic Throne since the founding of your Order? Can the

Church, can Peter's successor, still look to you as their truest and most devoted men-at-arms?"

The Pope went on to explain to his astonished audience that he was only prompted to ask this question because he had been receiving reports about the Jesuits and some of the other orders as well that had caused him both "pain" and "astonishment." There were four main tendencies or "deviations" that had caused particular concern:

The first was a tendency to think too much along "historical" lines—a diplomatic way of referring to the Order's early predilection for developing an independent theology of its own, which, according to these reports, appeared to be experiencing a revival.

The second was the tendency to neglect the contemplative life in favor of a more active involvement in worldly affairs, which was particularly aimed at those Jesuits who had proposed that the practice of the spiritual exercises be done away with.

The third was an especially dangerous tendency toward secularization: "Perhaps," the Pope observed, "there are those who are entertaining the delusion that the propagation of the Gospel would be facilitated by the adoption of a secular mode of life."

The fourth was a more generalized tendency toward autonomy and self-determination, which of course could only be realized at the expense of the principle of obedience: "The assumption seems to be that this principle of strict and manly obedience should be relaxed somewhat, as if it were harmful to one's character or to one's personal efficiency."

The shattering effect of the initial barrage was softened somewhat by the personal appeal that followed (along with its soothing implication that none of those present had themselves been infected by any of these tendencies): "The Church needs your assistance, since she is glad, and proud, to claim you as her upright and dutiful sons." And since no one, not even the Pope, seems to be able to speak of the Jesuits without lapsing into military metaphor, the delegates were finally assured that "new weapons will be forged to replace those that have lost their edge, in the old spirit of self-denial and spiritual self-mastery."

The last organ notes of the recessional had scarcely died away when the teleprinters began to clatter all over Europe. A number of papers (which apparently maintained their clipping files in excellent order) were able to point out that Pope Clement VIII had addressed a similar rebuke to the Fifth General Congregation in 1594: "To speak quite candidly, you must beware of the sin of pride, above all." Others took the view that Pope Paul had only spoken so sternly because he was especially disappointed to find that these "deviations" had taken root among the Jesuits (and if it had been any other order he would scarcely have mentioned it).

General Arrupe finally held a press conference at which a mimeographed statement was distributed that neither sought to contest these charges nor to furnish additional proof of their accuracy but merely pointed out that His Holiness had only been referring to the errors of a few specific individuals and that his "loving and fatherly words" were in no way to be interpreted as an indictment or a rebuff. (Finally, having discharged his duty to the Apostolic Throne and the principle of strict obedience, the General went on to add that though he had no intention of defending these specific individuals, in his view the most destructive error of all was committed by those who *remained inactive* for fear of finding themselves in error, and in this respect, he assured the journalists present, the Jesuits were not to be faulted nor were they ever likely to be in the future. This final pronouncement was not for the benefit of the public but rather for the consumption of the conservative faction within the Church, and the tone of the General's remarks did not suggest that relations between them were likely to improve.)

THE ORDER TAKES INVENTORY—THE POPE, THE JESUITS, AND THE JEWS

These events had come as that much more of a shock to many Jesuits because Paul VI, a graduate of the Gregoriana, had initially seemed to be rather well disposed toward the Order. In 1965 he had entrusted an elite task force of two hundred Jesuits with the conduct of his apostolic campaign against atheism (which will be the subject of the next chapter), and in the first year of his pontificate, 1963, he had chosen four Jesuit delegates from Italy, Germany, France, and the United States to prepare a collection of Vatican state papers for publication as a way of replying to the persistent charges that Pope Pius XII had been fully aware of the extent of Nazi wartime atrocities—particularly the roundup of the Jews—but had nevertheless refused to speak out against them. Normally these materials would have remained in the Vatican archives for a century or more, but Pope Paul was particularly anxious to clear the memory of his predecessor, and an additional reason for this untimely haste had been presented by the controversial success of Rolf Hochhuth's play *The Deputy*—a controversy that burned nowhere more brightly than in Rome, where all performances of the play had tactfully been forbidden.

The protagonist of *The Deputy* is a young Jesuit, Father Riccardo Fontana, who has witnessed the Nazi persecution of the Jews in Berlin and been sickened by it; he finally arranges to take the place of a Jew who is about to be deported to Auschwitz after he fails to persuade Pope Pius XII to speak out publicly against the Nazi Final Solution. (The title of the play is taken from a passage in "an underground Polish pamplet": "The world is silent. The world knows what is going on here—it cannot help but know, and it is silent. And in the Vatican the deputy of God is silent, too." *)

The character of Father Fontana is based on two historical figures, Father Bernhard Lichtenberg, provost of Berlin Cathedral, and Father Maximilian Kolbe, a Polish Franciscan who sacrificed his life at Auschwitz to save a fellow inmate. Neither of these men was a Jesuit, of course, and no actual Jesuit is known to have performed such an act of self-sacrifice, so perhaps Hochhuth was casting to type, in accordance with the maxim that the Jesuits are capable of anything, in the best and the worst sense of the term. It is a bit surprising that *The Deputy,* which was an enormous success onstage, was never made into a film. Perhaps would-be producers were scared off by the "controversial" subject? In fact, the rights were secured very early in the game by a French production company; the film itself remains in limbo. (*Honi soit qui mal y pense.*)

The actual task of sifting through the documents in the case was performed by an international team of Jesuit scholars—Fathers Pierre Blet, Robert A. Graham, Angelo Martini, and Burkhart Schneider. The archive included all official communications between the German government and the Vatican, memoranda of conversations, the collected correspondence of Pius XII, transcripts of the broadcasts of the Vatican radio station, plus a great deal of other material that was judiciously supplemented with reliable information from foreign sources. Three of the projected ten volumes had appeared by 1967; the series was collectively entitled *Records and Documents of the Holy See Concerning the Sec-*

---

*Quoted from the Grove Press edition, translated by Richard and Clara Winston (1964).

ond World War, and several of the 606 documents that were published in the first installment did indicate that Pius XII had had a much clearer idea of what was actually going on than his partisans were at first disposed to admit.

But even Hochhuth was not prepared to accuse Pius XII of anti-Semitism as such, but rather of the crime described by General Arrupe as "deliberate inaction"—though certainly the record of the Church in our century is tainted with a great deal of both. Theologians have even coined the term "anti-Judaism" to distinguish purely religious prejudice (of which Luther's is a notorious example) from race hatred of the Nazi variety. The term has not achieved much currency, since in practice the two are not always distinct, and in any case the development of political anti-Semitism in Europe in the twentieth century is inconceivable without the background of religious "anti-Judaism" that is virtually as ancient as Christianity itself. During the Nazi period certain Catholic writers even attempted to insure the "racial purity" of the principal figures of the New Testament by various ingenious dialectical exercises. Alfred Mirgeler solemnly explained in a publication called *Catholica* in 1933 that the doctrine of the Virgin Birth "has freed our Redeemer from any biological connection with his people on his father's side," and similarly the doctrine of the Immaculate Conception "has lifted up His Mother from amidst the corruption of Original Sin, which was decreed for the Jews and the pagans, and at the same time freed her from the imprint of this corruption which is particularly apparent in Jewish secularism." Even the Jesuit paper *Voices of the Times* contained an occasional echo of this sort of turgid nonsense, as when a telltale phrase like "for the sake of the racial purity of its posterity, the Church was always the most vigilant guardian of the purity of the Roman and later the Germanic races" turns up in an article entitled "Judah and Rome" (written by a popular religious writer, Hugo Rahner, the brother of Professor Karl Rahner, S.J., in 1934). But in those days it was actions rather than words that counted most, and a surprising number of Jesuits risked their lives to help save Jewish refugees and fugitives from Hitler's Final Solution; they received too little recognition when the need for secrecy was finally at an end, but the name of Father Ludger Born, who set up a way station in Vienna to assist Jewish fugitives from the Nazis (at the request of the bishops of the archdiocese), at least deserves to be mentioned in this connection.

Curiously enough, the Order has always had a reputation as a refuge for Jewish converts; Ignatius's secretary, Juan de Polanco, was accused by his adversaries within the Order of being a "New Christian," as baptized Jews (especially those whose conversions were less than sincere) were called in Spain and Portugal. Ignatius himself was hardly likely to have been troubled by such an accusation. "What a stroke of luck," he once said, "to be related to Christ our Lord and His Holy Mother, the Blessed Virgin." (Perhaps this is what led the French writer Roger Peyrefitte to suggest that Ignatius himself was of Jewish descent, since he offers no other evidence for this conjecture.) Ignatius's successor as General of the Order, Diego Lainez, was descended from a prominent New Christian family, as he makes clear in his autobiography; no one seems to have thought very much about this at the time, but in 1620 (when Lainez had been dead for over fifty years) General Vitelleschi received a petition from a group of Jesuits in the province of Toledo who felt "it would be accounted a great shame, as well as a sin, to suffer a General of the Order and one of its founders to be branded with this mark of infamy." They suggested, however, that the "stigma" might be retroactively removed, or in other words "that that which is written in the second volume of the history of the Society concerning the ancestry of Father Diego Lainez should be struck out."

This suggestion was not adopted, but for a time the descendants of New Christians or converted Muslims were not permitted to join the Order—and, according to Father Hubert Becher in his history of the Jesuits, a rigid genealogical search was actually carried out in disputed cases as far back as five generations. Nevertheless, by the end of the seventeenth century the Jesuits were being accused of having "defiled" the purity of Christian doctrine with their "rabbinical-pharisaical mentality" and obscured the clarity of New Testament morality with "subtle Talmudic incantations." (This is somewhat reminiscent of the fictional Jewish Jesuit Leo Naphta, the cold-hearted, caustic rationalist whom Hans Castorp encounters in Thomas Mann's *The Magic Mountain*.) Even after the restoration of the Order in 1814, when a particularly benighted anti-Semitism had become the official policy of Jesuit publications like *Civiltà Cattolica*, more traditional-minded thinkers like Kaiser Wilhelm I were still hinting darkly that "the Jews and the Jesuits always flock together" (in the course of a conversation reported by Bismarck), just as the Order was routinely described in hostile political pamphlets of the period as "a catch basin for rich Jewish brats." In recent years one has been more likely to hear it asserted that Jewish converts were not permitted to join the Order until 1945, which is not strictly correct—the sons of baptized Jewish parents have always been eligible for membership in the Order in modern times at least, though formerly by special application, a fact that is unhappily borne out by the Jewish surnames of the Jesuit fathers who were expelled from Germany in the days of the Third Reich.

"THE PRECIOUS GIFT OF FAITH"—THE JESUITS AND THE CRUSADE AGAINST ATHEISM

Like many of the later and lesser-known crusades of the Middle Ages, the campaign against atheism began, on May 1, 1965, with a stirring papal proclamation and was almost immediately forgotten. "To you of the Society of Jesus," Pope Paul told the two hundred Jesuits in a special audience, "we entrust the task of combating atheism with all the courage and all the strength that you can muster—to you whose duty it is to defend the Church and our holy faith in times of need." Certainly the Jesuit task force had been given what is usually called a sweeping mandate, since, as the Pope had informed them during this introductory background briefing, atheism "in our times is sometimes paraded openly, sometimes hidden, sometimes masked, it may have many faces, and it may be concealed beneath the mantle of progress, whether economic, cultural, or social." The announcement of the campaign against atheism was totally ignored by the press until four months later, when the original Vatican communiqué was hastily disinterred from the files. The reason for this belated surge of interest was a statement that General Arrupe had made in his first address to a full council of the Church; speaking to an audience of over two thousand Catholic bishops, he suddenly launched into a discourse on the papal crusade against atheism that was phrased in a way that clearly implied that the Holy Father had sent out a call to arms to all of Christendom (instead of issuing a set of rather vague instructions to a hand-picked Jesuit battalion).

This announcement was greeted with what one observer described as "silent astonishment," as General Arrupe plunged straight into his next topic—the "perfectly conceived strategy" by which atheism, in its various guises, "has poisoned the minds of devout Catholics and even priests themselves by inciting mistrust and dissension within the Church."

Atheism, the General went on to say, also wields "almost unlimited power in international organizations, in the financial world, and the mass media: television, film, radio, and in the press." There are those who believe even today that the General's intentions here were purely malicious, that they were actually meant to embarrass the Pope, who was scheduled to address the foremost of these "international organizations"—the UN General Assembly—in a couple of days' time.

In fact, it became clear enough before long that, in spite of the inflammatory tone of General Arrupe's remarks, the Jesuits' campaign against atheism was not likely to amount to very much—a suspicion that was partially confirmed when it was announced that a special investigative committee had been set up to study the problem more closely, or in other words, to provide a workable definition of atheism that would allow the two-hundred-man Jesuit task force to begin closing in on their quarry. This in itself proved to be no easy task, however. Jesuits from the Slavic countries expected that the battle against the godless Marxists would be joined immediately, while the German faction, led by Professor Karl Rahner, decided to set up a series of roundtable discussions with Communist party officials in Salzburg on the theme of atheism as a political ideology; the editors of *Civiltà Cattolica* in Rome were scandalized by this, of course, and refused even to sit down at the same table with Communists.

Those who were familiar with the history of the Order expressed some surprise that the Jesuits had been chosen to lead the fight against atheism in the first place, which seemed a bit incongruous—"like sending the monkey to guard the peanuts," as Nikita Khrushchev used to say—since for centuries the Jesuits have had to contend with the charge that they were little better than atheists themselves and that not even the Good Lord knew what they really thought and what they really believed. Perhaps they were simply reluctant to reawaken these ancient slanders, but in any case this was the last that was heard of the crusade against atheism for another ten years—until the Pope reminded them once again that it would be "a timely expression of your vow of obedience with respect to the Pope" if they rededicated themselves to the task with renewed vigor. Five years after that, in 1979, General Arrupe sent out a seven-page circular letter instructing his fellow Jesuits not to hang back in the fight against atheism and reminding them that after all they had "been presented gratis with the precious gift of faith," which seems to strike an oddly materialistic note in the midst of this antimaterialist exhortation. Perhaps as a way of making the task seem more congenial he

---

ARRUPE ON ATHEISM

The battle against atheism can be identified, at least in part, with the battle against poverty, since poverty was one of the reasons that the working classes have abandoned the Church.

—1965

The prevailing injustice which seeks in its various forms to deny the rights and dignity of mankind as a creature that is made in God's image and as the brother of Christ—that is the practice of atheism, that is the denial of God.

—1976

---

also provided them with a new and highly subjective definition of atheism: "They should not be counted among the unbelievers who do not share our faith in Jesus Christ if they can receive God into their hearts and reserve a place for him in their lives." This seems about as far as it is possible to get from the Counter-Reformation spirit of the statue of Ignatius in St. Peter's who is treading the dragon of "unbelief" beneath his right foot. *Tempora mutantur, nos et mutamur in illis.**

Arrupe's letter goes on to extend his progressive, post-Ignatian definition of "unbelief" a little further by emphasizing the need for greater candor and increased self-criticism among Catholics (not just among Jesuits), since, for example, he finds that the *potential* for unbelief is more widespread among Sunday Christians than among dissident religious sects. Next, the General reminds his fellow Jesuits, "We must confess that we are all more or less beginners (intellectuals not excluded) as far as this new subject of unbelief in its current form and its currently widespread dispersal are concerned." The letter closes, however, with a recommendation that is straightforward and pragmatic enough to be called Ignatian in the best sense of the word.

What we need above all is a change of style and method, a change of approach and content. In order to make genuine

---

*"The times change, and we change with them."

281

contact with those who do not believe or who doubt their own faith, it would be well worth our while to discover a way of seeing that will be new to many people and to teach them a way of talking about God that will have as little as possible to do with the conventional, the stereotyped, and the anachronistic, but will be able to make a connection with their own experiences of reality and to address itself to their most personal problems.

ORA IN ACTIONE—WORKER PRIESTS AND WAR RESISTERS

The first step toward "genuine contact" of the kind recommended by General Arrupe was actually taken while his predecessor, General Janssens, was still in office. The first of the so-called "worker priests" exchanged their soutanes for the traditional blue coveralls of the European working class and stood shoulder-to-shoulder with their fellow workers on the picket lines as well as the assembly line; this was simply the ultimate logical extension of the Benedictine *ora et laborae* ("prayer and work"), which was transformed by Ignatius into *ora in laborae* ("prayer in work"). During their student days in Paris, Ignatius and three companions had taken up residence in a kind of municipal shelter for homeless vagabonds, sold their textbooks, and split the proceeds with the inmates, but the college authorities called out the watch to restore them to their dormitories by force.

Later, but before the Order was officially chartered, a number of Ignatius's disciples chose to live among the poor, but the worker priests of our own era were inspired by social and political (rather than ascetic or symbolic) motives. The fear was expressed by many that these worker priests would be so seriously distracted by their factory jobs and their gritty proletarian surroundings that they would lose contact altogether with the spiritual ideals of the Order. Pius XII was most unsympathetic to the aims of the worker-priest movement, whose activities were so severely restricted during his pontificate that it could scarcely be said to exist at all—though even this was too much for the editors of *Civiltà Cattolica,* who commented with their usual asperity, "The priests have learned nothing from this experience while their life among the workers has made a mockery of their vows of chastity." But when the campaign against atheism was proclaimed by Pope Paul, the critics were overruled, the restrictions lifted, and the worker-priest movement was given its head, which immediately resulted in a sharp swing to the left. A note of social protest was rarely absent from their reports on conditions in the factories in which they worked, as when, for example, a French Jesuit who was working alongside foreign "guest workers" in a German factory noted sardonically in May 1975, "My colleagues here in the factory are Turks, Italians, Spaniards, Yugoslavs, and Greeks. German workers turn up, like meteors, and permit us to get a glimpse of them from time to time." (In France, the cradle of the worker-priest movement, their current headquarters is located on the Rue Lénine in Paris, though I was assured by the Jesuit fathers on duty there that this was purely a coincidence.)

Other Jesuits attempted to make "genuine contact" with doubters and unbelievers by sharing their living conditions as well as their working conditions. Thus, until June 1981 three young Jesuits lived in a building in Innsbruck that had originally been intended as a barracks, had later seen service as a prison, and was currently being used as public housing. The report of their experiences that appeared in the June 1980 issue of *Entschluss* (*Decision*), the Austrian Jesuit newsletter, made it clear that the lack of spiritual comfort was hardly the root of the problem. There were two hundred people, seventy of them children and adolescents, living in the former barracks complex. Thirty-five of these children belonged to just three families; there were three-year-olds who had not yet learned to talk. The apartment occupied by the Jesuits was one of the largest in the complex: a long "culvert," like a Quonset hut, about seven feet by fourteen, divided by two doors into three tiny rooms, "running water and toilet about thirty yards away from the corridor; an additional special feature, it was only possible to get outside by climbing over a balcony."

If the conservative Jesuits were concerned that these social experiments would eventually lead to the total secularization of the rising generation of Jesuits, then the younger progressives were equally anxious to escape the "cloistered" "ghetto mentality" of the traditional Jesuit residence. In 1969, for example, a Jesuit father and four brothers who had not yet taken their final vows rented a house on the outskirts of Munich where they intended to live "communally" until they had completed their studies. It seems especially significant that this anecdote of the alienated "uncommitted" sixties has a conventional petty-bourgeois happy ending—although the four brothers eventually left the Order, the Jesuit father has since risen to the rank of provincial and now holds the office of chairman of the German provincial conference. In this connection two points seem to be worth noting: first, that this particular Jesuit father's penchant for social experimentation has obviously not done any harm to him in his subsequent career in the Order, and, second, at the height of the age of protest a 20 percent rate of recovery—one in five— does not seem so bad in the circumstances.

The left wing of the Order had taken so much encouragement from Pope Paul's crusade against atheism, as the term was helpfully interpreted by General Arrupe, that the "Jebbies" in the United States were soon making headlines almost every week with some new and ever more spectacular protest against oppression and injustice. One of the best known of these leftist enfants terribles was Father Daniel Berrigan, one of a group of priests who had interrupted the bishop of Cleveland while he was saying mass as a way of protesting Cardinal Spellman's defense of the bombing of North Vietnam, which they considered to be a form of "religious observance." As Father Berrigan commented at the time, "When everything's going downhill, then cardinals start to talk like generals and generals start to give sermons and march up and down in church."

Cardinal Spellman was not amused, and Father Berrigan was reassigned to a post in Central America at the cardinal's request. Berrigan himself submitted to exile dutifully. All his followers and partisans were not to be dispensed with so easily, and a number of fellow Jesuits—in the true spirit of postconciliar parliamentary democracy, even in America—threatened to resign from the Order if a satisfactory reason for his "reassignment" was not forthcoming. His superiors were forced to yield, and Father Berrigan was recalled from exile. As soon as he was back in New York, he gave a press conference to clarify his position publicly— which would have been no less unthinkable a decade or so earlier. During the 1950's the celebrated Jesuit evangelists Father Leppich and Father Riccardo Lombardini had both had their public-speaking careers terminated as the result of comparatively minor peccadillos. Father Berrigan continued to turn up at at every antiwar demonstration of any consequence, and the Order continued to look the other way. Should this be interpreted as a sign of weakness? It would be safer to say that the internal balance of power of the Order had simply shifted, and Father Berrigan's antiwar activities were only interrupted by the intervention of the secular arm.

He and a group of fellow activists were charged with setting fire to a bundle of induction orders in a United States Army induction center and sentenced to three years in prison. His provincial had been informed that the Order was not prepared to post bail, and his superiors might have been tempted to regard it as still another divine dispensation when this hotheaded, unruly Irishman was finally put behind bars. Then something quite unexpected happened—General Arrupe himself came to visit Berrigan in prison. This was a cardinal work of mercy that required some personal courage, since Father Berrigan had already been disavowed by the Vatican and the hierarchy of the Order. Perhaps this gesture on General Arrupe's part was meant to express his conviction that in a self-policing, self-reforming order like the Jesuits, the dissidents and the adherents of unpopular causes should always have a certain sense of esprit de corps to sustain them.

Since then Father Berrigan has served his original stretch and is back behind bars again. In mid-1981 he was convicted of sabotaging nuclear warheads in a missile assembly plant (by drenching them with animal's blood) and was sentenced to another ten years in prison.

THE OTHER SIDE OF THE COIN—THE CONSERVATIVE JESUITS

While General Arrupe was trying to rally the Order with his call for "a life of poverty, simplicity, relentless activity, a life spent among the poor, a life of obedience, utility, and chastity," the Jesuits, however, were not necessarily forming up in a solid phalanx behind him. The Order was no longer such a tightly knit cadre as it had been in the past, and apart from the progressive Jesuits manning the advanced outposts of social reform there was still a staunch derrière garde of conservatives who might have endorsed the General's objectives in theory but whose actual approach to the problems of the day would have differed considerably both in form and content. While French Jesuits were taking part in protest demonstrations against the deployment of the neutron bomb in Europe, American Jesuits were drawing up a position paper of their own in which they dryly asserted that a thermonuclear bomb was not inherently more reprehensible than a Stone Age flint ax. And despite the activities of Father Berrigan, the "official" position of the Order on nuclear weapons still falls short of absolute pacifism; it would probably come closer to that expressed by Professor Gustav Grundlach, S.J., former rector of the Gregoriana, in 1959: "The application of atomic weapons in warfare is not unconditionally an immoral act."

And certain old-line Jesuits seem to be hanging back as far as General Arrupe's exhortation to create a new language that avoids anything that savors of the "conventional, the stereotyped, or the anachronistic" is concerned. A remarkable though perhaps unintentional example of this was furnished by a report of the German provincial conference in April 1981, which contained the sentence "In other words, the necessary 'contractions of the front' will have to be considered jointly." This expression, "contractions of the front" (which more usually appeared as "rectifications of the front," Frontbegradigungen) began to appear in Wehrmacht communiqués in 1943 as a stylish euphemism for "retreat," the mere mention of which had been strictly forbidden by the Supreme Strategist. Even considering the Jesuits' long tradition of martial metaphor, the use of National Socialist jargon like this in a German-language Jesuit publication does not seem highly appropriate. And, as with any large organization with long traditions and conservative tendencies, the Order has come to harbor a number of oddities and ancient vestiges that are not, strictly speaking, either progressive or conservative but simply archaic and outlandish. Father Adolf Rodewyck, for example, is involved with a kind of anachronism that partakes more of the spirit than the letter—he is an exorcist, in fact, the first Jesuit known to have practiced this calling since the year 1583, when a certain Father Scherer is said to have cast out precisely 12,652 demons who had taken possession of a young girl.

The unconventional career of Father Mario Schoenenberger provides a closer parallel to that of Père LaValette and some of the more shameless Jesuit entrepreneurs of the eighteenth century. Born in Switzerland, Father Schoenenberger had attained the position of regional assistant for East and West Germany, Switzerland, Austria, Holland, and Hungary in 1965—the Jesuit equivalent of a cabinet-level post. Everything went smoothly until 1968, when he decided to cash in on the financial expertise and the numerous useful contacts he had acquired in the service of the Order—by putting together a multimillion dollar commodities deal.

He approached the West German agricultural minister, Hermann Höcherl (a member of the Christian Socialist Union), with an appealing proposition; he was in touch with a prospective purchaser for the ministry's twenty-two hundred tons of surplus butter (which was just about to turn). In view of these special circumstances, Father Schoenenberger's broker's commission of a million Deutschmarks (out of a total purchase price of about DM 5.7 million) was not thought to be excessive, particularly since the entire sum was to be donated to various development programs in the Third World. Later, however, when the West German federal accounting office requested verification of the claim that the entire million marks actually had been disbursed in this fashion, Father Schoenenberger was unable (or merely unwilling) to comply. A year after the deal had gone down, Father Schoenenberger resigned from his post as regional assistant and left the Order altogether: At the time he was said to have done this in order to protest the official harassment of a group of Dutch Jesuits (whose activities are discussed in the next chapter), but it seems much more likely that the principles that were really at stake were those of laissez-faire capitalist entrepreneurship (of which Father Schoenenberger was heartily in favor) and total financial accountability on the part of high-ranking officials (to which he was heartily opposed).

"THE THIRD WAY"—THE DUTCH CHALLENGE AND L'AFFAIRE DANIELOU

The news from Amsterdam in the late 1960's was disturbing enough to shake the political foundations of the Order and even to threaten the dissolution of all formal ties between the Dutch Catholic Church and the Vatican. The possibility of founding an autonomous Catholic community was being seriously discussed in the Netherlands, the Curia was in a state of permanent red alert, but the burning question that had touched off this crisis was not that of papal infallibility, nuclear disarmament, the Pill, or abortion, but the relatively "technical" issue of priestly celibacy*

*First declared to be obligatory for the entire priesthood by Pope Gregory VII in 1085; the current regulations governing clerical celibacy were incorporated into the *Codex juris catolici* (the authoritative compilation of the canon law) in 1917.

—more precisely, it was the celibacy of one particular Dutch priest, Father Jos Vrijburg, that was originally at issue. Father Vrijburg was a Jesuit and a probationary preacher who had decided to get married after seventeen years in the Order; he knew perfectly well that he could hardly expect to remain a Jesuit after his marriage, but he saw no reason why he should not continue to be a priest. Two of his fellow Jesuits, Fathers Oosterhuis and van der Stap, publicly supported this demand, which prompted an immediate response from General Arrupe—either they would have to accept the vow of chastity as binding on all Catholic priests, or they would have to leave the Order altogether. They chose to leave the Order, which simplified matters considerably for the Jesuits; now it was up to the Dutch bishops to decide whether—as Father Vrijburg and his colleagues had strongy suggested—the issue of priestly celibacy was really crucial enough to justify a complete break with Rome. After a few tense moments the bishop reached a decision of Solomonic simplicity—Father Vrijburg was permitted to preach, even after his marriage, as long as his sermons did not accompany the celebration of the mass or the administration of the Eucharist. An elegant if somewhat anticlimactic solution.

At about the same time American Jesuits had come up with the theory of the "third way," which embodied an entirely different sort of compromise. Of the three ways referred to, the first was the traditional state of Christian marriage, the second was clerical celibacy, the third—which was recommended for Jesuits before they had completed their education and been ordained—would have permitted seminarians to strike up platonic friendships with women at their discretion—except that the "third way" was promptly and categorically ruled out by General Arrupe. It is certainly not clear how long this prohibition will remain in force. The Chinese have a proverb to the effect that predictions are always dangerous, all the more so if they concern themselves with the future, but it seems permissible to predict in this case that no simple and unambiguous solution will be found for this "problem" of the priestly celibacy in the next hundred years.

A more recent incident that was noteworthy in this connection (though it did not make much of a contribution to the theoretical side of the question) was the death of Cardinal Jean Danielou in May 1974, remarkable in particular because it occurred in the Paris apartment of a nightclub hostess called Madame Santoni. Cardinal Danielou was a Jesuit, a brilliant intellect who had played an important role in the reform of the liturgy during the 1960's (although for some years before Vatican II he had been forbidden to write for publication). The Parisian popular press, no great respecter of the cloth, was most interested in the circumstances of the cardinal's death, of course, and the dearth of actual, authenticated details was more than made up for by a wealth of innuendo.

A year later a transcript of the official police investigation of the cardinal's death, along with a statement by the French provincial, was circulated by the Order, and it is worth noting that this was an internal document, not intended for the general public, which suggests that this kind of ribald speculation about the manner of the cardinal's death was not strictly confined to the French popular press. At any rate, it was still considered to be necessary to scotch whatever rumors were still in circulation, and the original police report was not necessarily all that helpful in this respect. Mme. Santoni's profession of "nightclub hostess" was not normally the sort of work that she could have done at home in her apartment; her husband had been arrested only three days earlier on a charge of procuring, though whether or not on her behalf was not specified in the report. Finally, the cardinal had brought three thousand francs with him to Mme. Santoni's apartment—the provincial's commentary immediately forestalls any irreverent speculation on this theme by asking innocently "Did he want to help her?" and then providing the answer: "This is the obvious hypothesis. In any case it is clear that the cardinal occasionally took a personal interest in helping prostitutes and other women who had gotten themselves into difficulties."

Meanwhile a blue-ribbon panel of prominent laymen was formed in Paris to conduct a further investigation and clear the cardinal's name, and perhaps in ten years' time historians of the Order will be pointing out the uncanny parallel between the circumstances of the cardinal's death and a remark that is actually attributed to Ignatius, that he would have given his life if in so doing he might have saved a harlot from the sins that she might have committed in the course of a single night. Like Cardinal Danielou, Ignatius and his comrades took a particular interest in helping women, particularly married women who had fallen into the hands of pimps and procuresses; Ignatius even founded a refuge for "fallen women" in Rome, where the repentant magdalenes, once admitted, were obliged to stay on until it was felt that they were sufficiently rehabilitated to take up their former places in respectable society.

A Bitter Pill—The Jesuits and the Encyclical *Humanae Vitae*

The Jesuits were asked to revive another old Ignatian practice in 1968—that of "making black seem white"—and in addition this spiritual sleight of hand would have to be performed before the eyes of millions of believers without their losing face or sacrificing their credibility as priests and interpreters of Catholic doctrine. The occasion of this ultimate test of loyalty was the publication of the encyclical *Humanae Vitae,* in which all forms of artificial birth control were expressly forbidden. Clearly this was an issue of much more than academic interest to the vast majority of Catholics, and the initial reaction of the community of believers was hardly favorable, ranging as it did from blank incomprehension to howls of outraged protest. Paul VI was probably the first Pope since Pius IX to be given a nickname—"Pope Pill," "*Pillen-Paul.*"

The Jesuits, particularly those in Third World countries, had made no secret of their approval of the Pill as an efficient and reliable means of birth control, but, as Jesuits, they were sworn to put obedience ahead of consistency. In case anyone had forgotten, General Arrupe issued several reminders in the form of two separate circular letters addressed "To the entire community":

> Criticisms of the encyclical have begun to crop up in so many different quarters that I can no longer restrain myself from issuing still one more reminder of what our task as Jesuits consists of. As far as our relationships with the successor of Peter are concerned, there can be no question of any other than unswerving and decisive loyalty, which should be accompanied by love, candor, and creative thought and is by no means easy or convenient.

Thus, with all possible avenues of escape or evasion blocked off, the General went on to specify more precisely what he meant by "creative thought"—not just the servile repetition of the verbal formulas employed in the encyclical but rather "a willingness to embark on an intensive course of study in order to discover its meaning and intent, both for oneself and for others." And next the General makes a third pass at the subject; this time he seems to be saying that the encyclical is to be regarded as an artifact of some transcendental realm of dogma where, perhaps, black really *is* white: "These views [expressed in the encyclical] may not at first be compatible with one's own, but it is only by transcending one's own individual perspective that their correctness will be revealed." Finally the problem of public recantation is to be approached in the same straightforward fashion: "We must not be afraid to publicly proclaim, where necessary, that we have since adopted an opinion that is completely different from those which we may have formerly held."

Certainly General Arrupe is not to be reproached for his lack of firmness in this particular matter, but nevertheless these letters were almost immediately repudiated by the spiritual elite of the Order, including the provincials of both German provinces, Father Krauss in Munich and Father Ostermann in Cologne. Unlike the antiwar protests in America and Father Vrijburg's campaign against celibacy in Holland, which began at about the same time and only involved a handful of activists in each case, this was a broadly based protest movement—palace rebellion might be the better term—which involved at least a sizable minority of the Order. The German protesters, for example, drafted a reply to the General's circular letters that was signed by over a hundred Jesuit fathers who attended a protest meeting at the St. Georg high school in Frankfurt—and in which the General was crisply informed that "the Society of Jesus cannot accept the position which you have made it our duty to adopt in both your letters."

The General had already been acquainted with the theoretical basis for their refusal (as had a number of others), which was contained in three position papers that had been prepared by leading Jesuit theologians; one of them stated the problem, tendentiously but neatly, like this: "Once it is granted that the sort of candor which the Superior General requires of us can only result in an unqualified affirmation of the doctrine under discussion, then the question of the relationship between truth and obedience seems to define itself with particular clarity." The petition drafted by the German provincials added their own commentary on this passage; they felt that too much stress had been placed on the duty of obedience "which has only served to confirm the suspicion that has been steadily growing among outside observers over the last few decades that it is not the objectivity of scientific research or a genuine search for the facts that really decides a question for the Jesuits, but rather an authoritative pronouncement from on high. It is this that has put our credibility in danger."

After flagrantly violating so many of the Order's most venerable taboos, the protesters must have found it quite a relief to catch their General out on an old-fashioned point of theology. In one of his original letters General Arrupe had incautiously observed that the encyclical *Humanae Vitae* was "universally binding not only by reason of the foregoing arguments but also by virtue of the participation of the Holy Ghost." However, as the Jesuits were quick to point out, the encyclical was merely intended as an authoritative summary of the Church's previous teachings on the subject—which *in itself* is not "universally binding" for precisely the reason that such compilations are *not* thought to be prepared by the Holy Father with "the participation of the Holy Ghost." Certainly this was not the central point in controversy, but at least the Jesuits had demonstrated their versatility once again by making such a success of their first serious venture into the realm of disobedience.

The protesters and the critics of the encyclical received two different answers from Rome. The Pope's was the more effective of the two—he remained silent, but his silence was nonetheless extremely eloquent, since he managed to convey the full measure of disappointment he felt in this betrayal by the Jesuits, who had been his preceptors at the Gregoriana and his trusted "men-at-arms." It was the General who would have to back down, and he sent out still a third circular letter in which he assured "the community" that his first two letters had apparently given rise to serious misunderstandings, since he had not intended "in any way to limit or foreclose the scientific and objective discussion of the questions raised by the encyclical." In fact, the discussion that ensued went far beyond the bounds of the objective and the scientific in an all-out campaign to prove that the arguments advanced in the encyclical were, in the words of Professor Rahner, "actually, materially, and substantially false, and yet," he added, "one might still say eventually, Thank God the Church has chosen to take a stand against blind, unbridled hedonism." Professor Rahner had helped to draft a response to the encyclical that was adopted by the Conference of German Bishops as their own official position on the subject, and the following excerpt from an interview that appeared in *Der Spiegel* in 1968 makes it clear exactly how far Professor Rahner's own position might have strayed from "objectivity":

INTERVIEWER: Can you imagine a situation in which a Catholic wife might be on the Pill and, after having examined her conscience, still feel that she was being obedient to the Pope?

RAHNER: Yes, I can imagine that she might feel that way subjectively. Whether she is objectively correct is still another question.

INTERVIEWER: But as far as both this woman and the Church are concerned, would it be enough that she felt this way subjectively?

RAHNER: Yes.

INTERVIEWER: And this woman would not be under any obligation to consult with her confessor about this as often as possible to make certain that her opinion is correct?

RAHNER: No. There is no need for her to mention it every time she goes to confession. If I am subjectively convinced . . . according to the subjective dictates of my conscience—and you can't get around your conscience, after all—that I've done the right thing, then whatever it is I've done is not something that I need to take up with my confessor.

You may recall the proverb quoted earlier that recommended that one choose a Jesuit confessor because "the Jesuits always put pillows under your elbows"; even today, in this age of anxiety and moral complexity, Jesuit morality still seems to be designed to enable an independent-minded Catholic with a tender conscience to rest a little easier.

PRAXIS MAKES PERFECT—THE JESUITS AS MARXISTS

No organization has occupied itself so intensively with the study of Marxism since the days of the old Socialist First International, and certainly no Catholic order has a more legitimate right to concern itself with social issues—and the problems of socialism—than the Society of Jesus. The biography of Ignatius Loyola does not have to be tampered with in the interests of trendy revisionism to make him out to be a "social reformer," since he already was one to begin with. He rejected the medieval idea that man can best serve God through a life of prayer and contemplation, since if that were so, as he put it, "then all prayers would be too short that took up less than twenty-four hours of every day." He wanted his followers "to serve God in all their actions." The founders of the contemplative orders had left splendid, lonely cloisters as their monuments; Ignatius drew up plans for a model shelter to house the beggars and homeless vagabonds who thronged the streets of the cities. He also took an interest in such progressive schemes as an employment service for the unemployed, a retirement home for old men who were unable to look after themselves, and a shelter for abused or neglected children.

It was not long, however, before the original program of the founder gave way to more urgent projects such as the Counter-Reformation, and Ignatius's agenda for social action has only found its way back to the top of the pile in the last couple of decades. It was Karl Marx—or rather his writings and the various schools of interpretation they have inspired—who was largely responsible for this turn of events. The intellectual elite of the Order has taken up the challenge posed by Marxist theory, belatedly but intensively, and the Jesuits who are involved in some sort of social action, particularly in the Third World, are likely to be confronted with Marxist-Leninist praxis in any one of its infinite varieties (some of which may be considerably less radical or progressive than the ideology espoused by the Jesuits themselves).

This was the "theology of liberation," first championed by the Jesuits of the Third World in the 1960's, who have since come to play an increasingly important role in the affairs of the Order. In Latin America especially, the Church as a whole began to make its influence felt in the political arena, even though the distinction between social action and political agitation was not all that easy to draw. Both the Jesuits and the defenders of the *status quo* have experienced some difficulties with this, since, as Professor von Nell-Brenning puts it, "human rights are still tainted with the suspicion of Marxism." On the other hand, Jesuits and leftist *guerrilleros* were continually thrown together in the headlines of the international press, and even the reports of their less inflammatory activities—"In Mexico City the Jesuits have closed their college for the children of the rich and gone out on the land to teach the peasants free of charge"—still left us with the impression that Latin America was nothing more than a vast progressive school for radical priests. (Perhaps Father Berrigan was exiled to Central America for the same reason that the mad Hamlet was to be sent to England—since he would be less likely to be noticed among so many others of his own kind.)

But this, as we now know, is only part of the story. In recent years the Jesuits have published a series of volumes entitled *The Persecution of*

Christians in South America. The 1981 edition gives a detailed account of the dangers faced by practicing (though not necessarily radical) Christians even in countries "whose rulers attend mass," a phenomenon that many of us may recently have become aware of in connection with El Salvador but whose extent is not generally realized: "How many already know that in the ten years between the assemblies of Latin American bishops in Medellín [Colombia] and Puebla [Mexico] on the 'Catholic' continent of South America . . . far more than 1500 Christians have been arrested, tortured, or murdered simply because they wished to live as Christians?"

But in spite of this ominous trend, the Church has remained steadfast in its determination to "speak out for those who have no voice," irrespective of what the political consequences may be—"There is very little that is inherently 'socialistic' in denouncing a social evil, in the same way that certain forms of anticommunism often consist of nothing more than an attempt to conceal the evidence of injustice." This last is a quotation from an essay written by General Arrupe entitled "On the Marxist Analysis of Society," which was specifically intended as a kind of position paper for the benefit of the provincials of Latin America and the Jesuit hierarchy in general. It is interesting that the General points out a number of propositions that Marxism has in common with the traditional position of the Church on social issues: "There can be no doubt that an inequitable distribution of wealth . . . creates or facilitates exploitation," a state of affairs that has been "analyzed by Karl Marx as well as denounced by the Church." However, the General does point out the dangers of staking out too much common ground with the Marxists, in terms that seem especially ironic, considering the source: "Those Christians who had sought for some time to adopt a Marxist analysis of society . . . have had to acknowledge that they have gradually come to accept the point of view that the end would invariably justify the means."

In the 1960's and early 1970's the "theology of liberation" undoubtedly presented an alternative that many regarded as far superior to the complacency and conservatism of mainstream Christianity; in short, as Professor Rahner expressed it, it offered a chance to pursue "the spirit of the new and unexplored beyond the farthest frontiers." As far as Pope Paul was concerned, the chase had already overrun all permissible bounds by 1973; he issued a warning to Jesuit activists that spoke of "dangerous experiments," as well as of the "sorrow," "grief," and "dissatisfaction" that he himself had been made to feel. When the critical barrage emanating from the Vatican still had not let up after a year's time, Arrupe decided to convene a General Congregation of the Order in December 1974—one of only four that were occasioned by some crisis other than the death of a Superior General.

SILENCE IS GOLDEN—THE THIRTY-SECOND GENERAL CONGREGATION

The announced purpose of the General Congregation, which remained in session from December 3, 1974, until March 7, 1975, was that of "general stocktaking and discussion of alternatives for the future." General Arrupe was only slightly more informative when he spoke of the Congregation as the prelude to a forthcoming "root-and-branch reform of the Society of Jesus." It was left to Pope Paul, in his opening address to the delegates, to define the nature of the crisis; he urged them to shun "innovation for its own sake, innovation that calls everything into question," and warned them to "leave such reforms to the relativists who want to destroy today what they have built up yesterday." And finally, the delegates were reminded, they had chosen to assume certain obligations when they joined the Order, not the least of which was obedience: "The relationship between the Pope and the members of the Society has always been a free and voluntary association." The 239 delegates present from 80 different countries could consider themselves warned; "obedience" was to be the watchword. The delegates chose to disregard this timely warning, however, and the more than one thousand *postulata* that made up the agenda of the platform of the Congregation contained a number of highly inflammatory proposals, including a request that all distinctions of rank within the Order (and the accompanying privileges and perquisites) should be abolished. More than two thirds of the delegates voted for a preliminary proposal that involved a drastic restructuring of the Order. The fourth vow would be administered to all members of the Order, but in somewhat modified form—namely, it would only be applicable to "apostolic commissions" that the Pope had specifically entrusted to the Order for the benefit of the Church. This would not automatically compel the members of the Order to give their assent where questions of doctrine were concerned—in other words, a legitimate difference of opinion between a Jesuit and the Pope on a point of doctrine would not necessarily be a violation of the principle of obedience.

In addition, the delegates demanded a return to the "holy poverty" of the Apostles, this time to be guaranteed by a strict system of accounting. The real watchword of the Congregation was a slogan devised by Ignatius—"Preach in poverty"—and, recast in the jargon of the theology of liberation, it emerged as "Show solidarity with all the oppressed and underprivileged everywhere." (Perhaps it should be mentioned at this point that the *postulata* that were approved by the delegates did not go into effect as statutes of the Order until they had been approved by the Vatican, so that tne vast majority of them, which were not calculated to win the approval of Pope Paul VI, were presumably intended purely as symbolic resolutions or expression of intent.)

"Presumably" is the operative word here, since no explanation was to be forthcoming, at least for the time being. On February 14, 1975, the Pope imposed what in slightly less august circumstances would be called a gag order on the delegates; no further transcripts of the proceedings were to be published, nor the texts of any of the resolutions adopted, and the ban was even extended to include the summaries of the proceedings that had been prepared entirely for internal distribution (that is, to the various Jesuit houses around the world that were represented in the Congregation). Naturally the plan for the reorganization of the Order that the delegates had adopted received a firm papal veto at the same time. Pope Paul VI made it clear that he felt that the Order was in fact due for a wholesale reorganization, though scarcely of the kind that the delegates had in mind; or, as he put it, "the Society" would be "refurbished, renewed, and suffused with a new vitality" without being "radically transformed or distorted." General Arrupe—not for the first time, of course—was willing to deflect a great deal of the blame onto himself for what he acknowledged to have been his own failure of leadership; the whole episode was considered to have been nothing more than a temporary breakdown of discipline, now that order had finally been restored. At the final session of the Congregation he told the delegates, "We have understood the Holy Father. All Jesuits must abide by the Pope's decision. . . . We are sure that the Holy Father is the truth." This was on March 7, 1975; none of the controversial resolutions that the delegates had adopted had been ratified by the Holy Father.

After a month had passed, the ban on publication was lifted, and the resolutions that had actually been approved by the delegates were finally published, some of them with certain annotations and amendments that restricted even their symbolic ambit. (The proposed revision of the fourth vow had not even been adopted by the delegates, as it turned out.) The only question that remained was, How long would it take the Order to work its way through its collective identity crisis, the symptoms of which had only been temporarily arrested by this papal intervention? (Neither shock treatment nor corporal punishment, however resolutely applied, appeared to be the answer.) Writing a few months after the event in an official publication of the German provinces, Father Friedrich Wulf made use of a more decorous metaphor but reached eventually the same conclusion: "The lack of communication and the language difference between the Holy See and the Society were not even resolved by papal intervention and the obedient submission of the Congregation." Everything was in readiness for the next crisis, which would not be too long in coming.

GENERAL STRIKE—THE ERA OF PEDRO ARRUPE

On August 11, 1981, the Catholic News Agency reported from Rome: "The Superior General of the Jesuit Order, Pedro Arrupe, who has recently suffered a cerebral hemorrhage and is now embarking on what is likely to be a lengthy hospitalization, today confirmed the appointment of the American Jesuit Father Vincent O'Keefe as his temporary deputy for the duration of his convalescence. O'Keefe had been previously designated 'vicar pro tem' . . . . Father Arrupe, who will be seventy-four on November 14, had already offered his resignation to the Pope in April 1980 on the grounds of ill health and old age, but John Paul II requested him to remain at his post for the time being." This was a step that General Arrupe had been trying to avoid ever since he had taken office; the twenty-eighth Jesuit General, like the first, was determined to serve out his term of office, even when his physical and mental endurance was no longer adequate to the task. It had been decided at the Thirty-first General Congregation, in 1965, that a General could be prematurely relieved of the burdens of office "for reasons of the utmost seriousness."

As mentioned in the Vatican communiqué, General Arrupe had tried to invoke this new regulation on several previous occasions (the Order's official explanation of this being that "Father Arrupe merely wanted to ensure that this newly enacted provision could be inaugurated in a satisfactory manner"). Father Arrupe himself had suggested a different explanation—"the consequences of advancing age."

There is a third possibility that also suggests itself—this one political rather than procedural or physiological. General Arrupe was really more of a diplomat by temperament than a commander-in-chief, and he was constantly striving to achieve some sort of balance between the right and left wings of the Order. This was particularly resented by the ultraconservative faction, most of whom were Spanish; Father Ludwig Volk is a German Jesuit who apparently shared their views but had picked up from his progressive colleagues the habit of confiding the most indiscreet of his opinions to the columns of *Die Welt:*

> Rather than the more traditional conception of his post [General Arrupe] seems to have been inspired by the ideal of those recreational *agents provocateurs,* or activities directors, that are to be found at Mediterranean vacation resorts—a profession, admittedly, that is still in its infancy. They take on the Herculean task of inciting the complacent or the merely sulky vacationer to undertake a more physically taxing form of relaxation, an exercise in persuasion that requires one to be charming, cunning, and *simpático.* No solitary great captain, in short . . . but rather a popular commander with the common touch that it takes to galvanize his devoted soldiery into action.

The fact that Father Volk had benefited from the relative permissiveness of the Arrupe regime (in that he was able to give public expression to his views) seems only to have embittered him all the more.

There was even some speculation that General Arrupe had personally engineered the clash between the Pope and the progressive delegates to the Congregation as a way of forcing the issue of his resignation from the office (possibly because he was reluctant to expose himself to any further polemics by the likes of Father Volk). As ingenious as this analysis may have been, Father Arrupe remained in office, showed no apparent signs of bitterness, and even had the satisfaction of developing an increasingly close, almost affectionate relationship with Pope Paul VI during the last few years of his pontificate.

When John Paul II ascended the papal throne, the possibility of a rapprochement between the new Pope (generally reckoned to be even more conservative than his predecessor) and the progressive wing of the Order began to seem even more remote. General Arrupe persevered until April 1980, however, when, as mentioned earlier, the deteriorating state of his health made it impossible for him to defer his resignation any longer. (The news of his request to be relieved of his office was given even more play in the press than the mass resignation of the group of Portuguese cabinet ministers, which meant that, journalistically at least, the Order had risen once more to the level of a European power.) His request would have to be accepted by the Pope, of course, and his resignation would also have to be confirmed by a General Congregation of the Order—preparation for which had gotten under way almost immediately.

Protocol required the General to notify the Pope in person of his intention to resign, but it was not until four months later, August 1980, that Arrupe was finally granted an audience by John Paul II. The audience only lasted for ten minutes; the papal communiqué was correspondingly brief—the Holy Father had requested the General to defer his resignation once again "for the greater good of the Society and the Church." Arrupe meekly acceded to the Pope's "request," the preparations for the Thirty-third Congregation were canceled, and Arrupe remained in office for another year, until he suffered a stroke that left him quite incapable of discharging his duties any longer.

Although the policy of voluntary retirement that General Arrupe had tried unsuccessfully to take advantage of was a very recent development, there were a number of precedents for the appointment of a "vicar pro tem" to serve out the term of a General who had been incapacitated by illness. Two of these past vicars had been elected General on the death of the incumbent—Giovani Paolo Oliva in 1664, after three years' service as vicar, and Anton Anderledy in 1887, after four years' service. If Arrupe's chief assistant, Father Vincent O'Keefe, who was then fifty-six years old, were to succeed him in his turn, he would be the first non-European to be elected General in the history of the Order; it would make an appropriate symbol of cautious and unhurried progress for a

TRAGEDY NARROWLY AVERTED

In the middle of June, a false alarm at Fiumicino Airport, near Rome. The drug-sniffing dogs of the airport security staff, whose infallible noses have made them the terror of the international narcotics-smuggling syndicates, displayed unmistakable signs of agitation in the presence of a piece of hand luggage belonging to Father Arrupe, who was just returning from a trip to India and a meeting with regional superiors in Kuala Lumpur. The police showed even greater signs of agitation when they realized whom the suitcase belonged to. They began to entertain visions of a truly epochal drug bust, but the visions faded when it was explained that Father Arrupe had brought back a splendid garland as a memento of the cordial reception that was afforded him in the Orient—the garland contained cardamom seeds and small pieces of sandalwood.

from *The Jesuit Yearbook*, 1980–81

native of the New World, if not precisely the Third World, to occupy the Order's highest post.

Before long it began to seem that the Old World was not quite willing to relinquish the reins of power without a struggle. On September 12 Pope John Paul II named Father Paolo Dezza as his "personal delegate" for the duration of the General's convalescence. This was totally unexpected, and no explanation was offered, perhaps because it was felt it would be useless to try to disguise the purpose and the obvious implications of such a step—the delegate was eighty years old, a senior member of the conservative wing of the Order, and a trusted councillor of both Paul VI and John Paul II. (As far as the question of postecumenical progressivism was concerned, it may be assumed that he told these pontiffs exactly what they wanted to hear.) The installation of a special papal overseer (an event that was without precedent in the history of the Order) did nothing to ease the existing tensions between the conservatives and the progressives. In addition there was a second split within the Order—this was basically psychological rather than ideological—that was only indirectly affected by these developments but nevertheless continued to grow more serious of its own accord.

This was the disparity between the Jesuits of Europe and North America, who had grown accustomed to living in a world of middle-class privilege, who had perhaps unreflectively come to adopt the prejudices of the managerial or professional class, and for whom Christianity was little more than a profession, on the one hand, and the Jesuits of the Third World, on the other hand, for whom Christianity was little more than a prelude or a pretext for political activism. General Arrupe, for one, regarded both of these tendencies as basically antithetical to the real mission of the Order, as he made clear in an address to the General Congregation in 1974:

> How are people going to react to our fine speeches about justice and righteousness when they can see that we enjoy a standard of living that is superior to a great many of our fellow citizens, when all that we do positively reeks of privilege, when all of our social relationships just bind us more closely to the rich, the oppressors, the ruling class! And there is another side to this: How can anyone still recognize the evangelical nature of our mission when we resort to guerrilla tactics and the use of force, agitate for radical revolution, and corrupt our task of spiritual education with atheistic methods and ideologies?

Still, problematical though they might be, these contradictory tendencies are unlikely to prove fatal to the future development of the Order—especially since both can be traced back directly to the writings of Ignatius himself, who placed a higher value on what we would call "social action" than formal religious observance and who, of course, did whatever was necessary to cultivate the goodwill of the privileged classes. The last few chapters may have given a somewhat exaggerated impression of the Order reduced to fragments, riven with dissension, but in fact by more objective standards things still seem to be going very well indeed. A few statistics cited at random may make this clearer: Of the 140 universities and other centers of higher education that are run by the Catholic Church, fully 40 are run by Jesuits. (One out of every ten lawyers in

America is a graduate of a Jesuit college.) Twenty-four Catholic radio stations are also run by Jesuits, of which the most notable of course is Radio Vatican, which beams out programs in 33 different languages to listeners all over the world—270 programs for Europe, 130 for Africa, 50 for America, 40 for Asia and Oceania. The Japanese program has one of the largest audiences in the Far East, and the first broadcasts in Chinese went out in April 1980.

THE GREGORIANA TODAY

The Collegio Romano was renamed the Papal Gregorian University in honor of Pope Gregory XIII (1572–1585), who helped the Jesuits build new quarters for their college when they were forced to abandon the original site.

In 1980 there were 152 Jesuits from 29 different countries on the faculty, as well as 49 other instructors (15 secular clergy, 25 members of other religious orders, 11 laymen) from 15 different countries.

In 1980 there were 2,376 students from 85 different countries enrolled at the Gregoriana. Seven hundred thirty-two students listed Italian as their first language, 619 English, 398 Spanish, 154 French, 151 German, 80 Portuguese, and 252 none of the above. (This figure also includes 635 women students, who have been eligible for admission since Vatican II.)

Six different periodicals are published by Jesuits in the German-speaking provinces, varying in tone from popular to highly theoretical. Fourteen periodicals are published by the Order (or edited by individual Jesuits) in France, of which two, *Símvol* (*"Symbol"*) and *Plamyá* (*"Flame"*), are primarily concerned with the subject of religion in the Soviet Union. (*Plamyá* also deals with Marxist subjects and Soviet studies.)

The Jesuits' oldest calling, service in a foreign mission, continued to flourish and still has the same prerequisites of courage and self-sacrifice.

Although the realm of the Indies may be called the Third World today, the profession is no less dangerous than it was in the days of Francis Xavier and Father Ricci. Four Jesuits had already been murdered in the first few months of 1980, in India, Bolivia, and El Salvador.

This has merely been intended as a brief reminder of the fact that Jesuits do have other preoccupations besides polemics, political intrigue, and talking to the press. The real question facing the Order today is whether the current membership can perpetuate itself by persuading several thousand like-minded young men to devote their lives to the pursuit of one particular brand of Christian activism. The alternative seems to involve either slow extinction by attrition or outright absorption into the anonymous milling herds of secular radicalism.

BETWEEN THE OLD-BOY NETWORK AND THE AVANT GARDE— THE JESUITS PUT TO THE TEST

This extract from the "Confessions of an Ex-Jesuit" (actual title, *The Jesuits,* by Alighiero Tondi, published in East Berlin by Aufbau-Verlag in 1961) describes the horrors of the author's novitiate some time during the late 1940's—and perhaps also bears out the truth of Father Rahner's observation about the highly subjective nature of confession: "Kneeling on the bare floorboards, his hands clasped before him, the novice listened while his brothers criticized, abused, and reprimanded him for a quarter of an hour. . . . The master handed out the scourges to the novices, iron chains with long barbs on them, a hard, cruel whip with five tails. And the poor boy had been scourging his flesh with such a device every week since he was fifteen years old, not infrequently until he had drawn blood." The novice, according to Alighiero Tondi, needed explicit permission to do almost anything, even had to make a special "request" to get a piece of paper. Special permission was also required to send a letter or even a postcard; the novices were forbidden to have stamps in their possession, and the incoming as well as outgoing mail was censored. Even after they had taken their vows, brothers were not permitted to go out by themselves; the rules of the Order prescribed that "one must always have a companion with one at all times."

I did not encounter any novices while I was doing the research for this book, but the Jesuits that I met did not seem to be subject to any of these restrictions, were not the slightest bit secretive, and certainly had to ask no man's leave for a piece of paper—on the contrary, no other librarians were so helpful in enabling me to make copies of relevant materials. (As for instruments of torture, I saw none—with the possible exception of telephones and typewriters.) At least it is true that the Jesuits who came to visit me always seemed to travel in pairs, in an old Volkswagen beetle, though this was simply to save on gasoline rather than to keep tabs on each other. They were always right up to date on cultural and scientific subjects, and naturally they had read the reminiscences of their ex-brother Tondi and had put them aside with a rueful shake of the head. They were well informed and responsive, and though our opinions did not always coincide, theirs at least were always well thought out and often highly original as well. On one occasion, when we happened to be discussing some aspect of the sexual revolution, one of them quoted a remark of Clement of Alexandria, a Greek Church Father of the third century A.D.: "Let no man despise what God did not disdain to create."

This shift in the collective personality of the Order, from urbanity to downright worldliness, has also been reflected in various external ways, no less distressing to traditionalists. The clerical shovel hat (which owed its distinctive shape to a stiffening of twisted cord running around the brim) has generally been discarded, the soutane exchanged for more conventional garb, and among the younger Jesuits the Roman collar—once the last refuge of clerical respectability—has given way to the rolled-up turtleneck. Still, this is serious business not only to the conservative wing of the Order itself but also to a substantial body of "fellow-travelers" among the Catholic laity who have admired the elite, ascetic traditions of the Order and have always imagined these to be as solid and unwavering as the rock on which the Church of Rome was founded. (Or, to put it in a different way—*Sint, ut sint, aut non sint.*) Once these traditions have been abandoned, they feel, the Order has forfeited its right to existence.

Still, it seems incredible that the Catholic Church could exist without the Society of Jesus, or that the Order could have survived so many persecutions and prohibitions simply to become a victim of obsolescence. While this is not an absolute impossibility (177 of the 276 male religious communities founded since the fourth century A.D. are still in existence), it does seem more likely that the Order might be able to exist without the Catholic Church. In the United States the question of whether the Jesuits are really the Protestants of the future is already being discussed, and it must at least have occurred to the progressive-minded padres of Latin America that the kind of social engagement that they envision for the Order would be much easier to achieve without the restraining hand of the Vatican to contend with. The author of this extract from the official bulletin of the German provinces for May 1975 has clearly considered the possibility and rejected it (presumably while crossing himself and murmuring "God forbid!"): "Without the Church and, in particular, without its special relationships to the Pope the Society of Jesus no longer embodies the legacy of St. Ignatius and would be severely restricted in its potential for apostolic activities. By the same token the Church, the Holy See, cannot dispense with the Order. . . ."

D'Alembert was just as firmly convinced in 1772 that the Vatican would never permit the Order to be dissolved, since "such an outcome would be very like a treaty between the sheep and the wolves whose first article enjoined the sheep to give up their watchdogs to the wolves." D'Alembert's prophecy (certainly not a case of wishful thinking—he believed the Church and the Jesuits deserved each other) was disproved within a couple of months, and our modern prophet's has been tested but left basically intact by the events of almost a decade, though this certainly does not imply that the Order is any more "indispensable" to the Church than it was in 1772. The Order has chosen new tasks for itself and no longer derives its strength from its steadfastness and inflexibility; instead—to exchange D'Alembert's pastoral metaphor for the more conventional military one—it must be deployed on "a long, tortuous front of partial advances and retreats and various subsidiary operations"; this last phrase was written by Father Peter Lippert, a very clear-sighted prophet indeed, in 1912.

And apart from these strategic complications, the ranks have been thinned out quite a bit by death and desertion in recent years—from thirty-three thousand in 1964 to twenty-six thousand in 1975.* This has perhaps less to do with the Order itself than with the age we live in, which Professor Rahner has likened to "a heathen country with a Christian past and a few Christian remnants." General Arrupe presented a

---

*The latest available figures for 1981 show that the Order has held firm at 26,622 members (though this is about 400 fewer than in 1980). This total includes 19,574 fathers, 3,277 "scholastics," and 3,771 brothers.

somewhat more complex analysis of the problem to the Third International Congress of Religious Orders in Montreal in 1977: In the industrialized nations a surplus of material goods has created a new subspecies of mankind, *Homo consumens,* who is exclusively concerned with having at the expense of being, who is enslaved by his own self-induced cravings to *possess.* But if we intend to go on living together in this world for very much longer, then *Homo consumens* will have to be supplanted by a new type of human being, *Homo serviens,* who has some sense of solidarity with his fellow creatures and who yearns for a richer life rather than more possessions. It may be increasingly difficult to deny the force of the General's conclusions, and it is tempting to see the Jesuits as a kind of cadre for this cooperative, survival-oriented society of the future (since the qualities that are claimed to be necessary for our survival are scarcely to be found in any of our mainstream cultural institutions).

And here we return to one of the General's favorite themes—the corruption of organized religion, inasmuch as it has been allowed to become an apologist for the *status quo* and a bulwark of middle-class complacency: ". . . preaching the Gospel in the service of the Protestant values of liberty, property, and progress can seem innocuous enough and provide men with conscience balm, while at the same time making use of these values only to serve the interests of selfish materialism, exploitation, and enslavement of their neighbors." In other words, it is no longer enough simply to know how a Christian should behave in this world, since it has become the task of the true Christian to change this world for a better one.

VOX POPULI, VOX DEI—THE THIRD WORLD COMES TO THE FORE

Whether or not *Homo serviens* eventually inherits the earth, the spiritual direction of the Order is largely going to be determined by the Jesuits of the Third World before too long, a group that is more likely to be concerned with combating starvation and despair than complacency and overconsumption. Even at the General Congregation in 1974 the Asian, African, and South America delegates already constituted a solid bloc—at least for the purpose of contesting what was perceived as the arrogance and condescension of the European Jesuits. An Indian General

Assistant was appointed in the same year (his predecessor had been the only Italian in General Arrupe's inner circle)—the rough equivalent cf a cabinet-level post in the Jesuit hierarchy.

At the Order's seventh "Ecumenical Congress," held in Frankfurt in 1977, the confrontation was more sharply defined. While the European delegates were cautiously exploring fresh avenues of cooperation with Christians of other denominations, the Latin Americans explained quite bluntly that they had no interest whatsoever in righting the wrongs of the Counter-Reformation while there was so much social injustice in their homelands, "the poor people's continent," crying out for a Christian response. The Indian delegate pointed out that it was all very well for Catholics and Lutherans to arrange reciprocal privileges and preach the occasional sermon in each other's churches, but for him and his colleagues (as in the days of Father de Nobili) the real problem was to improve relations with the Hindus and the Muslims. The African delegates posed a question that was more reminiscent of the Chinese rites controversy, since they wished to "translate" the basic tenets of Christianity into traditional terms and concepts that their parishioners would already be familiar with. This emphasis on missionary work and closer "ecumenical" ties with non-Christian religions serves to underscore the point that the majority of Jesuit missionaries will be natives of the Third World countries in a few years if the present trend continues.

The preeminence of the Third World may be likely but it is not yet assured, a fact that is conveniently symbolized by the cover illustration on the *Jesuit Yearbook* for 1980–81, the Byzantine figure of *Christos Pantokrator,* Christ in Majesty, the Ruler of the Universe. This is probably not the image that the Jesuits of South America would have chosen to represent their conception of Christ as the friend of the poor and the consoler of the wretched of the earth. This, at least, is the vision of liberation theology—that the Christian message of salvation can be combined with a program of political and social change here below. It is important here, of course, that *combined with* should not mean *confused with;* the surest way for a religious order to lose its soul is to become exclusively preoccupied with the concerns of the material world. This seems to be the greatest danger that faces the Jesuit Order at present, and the Order has always had a dangerous disposition to allow itself to be possessed by the spirit of the times—whether this might be the fanaticism of the Counter-Reformation, the cynical worldliness of the Enlightenment, or the torpid conservatism of the nineteenth-century

Restoration. The Jesuits have often been charged with being too quick to alter their convictions to suit the intellectual fashions of the day; possibly so, but they have always "remembered their cloth," remembered who they really were—and frequently at the last possible moment. There seems to be no obvious reason why a turtleneck should not serve as just as effective a reminder as a soutane.

It is the peculiar fate of the Jesuits to be both a great hope for and a danger to the Church, which no doubt has something to do with the strange dual nature of the Order, whose field of operation has always been somewhere between action and contemplation, between heaven and earth—where, we may hope, it will always remain. But the Order will only have a future if it can abandon the practice of sanctifying every aberration in its history into a tradition, and when it is ready to ignore some of the precepts of its founder to concentrate on one that is the most important of all: "To find God in everything." But this simple precept has certain tactical corollaries as well: They must be more than a Vatican propaganda mill or a theological debating society. They must not try to set earth above heaven, or Marx above Jesus. They must not confuse novelty with progress—or endurance with virtue, for that matter. In order to be a source of hope rather than a danger for the Church, the Jesuits need only put that motto into practice that was adopted by the General Congregation in 1974: "For faith *and* for righteousness." For eternal life and for justice on earth—if the Jesuits can truly make this their purpose, then they can reply to their critics in the words of Jesus Christ: *"If you know how to interpret the look of the sky, can you not read the signs of the times?"*

BIBLIOGRAPHY

Appel, Petrus Maria. *Katholik, das musst Du wissen.* (Pamphlet). 1967.

Arrupe, Pedro. *Unser Zeugnis muss glaubwürdig sein (Ein Jesuit zu en Problemen von Kirche und Welt am Ende des zwanzigsten Jahrhunderts).* Ostfildern, 1981.

Autorenteam SJ. *Jesuiten. Wohin steuert der Orden?* Freiburg, 1975.

Bamm, Peter. *Frühe Stätten der Christenheit.* München, 1955.

Becher, Hubert, SJ. *Die Jesuiten: Gestalt und Geschichte des Ordens.* München, 1951.

Berrigan, Daniel. *The Trial of the Catonsville Nine.* Boston, 1970.

Bismarck, Otto von. *Gedanken und Erinnerungen.* Stuttgart, 1898.

Boehmer, Heinrich. *Ignatius von Loyola* (neu herausgegeben von Hans Leube). Leipzig, 1941.

———. *Die Jesuiten, eine historische Skizze.* Leipzig, 1913.

Brodrick, James. *Progress of the Jesuits, 1556–79.* London, 1946.

Brou, Pierre. *Les Jesuites et la légende.* Paris, 1906.

Campell, Thomas. *The Jesuits, 1534–1921.* London, 1921.

Canu, Jean. "Die religiösen Männerorden" in *Der Christ in der Welt, eine Enzyklopädie.* Aschaffenburg, 1963.

Chateaubriand, François-Auguste-René. *Le génie du christianisme.* Paris, 1802. [*Geist des Christentums.* Leipzig, 1870.]

Constitutiones Societatis Jesu. Rome, 1908.

Deschner, Karlheinz. *Abermals krähte der Hahn. Eine kritische Kirchenge-schichte von den Anfängen bis zu Pius XII.* Stuttgart, 1962.

Duhr, Bernhard. *Geschichte der Jesuiten in den Ländern deutscher Zunge.* 4 vols. Freiburg, St. Louis, 1907–28.

Fichtinger, Christian. *Lexikon der Heiligen und Päpste.* Wien, 1980.

Frederick the Great. *Historische und militärische Schriften, Briefe.* (*Ausgewählte Werke, 1. Band*). G.B. Volz, ed. Berlin, n.d.

Fridell, Egon. *Kulturgeschichte der Neuzeit.* 3 vols. München, 1927–31.

Fülöp-Miller, René. *Macht und Geheimnis der Jesuiten.* Leipzig, 1929.

Ganss, George E., SJ (ed.) *Constitutions of the Society of Jesus.* St. Louis, 1970.

Goethe, Johann Wolfgang von. *Die Reisen.* (2. Band der Sanssouci Ausgabe.) Potsdam, n.d. [*Travels in Italy,* tr. W.H. Auden. London, 1962.]

Gotto, Klaus, and Konrad Repgen (eds.). *Kirche, Katholiken und Nationalsozial-ismus.* Mainz, 1980.

Gracián, Baltasar. *Handorakel und Kunst der Weltklugheit,* tr. Arthur Schopen-hauer. Stuttgart, 1967. [*The Oracle.*]

Gregor, Joseph. *Weltgeschichte des Theaters.* Zürich, 1933.

Harney, Martin F. *The Jesuits in History.* New York, 1941.

Hochhuth, Rolf. *Der Stellvertreter.* Reinbek bei Hamburg, 1963. [*The Deputy.*]

Hoensbroech, Paul von. *Der Jesuitenorden, eine Enzyklopädie.* 2 vols. Leipzig, 1926–27.

————. *Vierzehn Jahre Jesuit.* Leipzig, 1910.

Hollis, Christopher. *A History of the Jesuits.* London, 1968.

Höver, Günter, SJ. (ed.) *Da riechts nach Jesuitenpulver.* Frankfurt, n.d.

Kierkegaard, Søren. *Tagebücher,* tr. Elisabeth Fenersinger. Wiesbaden, 1959. [*Journals,* tr. Alexander Dru. New York, 1959.]

Koch, Ludwig, SJ. *Jesuiten-Lexikon. Die Gesellschaft Jesu einst und jetzt.* Paderborn, 1934.

Koerbling, Anton, and Paul Riesterer. *Pater Rupert Mayer.* München, 1950.

König, Robert. *Deutsche Literaturgeschichte.* 2 vols. Leipzig, 1891.

Krebs, Richard. *Die politische Publiztik der Jesuiten und ihre Gegner in den letzten Jahrzehnten vor Ausbruch des dreissigjährigen Krieges.* Halle, 1890.

Lange, Martin, and Reinhold Iblacker (eds.) *Christenverfolgung in Südamerika.* Second edition. Freiburg, 1981.

Lay, Rupert, SJ. *Zukunft ohne Religion.* Olten, 1970.

Lesourd, Paul. *Entre Rome et Moscou: Jésuite Clandestin, Msgr. d'Herbigny.* Paris, 1978.

Lippert, Peter. *Zur Psychologie des Jesuitenordens.* Kempten, 1913. [*The Jesuits, a Self-Portrait.* New York, 1958.]

Loyola, Ignatius. *Briefe.* O. Karrer and H. Rahner, eds. Köln, 1942.

———. *Briefwechsel mit Frauen.* Hugo Rahner, ed. Freiburg, 1956.

———. [*Letters,* tr. and ed. William Y. Young. Chicago, 1959.]

———. [*Spiritual Exercises,* tr. W.H. Longride. London, 1950.]

Lützeler, Felix Franz Egon. *Hinter den Kulissen der Weltgeschichte.* 2 vols. Leipzig, 1937.

Marcuse, Ludwig. *Ignatius von Loyola.* Hamburg, 1956.

Melchers, Erna and Hans. *Die Heiligen. Geschichte und Legende* (bearbeitung Carlo Melchers). Augsburg, 1980.

Mir, Miguel. *Historia interna documentada de la Compañía de Jesús.* 2 vols. Madrid, 1913.

Mitchell, David. *The Jesuits, a History.* London, 1980.

Orthbandt, Eberhard. *Das deutsche Abenteuer.* Baden-Baden, 1960.

Pascal, Blaise. *Lettres provinciales.* Stuttgart, 1980. [*Provincial Letters.*]

Prause, Gerhard. *Niemand hat Kolumbus aufgelachet.* Seventh edition. Düsseldorf, 1976.

Rahner, Hugo. *Ignatius als Mensch und Theologe.* Freiburg, 1964.

Rahner, Karl. *Betrachtungen zum ignatianischen Exerzitienbuch.* München, 1965.

313

————. *Strukturwandel der Kirche als Aufgabe und Chance.* Freiburg, 1973.

————. *Toleranz in der Kirche.* Freiburg, 1977.

Ranke, Leopold von. *Geschichte der Papste.* Berlin, 1980. [*History of the Popes,* tr. Thomas Babington Macauley.]

Rauschning, Hermann. *Gespräche mit Hitler.* Zürich, 1939.

Rössler, Hellmuth. "Die Societas Jesu," *Jahrbuch III der Ranke-Gesellschaft,* 1957.

Rules of the Society of Jesus. Roehampton, 1926.

Schott, Ludwig. "Das Welttheater der Jesuiten" in *Münchner Alltag.* München, n.d.

Simon, Edith (ed.). *Ketzer, Bauern, Jesuiten.* Hamburg, 1973.

Spee von Langenfeld, Friedrich. *Trutznachtigal.* Leipzig, 1937.

Stark, Dr. Johannes. *Zentrumspolitik und Jesuitenpolitik.* n.p., 1932.

Stierli, Josef. *Die Jesuiten.* Frybourg (Schweiz), 1955.

Teilhard de Chardin, Pierre. *Genèse d'une pensée.* Paris, 1961. [*The Making of a Mind: Letters from a Soldier-Priest,* tr. René Hague. New York, 1965.]

Tondi, Alighiero. *La Potenza segreta dei Gesuiti.* Rome, 1953.

Wiegand, Friedrich. "Die Jesuiten," *Wissenschaft und Bildung,* 1926.

Wulf, Friedrich (ed.). *Ignatius von Loyola. Seine geistliche Gestalt und sein Vermächtnis.* Würzburg, 1956.

Xavier, Francis. *Briefe.* Elisabeth Gräfin Vitzthum, ed. Leipzig, 1941.

Zglincki, Friedrich von. *Der Weg des Films.* Berlin, 1956.

JESUIT PERIODICALS

An Unsere Freunde. Newsletter of the South German province.

Assistenz-Rundbrief. München.

Catholica. Quarterly review of theology. Reprint, Amsterdam, 1970.

Entschluss. "Zeitschrift für Praxis und Theologie." Published by the Austrian province.

Jesuiten. Jahrbuch der Gesellschaft Jesu. German edition, published by the General Curia of the Order.

Petrusblatt. Berlin.

Stimmen aus Maria Laach (after 1915, *Stimmen der Zeit*). Freiburg.

INDEX